Vitalistic Thought in India

Sai Garib Dass Oriental Series : 159

Vitalistic Thought in India

(A study of the 'prāṇa' concept in Vedic literature and its development in the Vedānta, Sāṃkhya and Pañcarātra traditions)

PETER CONNOLLY

Sri Satguru Publications
A DIVISION OF
Indian Books Centre
Delhi–India

Published by
Sri Satguru Publications
Indological & Oriental Publishers,
A Division of
Indian Books Centre
40/5, Shakti Nagar,
Delhi-110007
INDIA

First Edition : Delhi, 1992

ISBN — 81-7030-348-6

Typeset by
ABC *for* **DTP**
6, Rajdhani Enclave, Delhi-34

Printed at
D.K. Fine Art Press, Delhi-52

Printed in India

Contents

Preface

This work is a revised version of my thesis 'The Concept of Prāṇa in the Literature of the Veda and its Development in the Vedānta, Sāṃkhya and Pañcarātra Traditions', for which I was awarded the degree Doctor of Philosophy by the University of Lancaster, England. Consequently much of it is quite technical in nature. The general reader may therefore find it useful to read the introduction, conclusion and chapter summaries before working through the text proper.

The conversion of the thesis into a book could not have taken place without the assistance of others. I would particularly like to express my appreciation to the Research and Publications Committee of the West Sussex Institute of Higher Education for providing a grant to cover the cost of retyping and to Karen Woods, Sarah Pollard and Tracy Bruton for doing the work. I am also grateful to Dr. Andrew Rawlinson and Dr. David Smith of Lancaster University for their help and guidance whilst I was a graduate student. If other students of Indian religion find this work useful in the course of their own investigations I will consider my efforts to have been worthwhile.

This book is dedicated to my Mother and Father, who helped me return to education after a period of youthful disenchantment and rebellion.

Abbreviations

A.Ā.	–Aitareya Āraṇyaka
A.U.	–Aitareya Upaniṣad
A.V.	–Atharva Veda
B.A.U.	–Bṛhad-Āraṇyaka-Upaniṣad
B.C.E.	–Before the Common Era
B.S.	–Brahma Sūtra
C.E.	–Common Era
C.U.	–Chāndogya Upaniṣad
J.U.B.	– Jaiminiya-Upaniṣad-Brāhmaṇa
Kaṭh.U.	–Kaṭha Upaniṣad
Kauṣ.U.	–Kauṣītakī Upaniṣad
Mait. U.	–Maitrī or Maitrāyaṇīya Upaniṣad
P.U.	–Praśna Upaniṣad
R.V.	–Ṛg Veda
S.B.	–Śatapatha Brāhmaṇa
S.K.	–Sāṃkhya Kārikā
S.S.	–Sāṃkhya Sūtra
S.U.	–Śvetāśvatara Upaniṣad
S.V.	–Sāma Veda
V.S.	–Vājasaneya Saṃhitā

A note on sanskṛt words

Since the devanāgarī script has no capital letters and, as a matter of course, runs words into each other there is no universally accepted manner of reproducing such features in English. The principle adopted in this study is, by and large, to provide sanskṛt words with an initial capital letter only when they are clearly being employed as proper names or where an author who provides capitals for them is being quoted. With regard to word combination I have generally followed the text under consideration for nominative and accusative endings. Where sanskṛt words have been incorporated into a list the stem from is used. In some places, however, the original inflexion has been incorporated so as to convey more clearly the point being made.

Introduction

This study emerged from an earlier interest of mine in the subtle body (sukṣma or liṅga śarīra) as found in the sacred literature of India. Descriptions of the subtle body vary from tradition to tradition and from text to text. The reasons for the variations are not, however, readily apparent. One thing which did become clear as I examined the material relevant to this issue was that in some accounts, e.g. those found in Vedānta literature, prāṇa (breath, vitality) was a prominent component whilst in others, e.g. those found in Sāṃkhya literature, it found no place at all. It was this discrepancy, perhaps more than any other factor, which led me to focus on the development of the prāṇa concept. I was hoping thereby to go some way towards adducing reasons for the existence of two quite different accounts of an entity which performed an almost identical function in the different systems. The following discussion offers what I hope is a convincing answer to that problem and one which will constitute a working base for further elucidation of material relevant to this issue.

The study divides into three major sections. The first deals with the evolution of the prāṇa concept in pre-Upaniṣadic Vedic literature, the second with its treatment in the Upaniṣads, whilst the third examines its place in the world-views of three influential religio-philosophical traditions which claim to be in accord with the teaching of the Veda: Vedānta, Sāṃkhya and Pañcarātra. The Vedānta and Sāṃkhya systems are two of, if not *the* two most influential, indigenous world-views in Indian culture. The great epic Mahābhārata is permeated with concepts from both traditions. So too are those great compendia of mythology, cosmology and ethical guidance, the Purāṇas. Similarly, the various Vaiṣṇava, Śaiva and Śākta sects all display the influence of one or both these systems in the construction of their soteriological and cosmological doctrines.

In the modern period, due to the efforts of groups such as the Ramakrishna mission and the Arya Samaj, Vedānta has been presented to India and the world as India's great philosophical heritage, whilst Sāṃkhya has become virtually redundant as an independent system. Even so, its influence is felt everywhere, even in the Vedānta tradition which, like Rome did to Carthage, has eliminated it as a competitor.

The choice of Pañcarātra as the third system for investigation was largely determined by the fact that it is the most ancient Vaiṣṇava tradition and boasts a considerable and influential literature. Its philosophical basis is a reasonably clear synthesis of Vedāntic and Sāṃkhyan thought whilst its overall world-view is dominated by the most pervasive and influential force in Indian religious life: bhakti, the attempt to experience complete devotion and surrender to a personal god. It thus seemed an ideal system for inclusion into this study.

Other possible contenders were the Śaiva systems of Kaśmir which, in varying degrees, represent syntheses of Vedānta and Sāṃkhya teachings and the later Nātha Yoga tradition which emerged out of what might be called 'the tantric ferment' of medieval Bengal. However, neither could boast the same antiquity as the Pañcarātra and would therefore be less illuminating with regard to the earlier career of the prāṇa concept. Nevertheless, they contain much material relevant to this study and should provide fertile pastures for similar investigations in the future.

In the first chapter I argue that the pre-Upaniṣadic Vedic tradition displays the development of a world-view and soteriology which continues smoothly into the Upaniṣadic period. This is not to say that the pre-Upaniṣadic and Upaniṣadic pictures are the same, far from it. The tendency to present the source of existence as bi-polar or androgynous (prāṇa-Vāc; puruṣa-Virāj being, perhaps, the best examples) is almost completely absent from the Upaniṣads whilst notions of rebirth and criticisms of Vedic knowledge, almost unknown in earlier literature, find considerable prominence. Nevertheless, the material presented in chapter one provides sufficient evidence to regard Dasgupta's claim that 'The passage of the Indian mind from the Brāhmanic to the Upaniṣad thought is probably the most remarkable event in the history of philosophic thought,'[1] as a considerable overstatement.

Whilst the pre-Upaniṣadic conception of ātman may not have acquired the features which characterise it in the Upaniṣads it is clear that many of them were available to the pre-Upaniṣadic thinkers, having already been developed in association with the concept of prāṇa. In A.V. 11.4 prāṇa is presented as the source and foundation of all existence and the true identity of divinities such as Prajāpati, Sūrya and Virāj. At the level of the individual, according to texts like the Śatapatha Brāhmaṇa and the Aitareya Āraṇyaka, prāṇa manifests as the immortal essence of a person which, when known, bestows immortality. It enters the individual body by way of the head and pervades it. Once inside the body it manifests as the various breaths or airs (prāṇas): prāṇa, apāna, vyāna, udāna and samāna and as the faculties of speech, mind, breath and the senses; its activity generates mentation. All these characteristics are attributed to ātman or brahman or both in the Upaniṣads.

This description of the nature and function of prāṇa continued to be elaborated by some Upaniṣadic teachers. Other groups, however, were developing concepts of ātman and brahman which either absorbed the characteristics of prāṇa, thereby making it virtually redundant, or subordinated the prāṇa concept in such a way as to make it just one derivative of ātman/brahman. Some attempts to counter this process are in evidence, e.g. the Kauṣītakī Upaniṣad, but the dominant trend was towards the subordination of prāṇa.

In chapter three, the mechanism of this subordination process is laid bare through an examination of the evolution of the Vedānta tradition as it culminated in the Brahma Sūtra and the schools which accepted this text as authoritative, particularly those of Śaṅkara and Rāmānuja. In particular, it will be argued that both of these commentators stand squarely in the camp of the compilers of the Brahma Sūtra, one of whose aims was to rob the concept of prāṇa of any claims it might have to be regarded as the equivalent of ātman/brahman. Also evident in the writings, both commentarial and independent, of Śaṅkara and Rāmānuja is a willingness to substitute Sāṃkhya categories for Upaniṣadic ones, particularly where the latter are connected with prāṇa. It will thus be argued that, despite its claim to being an exegetical tradition interpreting the teachings of the Upaniṣads and its rejection of

Sāṃkhyan interpreations of the same, the Vedānta of Bādarāyaṇa, Śaṅkara and Rāmānuja sacrifices many Upaniṣadic concepts in order to develop a coherent system of doctrine which includes many Sāṃkhya notions not found in śruti.

The second part of chapter three will present a case for the non-Vedic origin of Sāṃkhya and seek to demonstrate that the concept of prāṇa has no legitimate place in the Sāṃkhya scheme and was only incorporated to give credence to its identity as a tradition whose teachings are consonant with śruti. In sum, these first two sections of chapter three argue that as the Vedānta and Sāṃkhya systems developed the concept of prāṇa was marginalized in the former and given greater, though extremely limited, prominence in the latter.

The final part of chapter three will sketch out the cosmological picture of the Pañcarātra tradition in both its primitive and developed forms and indicate how the concept of prāṇa was employed. In particular, it will be argued that an examination of the prāṇa concept in this scheme confirms its essentially synthetic nature, not least because the Pañcarātra treatment of prāṇa produces problems of coherence across the teaching as a whole. It will also be demonstrated that, despite exhibiting little concern for the prāṇa concept, the Pañcarātra actually preserves the pre-Upaniṣadic status of prāṇa better than either the Vedānta or Sāṃkhya traditions even though these lay claim to being authoritative interpreters of śruti.

1

The Concept of Prāṇa in Pre-Upaniṣadic Vedic Literature

Background

The literature of the Vedic Saṃhitās, along with their respective Brāhmaṇas, Āraṇyakas and Upaniṣads, constitutes the oldest body of literary evidence relating to the orthodox, i.e. brāhmanical or brāhmanically accepted, religion of India. These texts were composed over a considerable period of time, some Ṛgvedic maṇḍalas (e.g. 2-7, the family books) perhaps taking shape in the period preceding the Aryan migrations into India, whilst portions of the two oldest Upaniṣads, the Bṛhadāraṇyaka (which constitutes sections 4-9 of the 14th kaṇḍa of the Śatapatha Brāhmaṇa) and the Chāndogya (which constitutes sections 3-10 of the Chāndogya Brāhmaṇa), indicate, by references to Ajataśatru, that the Aryan peoples had reached at least as far eastwards as Kāśi (Banares/ Vārāṇasī). Not surprisingly, the religious concerns of these people changed considerably during this period of migration. In the earliest periods of Vedic composition the Aryans had been predominantly nomadic pastoralists. By the time of the early Upaniṣads, however, that nomadic pastoralism had given way to a more settled, agriculturally-based lifestyle. Consequently we witness a tendency towards more time-consuming religious activities. In particular we find increasing complexity in the sacrificial ritual-the Śatapatha Brāhmaṇa is a good witness to this - and the internalization of its essential features through contemplative practices. Throughout this period of migration and textual composition we witness a tendency on the part of the brahmin priesthood to systematize their view of the universe. Thus, although these works are not systematic expositions of religious belief and practice, their contents, by and large, being the actual hymns and chants employed in the sacrificial ritual along with guidelines on the performance and symbolic interpretation of that ritual, they do contain a considerable amount of material concerning the world-view of the Vedic people.

Nevertheless, information on any particular topic is not always easy to locate or interpret. Apparently descriptive material is often intermixed with the praises of various deities and symbolic connections between seemingly unrelated aspects of existence. Mythical accounts often convey profound truths through symbolic episodes and it is not always easy to ascertain the realities behind the symbols. Hence, some modern scholars have argued that a particular kind of hermeneutical sensitivity is required if one's reconstruction of any Vedic doctrine is to be of value. Two modern writers who have developed such a case are Jeanine Miller and Maryla Falk.[1]

Both of these writers have argued that most Western scholars have failed to appreciate the rich inner spirituality embodied in Vedic literature and that this has led to a gross distortion of early brāhmanical religion being promulgated. Miller, for example, points out that many recurring terms in the Veda have a dual meaning and that the meaning of sanskṛt words is significantly determined by the context in which they are used.[2] For her, many of the Vedic hymns are '...not merely symbolic but recondite or esoteric.'[3] In this connection she quotes the French scholar L.Renou, who writes, 'The Ṛgveda is much more than an adjunct to ritual... the aim was to compose on a given theme... not introducing direct accounts of the lives of the gods so much as veiled allusions, occult correspondences between the sacred and the profane... A large part of Sanskrit literature is esoteric.'[4] In other words, the Vedas, like the Tantras, are composed in a kind of code, what Falk calls a 'technical terminology'[5] and Miller a 'sacerdotal language'.[6] The Tantras call it 'sandha bhāṣya' (between or twilight language). If this is the case an essential requirement for Vedic exegesis is 'the cracking of the code' and this is where both Falk and Miller feel Western scholars have made very little progress.

The following extract by Edward Conze illustrates well the similarity between Falk's and Miller's understanding of Vedic hymns and Tantric material as well as revealing the vast perceptual gulf that can exist between those who know the code and those who do not. According to Conze, we find in the Tantras 'Thousands and thousands of pages... filled with statements about "cosmic tortoises" and "sky dogs", or about gods dressed in "fur coats" or "tiger skins" living in "iron palaces" or "copper fortresses", and "holding a black trident with four heads stuck on it and a blood-dripping heart, at which two black vipers are sucking"... What are we to make of all that?... we are at a loss to know what their jokes really meant. We can well imagine, to give a parallel case, an earnest Japanese anthropologist of the year A.D. 3242 pondering over a choice piece of ornithological information he has found in an English soldier's letter of 1942, "Two wrens went into the sea and four blue tits came out again." Some initiation into the lore of the English army would soon tell him the meaning of that statement. In its absence he would have to resort to wild guesses, without having much to go on.'[7]

Miller and Falk, however, do not see themselves as sharing the plight of the Japanese anthropologist for, according to Miller, although words like 'kine, rock, mountain, stronghold, rivers, water, serpent, sun, heavenly light (svar) are... part of a mythological inheritance with a peculiar significance of its own... the keys to their meanings (are) in the very verses where they appear.'[8] In Miller's view, the failure on the part of many Western scholars to recognise the multivalence of much Vedic terminology has led them to provide concrete interpretations of most terms and this in turn has led to many of the hymns appearing unintelligible. An appreciation of their intended import, however, reveals a coherent message concerning the spiritual development of human beings.

According to Miller, 'The recurring mythical theme central to the Ṛgveda takes the form of a primeval feat performed either by certain gods, or by mankind's ancestors, the sons of heaven (angirasaḥ), and described either as the slaying of a primeval monster, Vṛtra, which prevented the waters from flowing, or as the breaking asunder of the rocky cavern by means of mantras; the result in both is the same: the setting up of the sun, till then hidden, in the sky, the release of the waters of life, the giving of light as a permanent boon to mankind, the finding of the path to heaven.'[9] In the Vṛtra myths Indra (the great generator of tapas, the one who by 'the fervour of his meditation... was able to reach out even to the supreme light' - R.V. 10 32 1; 10 167 1[10]) defeats Vṛtra, who covers the rock and holds back the waters, thereby releasing the waters. The consequence of this is that the sun (sūrya), which is 'the great treasure to be won',[11] the deity 'whose all-illuming gaze makes of the "spiritual powers" that generate it the all-seeing, all knowing and all-wise gods',[12] is set up on high.

A variant of this theme is found in the Vala myths. Here, Brahmaṇaspati (called 'the brahman finding wealth' in R.V. 2.1.3),

> '....drove the kine forth and cleft Vala through by prayer [brahman], dispelled the darkness and displayed the light of heaven... All they who see the light have drunk their fill thereat: together they have made the watery fount flow forth.'[13]

Another version of this myth, R.V. 1.52, has Indra, the Vṛtra slayer, breaking open Vala's stronghold. The similarities are many, the obstruction is pierced, the waters are freed, the light of the sun is revealed. One apparent difference is the freeing of the cattle in the Vala version, but the fact that for interpreters as diverse as the modern Indian mystic Aurobindo and the American orientalist W.N.Brown the plural for 'cow' can also mean or be a metaphor for 'rays of light'[14] makes even this difference less marked than it might seem.

The freeing of the cattle may, on the other hand, be introducing more relevant information. The cow, as R.V. 8.100.11 inform us, is Vāc (speech). The cow's voice is pleasant and its gift is food and drink. 8.101.1, Miller explains, tells us that light projecting (jyotir agrah) speech milks the honey yielding udder, which is the nectar of heaven, the vision of the gods.[15] Like Agni, Vāc holds all the worlds together (R.V. 10.125.8),[16] and as Agni is born from the waters (R.V. 1.72.7; 2.1.1; 3.26.7) so Vāc has her home in the waters (Ṛ.V. 10.125.7-8). As Miller states, 'It would seem that vāc, the verbum, and agni, the flame, are two sides of the one power.'[17] Hence, the releasing of the cows and the setting up of the sun (a form of Agni) could be taken as a revelation of the light-sound nature of the supreme truth which lies hidden.

For Miller then, many of the prominent terms in the Vedas have meanings which refer to various aspects of the spiritual quest and the realizations associated with its accomplishment. The methods by which these realizations are acquired are discussed at some length in her section on 'Vedic Meditation' in *The Vedas.* Briefly, she divides Vedic meditation into three types: mantric, visual and absorbtive, though she acknowledges that they are all interlinked. Prayer (brahman) is the essential ingredient of the mantric meditation. Brahman is the steed (Ṛ.V. 2.2.10) or the charioteer (Ṛ.V. 3.35.2-4) of the chariot of visionary awareness which carries the worshipper towards spiritual realization. As she points out, 'Both the patriarchs and the gods share the use of the chariot (10.15.10) which in 10.63.4 and 1.140.1 bears the epithet of "light" or "luminous" (jyotīrathā) and facilitates the "crossing" to the other shore (pārāya gantave 1.46.7)... The ocean meant is not the sea but the intermediate region of Vedic cosmogony which stands between earth and heaven.'[18]

The importance of prayer (brahman) is, she argues, explained in A.V. 7.1.1 where we read,

> 'They, either who by meditation led the beginning (agra) of speech, or who by mind spoke righteous things (ṛta) they, increasing with the third incantation (brahman), perceived (man) with the fourth, the name of the milch cow.'[19]

For Whitney this is 'mystic, obscure and un-Atharvanic material.'[20] For Miller, however, 'Keywords are given showing steps in the progress of meditation, the idea of "increase" or exhilaration (vṛdh) being notable and pointing to that exalted fulfilment which contemplation brought to its practitioners ... meditation, thence absorbtion into the "third incantation" thence to the fourth where the supreme mystery is revealed, or the sun is found, or the name of the cow is known.'[21] The name of the cow, of course, would be the hidden or unperceived nature of Vāc.

In Miller's scheme the experience of the sun or the name of the cow is the experience of the ātman. In Ṛ.V. 1.115.1 the sun is called the 'ātman' of 'what moves and moves not' and is the splendid face of the gods. It '... is discovered as the loftiest light beyond darkness (1.51.10) in the fourth brahman (5.40.6)... That self in all which the Atharvaveda describes as "desireless, wise, immortal, self-existent, contented with the essence, lacking nothing, is He. One fears not death who has known him, the ātma - serene, ageless, youthful (A.V. 10.8.44 Whitney's translation) is the divine sun.'[22]

The principal foci for visual meditation are the gods, since they are the beings who have already crossed over and who inspire the prayer that can lead to the highest realization. The gods and the chariots they use are contacted through the cultivation of dhī (visionary insight), a term derived from the same root as the later yogic word for contemplation, 'dhyāna'. This combination of prayer and vision leads the Vedic seers (ṛṣi) to 'gaining insight into transcendental states.'[23] This is manīṣā (intuitive insight). It leads to an understanding of '... the nature of the all pervading light symbolised as the winged bird (suparṇah) or solar ray which in pervading the ocean has penetrated all things [and] is described in 10.177.2 as bright as lightning dyotamānā) as well as svarya ... The lightning-like flash of insight, whether caused by soma, the elixir of immortality, or by brahman, the Vedic prayer, revealing something hitherto unknown, grants an uplifting or ecstatic experience which elsewhere made the bards exclaim: "We have seen the gods, we have become immortal" (8.48.3)'[24] In Miller's view the consequence of attaining the highest realization was that the goal of the Vedic sages, immortality, was secured.

When the Vedic hymns are examined against the background of this goal and the abovementioned methods for achieving it, then the non-concrete meanings of many terms become apparent. Hence the cow (or cows) represent the audible dimension of the ultimate as the sun represents the visual. The wealth, so often requested by the ṛṣis, is not material but spiritual wealth and the courage (suvīrya) to get it, which is only available to those who strive after immortality (Ṛ.V. 3.25.2), is spiritual courage. Hence, as Miller points out, 'That light which is free from fear (jyotir abhayam) is thus revealed as the great goal of the Vedic seer, the prize to be won ... The harnessing of the chariot of prayer is done with a view to reaching svar, that wide world (uruṃ lokam) full of spacious freedom and splendour (svarvat), that ultimate light (jyotir uttaram) which the Yajurveda was to claim abides eternal in every creature (Y.V. 34.3), which the Ṛgvedic ṛṣi discovers beyond the darkness and identifies with the sun (Ṛ.V. 1.50.10), which the seer Atri found as the sun of illumination in the fourth degree of prayer (5.40.6). This "heavenly light" (svarvaj jyotih) the sages yearn to obtain as they proceed to the transcendent lord of the assembly for that "longed for gift" (kāmyam sanim) which is wisdom or enlightenment (medhā).'[25]

In Miller's view then, the spirituality of the Vedic tradition itself enabled humans to experience the highest levels of spiritual insight and attainment; there was no need for these to be brought in from the outside. Thus, the kind of claims by writers such as Pande and Zimmer[26] that Jainism and classical forms of Yoga and Sāṃkhya cannot be traced back either as a development of or as a reaction against the Vedic tradition do not mean that the whole karma-saṃsāra-mokṣa world-view associated with these traditions similarly originated outside of the Vedic fold.

However, in the later Hindu tradition, as in Buddhism and Jainism, the heavenly realms where dwell the gods are part of saṃsāra. This does not appear to be the Vedic view. In the Vedas heaven is heaven and is experienced by the immortal gods, who were once mortal, some ancestors, who were also once mortal but are now immortal, and ordinary deceased humans who are in danger of falling away.[27] The Vedas mentioned various ways of gaining immortality and both gods and ancestors had to exert themselves to obtain it. Those who have not exerted themselves in the same way are likely to lose that heavenly state.[28] In the later contemplative tradition, and Miller is at pains to explain that in the Vedas the spiritual practice for the attainment of immortality is essential contemplative, the highest spiritual state is beyond any kind of heavenly existence, thought of course we do witness later challenges to this from various bhakti sects, e.g. the Vaiṣṇavite claim that the supreme state is abiding with Viṣṇu in the Vaikuṇṭha heaven. In the B.A.U. we find evidence of the Vedic world view that those who do not return to further life as the human or animal reside in the world of brahma.[29] That such a view was by and large rejected in favour of a concept of liberation with more in common with Buddhism than the Saṃhitās can be seen from the nature of the accounts of the liberated state in the later Upaniṣads.[30] How do we account for this transformation?

If one views Vedic spirituality in a crudely materialistic way, regarding it as being essentially concerned with this-wordly benefits, plus a blessed existence in heaven after death, both of which are obtained through sactificial ritual, then one is almost compelled, as Pande demonstrates, to see the whole saṃsāra-mokṣa world-view as deriving from non-Vedic and probably indigenous sources. If, on the other hand, one accepts Miller's argument about the presence of an advanced kind of meditative spirituality informing the cosmology of the Vedic tradition, one has to think not in terms of the brahmins trying to squeeze an essentially foreign spirituality into their own inadequate mythical framework and then eventually conceding almost entirely to the new way, but more in terms of two recognisably developed spiritual traditions coming into contact and exchanging insights.

At the present time it is not possible to decide clearly one way or the other. There has been a growing body of evidence and argument presented in favour of the entire yogic picture of things having emerged in non-Vedic circles, see, for example, Reat 1980. Those who argue against such a view, like Miller and Falk, are few and far between. The material upon which they base their interpretations does not self-evidently support them and is highly controversial. What is in their favour is that this material is either highly opaque to scholars or their views on it are often even more unlikely or unintelligible than those of writers such as Miller and Falk. This state of affairs is well illustrated in the various interpretations that have been put forward of Ṛ.V. 1.164.

At the beginning of her introduction to this hymn W.D. O'Flaherty writes, 'This long and complex hymn has inspired many elaborate, detailed glosses and still remains largely obscure. The language, however, is not particularly difficult...'[31] What has been lacking in the interpretation of this hymn is a key to the imagery employed and the obscurity persists largely because the various 'keys' provided by some scholars have been found inadequate by others. As W. Johnson puts it, 'The primary desideratum for an adequate interpretation of the tenor of any parabolic language is to have a complete account of the image vehicle, especially when the image consists of an extended metaphor. Each element in the complex vehicle must be stated, and then accounted for in the reading of the tenor. For this an adequate translation of the vehicle language is required...'[32] Johnson himself does not offer a comprehensive interpretation of the whole hymn but of just three verses, 20-22, though of course he does make some attempt to explain the context in which these verses occur. Following Renou, he argues that the context in which this hymn would have been recited was sadhamāda (a drinking together) where the participants engaged in riddle solving, singing, drinking and staying awake. This, again following Renou, he calls a 'speculative symposium'. At these symposia special verses of an enigmatic nature called 'Brahmans' were used and these can be found in various places throughout the Ṛgveda. The verses in question read as follows :

> 'Two birds, inseparable [or paired] companions, embrace the same tree. One of them eats the sweet fruit; the other looks on without eating.
>
> Here where the birds (priests) in conclave flawlessly laud their portion of immortality,* the mighty herdsman of the whole world, the wise one (Agni), has entered me, the simpleton.
>
> That tree on which the birds that eat the sweet fruit all light and breed- no one eats the sweet fruit at its tip, they say, who does not know the father.'[34]

In surveying the literature on this material Johnson reveals considerable variation in the way exegetes understand this hymn. Thieme, for example, '... argues that the overall tenor of the entire image is the nighttime's sky.'[35] The two birds, in his view, symbolize the waxing and waning moon. For W.N. Brown it is'... a parable dealing with the attainment of immortality',[36] whilst K.N. Dave takes the birds to be golden eagles and golden orioles which, in turn, symbolize those who live on the tree of life and are aware of their dependence on the sun and those who do not know or cannot acknowledge their dependence. The former can enjoy the sweet fruits whilst the latter cannot.

Johnson's own view is that the tree is the contest or speculative symposium frequented by birds (contestants) some of whom are masters or 'fathers' (eaters of the fruit) whilst others are students (just looking on). Like Brown,[37] but unlike the Muṇḍaka Upaniṣad, the Śvetāśvatara Upaniṣad, traditional commentators like Śaṅkara and Sāyaṇa and more recent exegetes such as P.S. Sastri, Johnson argues that in the Ṛgvedic context it is the eater of the fruit rather than the one who looks on that superior. Given this proliferation of views on just one small portion of the hymn it is clear that an authoritative interpretation of the whole, which accords with Johnson's criteria presented above, is still not forthcoming and neither Miller's nor Falk's contributions[39] could be claimed to be sufficiently comprehensive. Given the present state of our

---

* Johnson (p. 249) suggests, following Boyer, that here, as in most Ṛgvedic passages, amṛta is better translated as 'lie' than as 'immortality'.

knowledge a definitive solution to this issue is unlikely to be available in the immediate future. All that can be said when reflecting on this quite general level of explanation is that a serious consideration of the arguments put forward by writers such as Miller and Falk makes one wary of accepting the picture of Indian religious history which has been quite pervasively expounded since the second world war and perhaps most well summed up by Pande and Reat.[40]

Although interpretations of Vedic material such as those offered by writers such as Miller and Falk need to be considerably strengthened before they attract any broad based support I would suggest that an investigation of the prāṇa concept in this literature leads to a conclusion which is supportive of rather than antagonistic to their claims about continuity between Saṃhitā, Brāhmaṇa, Āraṇyaka and Upaniṣad conceptions of the spiritual path. In particular, it can be seen that in pre-Upaniṣadic literature the seers repeatedly identify one principle as the source of all existence, though it is often referred to by different names, one of which is prāṇa. The prāṇa concept was a particularly useful one since, perhaps more than any other term employed to refer to the fundamental reality, it demonstrated the continuity between the cosmos and the individual. For the Vedic thinkers prāṇa was understood as the immortal, essential element in man which is detachable from the body. When outside the body it was thought to be unitary though once inside it was conceived as being diversified. Entering the body by way of the head, it was seen to be distributed throughout (perhaps along definite pathways). In addition it was thought to be the essential factor in the nourishment and vitalization of the body as well as the cause of mentation. As will be demonstrated in the next chapter, all of these notions can be found in the Upaniṣads, which can thus be seen to be more continuous with earlier thought than many writers, e.g. Dasgupta (1922) (1) p. 31, have been prepared to acknowledge.

Prāṇa and the Cosmos

The tendency to look for a unitary principle lying behind the world can be identified in even the earliest portions of the Vedic corpus. In the early Vedic hymns such unification took place primarily at the theological level, various deities being accorded supreme status or declared to be the true identity of all the gods. Hence Ṛ.V. 3.46.2 calls Indra the universal sovereign, whilst 2.27.10

makes Varuṇa sovereign over devas, asuras and mortals. In Ṛ.V. 2.38.9 we are told that not even Indra, not even Varuṇa, nor yet Mitra, Aryaman or Rudra break the high law of Savitṛ, yet 7.87.6 makes Varuṇa the 'controller' of this world. In places, all the gods are said to be manifestations of one god. Hence Ṛ.V. 2.1 makes the following statements about Agni:

> 'Hero of Heroes, Agni thou art Indra, thou art Viṣṇu of the Mighty Stride, adorable:
> Thou, Brahmaṇaspati, the Brahman finding wealth, thou,
> O Sustainer, with thy wisdom tendest us.
>
> Agni, thou art King Varuṇa whose laws stand fast;
> as Mitra, Wonder-Worker, thou must be implored.
> Aryaman, heroes' Lord, art thou, enriching all,
> and liberal Aṃśa in the synod, O thou God.
>
> Thou givest strength, as Tvaṣṭar, to the worshipper:
> thou wielding Mitra's power has kinship with the Dames.
> Thou, urging thy fleet coursers, givest noble steeds:
> a host of heroes art thou with great store of wealth.
>
> Rudra art thou, the Asura of mighty heaven: thou art the Maruts' host, thou art the Lord of food,
> Thou goest with red winds: bliss hast thou in thine home.
> As Pusan thou thyself protectest worshippers.
> Giver of wealth art thou to him who honours thee,
> thou art God Savitar, granter of precious things.
> As Bhaga, Lord of men thou rulest over wealth,
> and guardest in his house him who hath served thee well.'[41]

We even find an occasional reference with an ontological bent, e.g. Ṛ.V. 2.24.11.

> "He is the God spread forth in breadth against the Gods:
> he, Brahmaṇaspati, encompasseth this All.'[42]

In the later books of the Ṛgveda both of these tendencies are much more evident. Hence, in Ṛ.V. 1.164.46 we are told that,

> 'They call it (the One Real) Indra, Mitra, Varuṇa, Agni.
> Then there is the heavenly bird Garutmant (Sun).

The inspired priests speak of the One Real (ekam sat) in many ways.

They call it Agni, Yama, Mātariśvan.'[43]

A similar tendency can be identified in Ṛ.V. 10.90, the puruṣa sūkta, to be discussed below. These tendencies towards the identification of the great gods with each other and the tracing back of all existence to one primal principle is continued in the later Saṃhitā texts and in the Brāhmaṇas and Āraṇyakas. Prominent contenders for the status of primal principle are prāṇa, Vāc, puruṣa, Virāj, Brahman, Agni, Sūrya, Indra and Prajāpati. In a number of places identifications between two or more of these terms are made and, often, less well known terms are declared to be synonymous with one of more of them. That Vāc was, without doubt, understood as a primal principle is made clear by W.N. Brown, whose exegesis of Ṛ.V. 1.164 shows that she is the One Real (ekaṃ sat) who divided herself fourfold, all four parts being known to the immortals but only the fourth, in the form of Vedic deities, being known to mortals.[44] Yet we might also note Miller's argument that Vāc and Agni (including Sūrya) are two poles of the primal principle.

A more wide ranging treatment of this issue has been attempted by Maryla Falk. She suggests that if we take the puruṣa sukta (Ṛ.V. 10.9C c.f. V.S. 31.12) as our starting point, we read, in verse 5, that from puruṣa came Virāj; then from Virāj puruṣa was born. This she takes as indicating a conception of the initial and fundamental reality as androgynous, a conception prefigured in an earlier Ṛgvedic hymn, 3.38 (though neither Griffith's nor Miller's[45] translations bring this out), and in the more or less contemporaneous 1.164.41-2.[46]

In A.V. 8.10.1. Virāj is presented as the first principle of existence and, in Falk's opinion, Virāj is another term for Vāc (the goddess of speech), an identification brought out in Ṛg Veda 10.189.3, though again Griffith's translation does not make it apparent, in A.V.9.2.5. and, later, more explicitly, in Chāndogya Upaniṣad 1.13.2.. Vāc, in turn, is the serpent queen (sarparājñi) in the invocation to the deity in Ṛg Veda 10.189 and the radiant serpent (suruco hvāraḥ) in Atharvaveda 4.1.1, which she identifies with the queen of the ancestors (pitryā rāṣṭri) iṇ verse 2.[47] The queen, it seems, is the brahman mentioned in verse 1. Whitney's version runs as follows :

'The brahman that was first born of old (purastāt; in the east?) Vena hath unclosed from the well-shining edge (sīmatas; horizon?); he enclosed the fundamental nearest shapes (viṣṭhā) of it, the womb (yoni) of the existent and the non-existent.

"Let this queen of the Fathers (?pitrya) go in the beginning (agre) for the first birth (janus; race?), standing in the creation; for it (him?) have I sent (hi) this well-shining sinuous one (?hvāra); let them mix (śrī; boil?) the hot drink for the thirsty one (?dhāsyu).'[48]

If Falk is correct, and there are certainly indications in the above translation that she might be, then, here at least, Vāc and brahman are the same.

In support of this interpretation she cites Ṛgveda 10.114.8, where we read:

Vāc spreadeth forth as far as Prayer (brahma) extendeth.'[49]

We may also note Aitareya Āraṇyaka 1.3.8. which reads,

"As far as brahman extends so far does Vāc, wherever there is is brahman there is Vāc, wherever Vāc, there is brahman, is what is meant.'[50]

The other aspect of the cosmic androgyne is puruṣa, who is the bull in Ṛgveda 3.38. and 'he who abides in the living being' in Ṛgveda 1.164 (this is made clear in A.V. 4.1.2) as well as Indra or Indha in Śatapatha Brāhmaṇa 6.1.1.2 and 7.5.1.7. We are also informed, in Śatapatha Brāhmaṇa 6.2.2.5, that the puruṣa is Agni (who is identified with prāṇa in 10.4.1.23) and Prajāpati (who is identified with prāṇa in 6.3.1.9 and 11.1.6.17) and that Prajāpati created the waters out of Vāc, 'for Vāc belonged to him.' As one quarter of Vāc generates uttered speech so does one quarter of puruṣa generate physical form (rūpa). Rūpa or rūpas are, however, simply modifications of prāṇa.[51] Prāṇa, of course, is Vāyu (Ś.B. 9.1.2.38), āyus (Ś.B. 8.7.3.20) and vāta (Ś.B. 8.7.3.12) and hence the source of all gods and living creatures (Ś.B. 14.2.2.2-11). In some places Vāc and prāṇa are actually described as partners or co-principles (e.g. V.S. 8.37 and Ś.B. 7.5.1.7). We thus have a fundamental dichotomy present in the one supreme source, each side of which becomes diversified when, through creation, one quarter of itself manifests as the world of normal human experience. However, in the primal unity of the androgynous state all form is shapeless prāṇa-puruṣa; all sound is distinctionless Vāc-Virāj.

The equivalences outlined above can be represented in tabular form, masculine terms in one column, feminine terms in the other. We may note that, in general, where masculine and feminine terms appear together in the texts then either one is subordinated to the other (e.g. in Ṛ.V. 1.164 Agni is subordinated to Vāc and in A.V. 11.4 Virāj is subordinated to prāṇa) or they are presented as co-ultimates (e.g.puruṣa-Virāj in Ṛ.V. 10.90 and prāṇa-Vāc in Ś.B. 7.5.1.7). Thus :

TABLE 1

1.	puruṣa (m.)	Virāj (m.f.)
2.	prāṇa (m.)	Vāc (f.)
3.	Agni (m.)	brahman (m.n.)
4.	the bull (m.)	the cow (f.)
5.	Prajāpati (m.)	sarpa rājñi (the serpent queen-R.V. 10.189) (f.)
6.	Indra (m.)	suruco hvāraḥ (the radiant serpent - A.V. 4.1) (f.)
7.	Sūrya (m.)	pitryā rāṣṭri (queen of the ancestors - A.V. 4.2) (f.)

However, two of these terms present problems for a simple masculine-feminine division: the masculine or neuter 'brahman' and the masculine or feminine 'Virāj'. The term 'brahman' has many meanings and certainly arguments could be put forward to suggest that it could equally well be placed in the masculine column. For example, Ś.B. 6.3.1.17 equates prāṇa and brahman and the Śvetāśvatara Upaniṣad equates brahman and puruṣa. However, other early texts, such as Ṛ.V. 10.114.8 and A.Ā. 1.3.8, suggest an equation between Vāc and brahman. Like both puruṣa and Vāc, brahman has four divisions.[52]

At its lowest level brahman manifests, like Vāc but unlike puruṣa, as sound and hence the connection with Vāc seems stronger. In support of this we may note the observation of Bhattacharji[53] that Vāc, as Sarasvatī, is the manasa-kanya (born of the thought) of brahman, which means that she is the 'externalization of a latent characteristic.'

'Virāj' is, perhaps, even more problematic. Monier-Williams regards Virāj in the puruṣa sūkta as masculine though he does acknowledge a feminine usage in A.V. 8.10.24 and 11.8.30 where she is 'regarded as a cow.'[54] This, however, is a gross oversimplification amounting to distortion. At the beginning of 8.10 we read,

> 'Virāj verily was this [universe] in the beginning;
> of her when born everything was afraid, [thinking]
> "this one indeed will become this [universe]." '[55]

Clearly the Virāj referred to in this verse cannot be a cow in any ordinary sense of the term. A.V. 10.10.26 is worth noting in this connection for it informs us that 'the cow', here not connected with Virāj, is immortality, is death, is 'this all.' In other words, it is a symbol for the immortal source of all existence. 8.10.24 reads :

> 'She ascended; she came to men (manuṣya); men called to her : O rich in cheer, come. Of her Manu son of Vivasvant was young, earth [was] vessel; her Pṛthī son of Vena milked; from her he milked both cultivation (kṛṣi) and grain, men subsist; successfully by what is cultivated (kṛṣṭa), one to be subsisted upon, becometh he who knoweth thus.'[56]

When these two verses are considered together it is clear that we have here an instance of the metaphorical usage of the term 'cow' akin to that identified by W.N. Brown in connection with Ṛ.V. 1.164, only here it is Virāj rather than Vāc that is referred to. This use of a common metaphor provides further support for the placement of Virāj in the feminine column. In the context of this hymn the 'milking' of Virāj is the obtaining of certain kinds of knowledge or power from an entity recognised as creatrix.

The other verses of 8.10 support this interpretation for in them Virāj goes to a different group or individual and is 'milked' for a variety of benefits. The asuras 'milked' her for the power of māyā (creative energy, illusion); the fathers 'milked' her for svadhā (what the fathers subsist upon); the seven ṛṣis 'milked' her for brahman and penance; the gandharvas and apsarases 'milked' her for 'sweet odour'; the other folks (itarjana) 'milked' her for concealment and the serpents 'milked' her for poison. In other words, the various classes of beings acquired their characteristic features from Virāj. A.V. 11.8.30 is even less supportive of Monier-Williams' view. Although the meaning of the verse is unclear and there is no reference to Virāj as a cow or even to milking one thing which is certainly implied is that she is the possessor or companion of brahman.

Monier-Williams also points out that even in the Atharva Veda Virāj is identified with prāṇa, a masculine term in our list. With regard to this claim, the context again indicates a tendency towards misrepresentation in Monier-Williams' view. Though he does not provide a reference for this identification it can only be that presented in A.V. 11.4.12. This is a verse in the hymn praising prāna, where prāṇa is presented as the source of all, the controller of all, the foundation of all. It reads,

> 'Breath is Virāj; breath the directress; breath all worship; breath is the sun, the moon; breath they call Prajāpati.'[57]

The intention here is obviously not to suggest that prāṇa and Virāj are synonymous but to present prāṇa as the essence of all, including Virāj. Thus, although the terms 'brahman' and 'Virāj' do not fit into the right hand column quite so neatly as do the other feminine ones they would seem to be more appropriately placed there than in the left hand one, though it may well be the case that they require a separate column. Certainly, some texts subordinate all of these principles to just one of them and hence the usage is variable. 'Brahman' is clearly one such principle. The same could be argued with regard to Vāc who, in Ṛ.V. 1.164, is called the one real (ekaṃ sat) and equally, if not more strongly, in the case of prāṇa.

The classic reference to prāṇa as the ultimate source, ground and controller of all is A.V. 11.4. A.H.Ewing suggests that in this hymn we encounter 'the highest meaning of prāṇa' as the 'primeval cosmic principle.'[58] The particular passages where the primeval status of prāna is most clearly established are:

Vs. 1	'Homage to prāṇa in whose control is this all, who hath been lord of all, in whom all stands firm.'
Vs. 10	'Breath (prāṇa) clothes (anu-vas) human beings (praja), as a father a dear son; breath is lord of all, both what breathes and what does not.'

Vs. 12 'Breath is Virāj, breath is the directress, breath all worship, breath is the sun [sūrya], the moon; breath they call Prajāpati.'

Finally, in verse fifteen, we are told that:

'Breath they call Mātariśvan; breath is called the wind [vāyu]; in breath what has been and what will be, in breath is all established (pratiṣṭhita).'[59]

The first and last verses quoted clearly suggest that the whole of existence subsists in prāṇa and both verse one and verse ten make prāṇa the lord of all creation ('lord of all, both what breathes and what does not'–echoing, perhaps, an early Ṛgvedic verse, 4.53.6, where Savitṛ is said to be 'he who controls the world, what moves not and what moves').[60] We may note that prāṇa is identified, in verse twelve, as the source or true identity of a number of principles from the above table: Prajāpati, Virāj and Sūrya. We may also note Bloomfield's comment that the 'identification of Prāṇa in sts. 21 and 22 with the sun in the form of haṃsa ... is a roundabout way of saying that prāṇa (ātman) is identified with brahma, brahmā.'*

That prāṇa retained such an exhalted status, in the minds of some Vedic teachers at least, is clear from a much later work, the Aitareya Āraṇyaka. This is a complex text, being made up of five individual āraṇyakas. Of these the second and third together constitute what is sometimes called the Mahaitareya or Bahvṛca Upaniṣad. The more well-known Aitareya Upaniṣad constitutes just a small part of this larger work, comprising adhyāyas 4-6 of the second āraṇyaka. In addition, F. Max Müller has picked out adhyāyas 1-3 as constituting a separate Upaniṣad, though he does not provide a traditional name for it.[61] He also argues that the first three adhyāyas of the Āraṇyaka were probably composed by the same hand as that responsible for the Aitareya Brāhmaṇa, though Keith, whilst agreeing with Müller's general conclusions, points out that in Sāyaṇa's time the whole of āraṇyakas 1-3 were regarded as being the work of the compiler of the Brāhmaṇa. Müller regards the last two āraṇyakas as being the work of a different author or authors, who would be, according to Sāyaṇa, Śaunaka and Āśvalāyana.[62] These divisions can be represented schematically as follows:

TABLE 2
5 Component Āranyakas

<table>
<tr><td>1.</td><td>Deals with the Mahāvrata rite.</td><td></td></tr>
<tr><td>2.</td><td>Adhyāyas 1-3. Deals with the uktha.
Adhyāyas 4-6 = Aitareya Upaniṣad.</td><td rowspan="2">Mahaitareya
or Bahvṛca
Upaniṣad</td></tr>
<tr><td>3.</td><td>Deals with symbolic interpretations
of terms from the Ṛgveda Saṃhitā.</td></tr>
<tr><td>4.</td><td>(Śaunaka).</td><td></td></tr>
<tr><td>5.</td><td>(Āśvalāyana).</td><td></td></tr>
</table>

The material dealing with prāṇa comes almost entirely from āraṇyaka 2 adhyāyas 1-3. Keith claims that this section should be regarded as independent since it is not really connected with the first āraṇyaka and is later than it, though earlier than the Aitareya Upaniṣad proper (āraṇyaka 2 adhyāyas 4-6). Nevertheless, it is likely that with the text 2.1-3 we arrive at the beginning of the Upaniṣadic period.

To understand the views about prāṇa that are held by the author of this text one needs to begin with the story of the faculties trying to determine which of them is the hymn (uktha - the high chant of the Ṛgveda), this being employed as a synonym for the supreme principle (2.1.4). Speech, sight, hearing and mind all quit the body but it only falls when the prāṇa departs. Similarly, each in turn returns to the body but only on the return of prāṇa is it re-animated. At this demonstration of the prāṇa's supremacy the other faculties proclaim that:

> '... breath only is the hymn. Let men know that breath is the hymn. The gods said to breath, "Thou art the hymn, thou art all this, we are thine, thou art ours." '[63]

The identity of prāṇa and uktha can then, presumably, be read back into 2.1.2, where it is said that all existence springs from the uktha.[64] Certainly, the verses following 2.1.4 simply reiterate this view in a variety of ways, a reiteration that is continued throughout adhyāyas 2 and 3. 2.1.5 commences with the statement that, 'The gods carried him forward.'[65] The most logical identity of 'him' is the prāṇa-who-is-the-uktha and this is confirmed by Sāyaṇa, the only traditional commentator to comment on the entire

Āraṇyaka.[66] Also, in 2.1.5 there is a distinction made between prāṇa and apāna and each is placed on a level with other faculties (speech, etc.). So we read :

> 'Day is breathing forth (prāṇa), night is breathing down (apāna). Speech is fire, sight yonder sun, mind the moon, hearing the quarters...'[67] Then we are told that :
>
> '... this is the union of those sent forth.'[68]

'Those sent forth' are obviously the faculties, speech etc., which are regarded as the forms of deities residing in the body. 'This', as Keith points out,[69] is obscure but a reasonable interpretation, given the context, would be that it is the prāṇa-which-is-the uktha. Prāṇa and apāna would then simply be derivatives of this in the same way that speech etc. are.

In 2.1.6 we are again reminded of the ultimate nature of prāṇa when we are told that :

> '... all of this is covered by prāṇa. This ether is supported by prāṇa ...'[70]

Such a power is obviously a creative force and the remainder of this adhyāya and the whole of the next are devoted to establishing a link between, if not the identity of, prāṇa, the cosmic puruṣa and Prajāpati. The powers of prāṇa (which is called 'this person' in 2.1.7 and 'he who shines' in 2.2.11) are that he creates earth, fire, sky, heaven, the sun, the quarters, the moon, the waters and Varuṇa (lord of the moral order (ṛta) and the deep water). Furthermore, he is,

> 'all these verses, all these Vedas, all sounds (ghoṣa)...'[71]

a list which, presumably includes the thirty-six syllabled bṛhati metre, which is 'the whole self.'[72] Finally, we may note that in 2.2.3 Indra tells Viśvamitra that he is prāṇa, Viśvamitra is Prāṇa and all creatures are prāṇa.

We can thus conclude that in this part of the Aitareya Āraṇyaka, the only part dealing at all comprehensively with the topic of prāṇa, the vital force is considered to be the source of all and the ground or being of all.

Prāṇa and the Individual

In A.Ā. 2.1.8 we are informed that it is knowledge of prāṇa, of how it functions and how it exists in the human body, 'the hiding place of brahman', that brings immortality. Why this should be so can be inferred from a study of the Śatapatha Brāhmaṇa. In 1.4.3.8 there is a reference to the 'antasthā prāṇa' (the middle or central prāṇa) which Ewing regards as synonymous with the 'madhyama prāṇa' of the Upaniṣads.[73] He also suggests that here the clear intention of the verse is to present prāṇa as 'the controlling influence', the 'Inner Ruler' which is 'an active, conscious, even Divine Force which dominates the entire organism.'[74] Eggeling translates thus '... what central breath [antasthā prāṇa] there is (in the body) ... that one indeed is the internal motive force of the breathings ... And whosoever knows that internal motive force of the breathings, him they regard as the internal motive force.'[75] If Ewing is correct then we have here a concept which is almost identical to the Upaniṣadic antaryāmin (inner controller). The Śatapatha Brāhmaṇa also equates prāṇa with the immortal element in man (Ś.B. 2.2.2.8–15; 10.2.6.18)[76] and states that the prāṇas, which are 'the highest thing of all this universe' (8.7.4.21), are immortality (9.1.2.32). Mythically, this is presented in terms of the division of Prajāpati in Ś.B.10.1.4.1:

> 'Now at the beginning, Prajāpati was (composed of) both these, the mortal and the immortal–his vital airs alone were immortal, his body mortal...'

Such a division is also reflected in the human being; hence Ś.B. 6.7.1.11 informs us that,

> '... that part of the vital air which is immortal is above the navel and streams out by upward breathing; but that which is mortal passes by and away from the navel...'

A crucial part of this knowledge of prāṇa is, as was noted above in connection with the Aitareya Āraṇyaka, that it exists in two principal modes, a unitary one, when it is the foundation of all existence and the inner controller of the individual, and a diversified one, when it is the various cosmic forces and the breaths and faculties which exist in the body. Hence, 8.7.3.21 informs us that,

> '... this vital air [prāṇa] whilst being one only, extends over all the limbs, over the whole body.'[77]

and 11.1.2.3 explains that,

> '... this sacrifice is the blowing (wind) [vāyu = prāṇa]: he blows, as it were, as a single one, but when he has entered into man he is divided into ten parts.'[78]

Most statements about the number of prāṇas in the Ś.B. suggest that there are ten of them. However, some texts increase the number by varying amounts; hence we find references to eleven (8.4.3.8; 11.2.1.2), twelve (12.3.2.2.) and thirteen (3.8.4.1).

The unified prāṇa enters the body by way of the head[79] and then spreads throughout, infusing every limb.[80] In so doing it nourishes and vitalizes the body.[81] Those parts not reached by the prāṇa dry up and wither away.[82] The distribution of prāṇa appears to be effected by means of definite pathways, though the text is not clear on this. Ś.B. 7.2.2.18 tells us that,

> These vital airs (move) in lines (channels).'[83]

This is endorsed by 8.1.3.10, which informs us that the sacrificer,

> '... lays them [the alter bricks] both lengthwise and crosswise, whence there are here in the body (channels of) vital airs both lengthwise and crosswise. He lays them down touching each other : he thereby makes these vital airs continuous and connects them; whence the (channels of the) vital airs are continuous and connected.'[84]

The 'channels' interpretation is also supported by 8.3.4.1:

> '... these (channels of the, or, bricks representing the) vital airs are separated from each other by the width of a horse-hair (vāla).'[85]

Since 8.1.3.10. says that the bricks are all laid touching each other they cannot be a horse-hair width apart and it would only make sense to say this if, as Eggeling infers,the prāṇas are distributed along definite pathways. Two further references could be employed in support of this view : 10.3.5.5,

> 'And this course (guh) is space–this space which is inside the body–for along this space it (the breath) courses...'[86]

and 10.2.1.6 where there appears to be a reference to a prāṇa moving by a nāḍī from the body to the wing of the altar bird. This reference is, however, ambiguous since prāṇa is not directly mentioned. Eggeling translates it as follows:

> 'On that bending limb he places one brick: he thereby gives to it (the altar bird) that single tube (tubular organ - nāḍī) which joins onto (the body) from the bending limb of the flying bird.'[87]

In the notes he writes, following Sāyaṇa, 'The brick is apparently meant to represent symbolically the bone of the upper segment, or some tubular organ by which the vital air is supposed to enter the wing from the body.'[88]

The vitalization of the body appears to be the result of the activities of the five prāṇas: prāṇa, apāna, vyana, udāna and samāna. However, as was noted in connection with the Aitareya Āraṇyaka, the one prāṇa also manifests as the different sensory faculties. There are various lists of these in the Ś.B. The 'prāṇas in the head' or 'the prāṇas of Prajāpati' (7.5.2.6, 9.2.2.5 and 9.3.3.8) are mind (manas), eye (cakṣus), breath (prāṇa), ear (śrotra) and voice (vāc). The eyes, ears, nostrils and mouth are the seven prāṇas mentioned in 7.5.2.8-12 and the same list, with speech substituted for mouth, is found in 9.3.1.10-12. Hence, when prāṇa diversifies in the body it manifests as both vital forces (the five prāṇas) and perceptual faculties.

This is not all, for, as we might expect from the inclusion of manas among the list of prāṇas, prāṇa is also the source, if not the substance of mentation. Thus,

> '... Savitṛ is the mind and the thoughts are the vital airs....'[89]

and

> '... the divine inspirers doubtless are the vital airs, for these inspire all thoughts...'[90]

A similar sentiment is found in A.Ā 2.3.5, where we are told that,

> '... the self that is speech is imperfect, since a man understands if driven to thought by breath (prāṇa), not if driven by speech.'[91]

This connection between mind/thoughts and prāṇa is a consistent feature of the orthodox world view in much subsequent literature; C.U. 6.8.2, for example, affirms the mind's dependence on prāṇa whilst a much later yogic text, the Haṭhayogapradīpikā, declares the breath (samirana i.e. prāṇa) to be one of the two causes of mental activity, the other being vāsanā (memory deposits) (H.Y.P.4.22). Hence, Reat's claim (1980 p. 130) that 'the universe lives, but apparently is not conscious' cannot be applied to the entire pre-Upaniṣadic Vedic tradition.

In fact, it would be more correct to regard the pre-Upaniṣadic view as being that consciousness is but one manifestation or expression of vitality. Admittedly, Reat's observations are based on the Ṛgveda alone since he regards all later Vedic material as being subject to the influence of his postulated indigenous yogic tradition. Whilst this may be true it also seems reasonable to assume an internally motivated development of the religion given the considerable changes in time and circumstance that occurred between the composition of the Ṛgveda, and, say, the Aitareya Āraṇyaka. What has been attempted in this chapter is a demonstration that the elaboration of the prāṇa concept, which could hardly be described as prominent in the Buddhist and Jain traditions, within mainstream brahmanism took that tradition much closer to the world-view of the Upaniṣads than many writers have been prepared to concede.

If we take all the abovementioned material together a fairly clear picture of the brahmanical concept of prāṇa begins to emerge. The supreme prāṇa is the self-existent source of everything; it is thus the ground or being of ephemeral mortal forms. It is locked or hidden in the body and is its inner controller. It is diversified as prāṇa, apāna etc., the perceptual faculties and, possibly, thoughts. One who knows this, who knows the deity, knows the supreme prāṇa, knows the immortal (which is, in fact, the true essence of a person) and attains immortality. Thus, we have here, in outline, the same salvific scheme that dominates the Upaniṣads, but with the difference that whilst the Upaniṣads make ātman the primary concept and prāṇa a secondary one, here the reverse is the case.

Prāṇa and Ātman

Scholars are divided in their opinions about the intentions of the pre-Upaniṣadic authors when they employ the term 'ātman'. Some, like H.G. Narahari, regard pre-Upaniṣadic uses to be essentially the same as Upaniṣadic ones. Others, such as, A.H. Ewing, think they are quite different. What I shall seek to demonstrate in this section is that whilst there are a few examples of Upaniṣad-like usage of the term 'ātman' in pre-Upanisadic literature, this is by no means the norm. In fact, this literature provides examples of a variety of meanings for 'ātman', ranging from 'body' through 'breath' and 'self' to 'Self', all of which are legitimate in different contexts. By and large, however, I find myself more in agreement with Ewing than with Narahari, whose general thesis I will attempt to refute.

In his doctoral thesis, *Ātman in Pre-upaniṣadic Vedic Literature,* Narahari's main aim is to demonstrate that there is a considerable body of evidence to indicate that in pre-Upaniṣadic literature, particularly the Ṛgveda, the adherents of brāhmanical religion had the conception of an immortal factor in man that is analogous to the Upaniṣadic concept of ātman. Such a conception, he argues, is directly or indirectly implied by the following terms in many of their occurrences: brahman, satya, ātman (and its shortened form tman), ajo bhāga, jīva, prāṇa, manas, suparṇa and asu. In particular, he seeks to demonstrate that this Vedic concept shares with the Upaniṣadic conception of ātman the characteristics of being 'the essence of the body... the "controller" [and] the source of happiness.'[92]

Narahari's procedure is to take each of the words in turn, indicate where they occur in the Ṛgveda and demonstrate that, in some instances at least, they are used in a way which, if not fully Upaniṣadic, is a genuine prefigurement of Upaniṣadic usage. An examination of this material reveals that whilst he has a case it is much less clearly demonstrated than he seems to think. One of the significant weaknesses is that his interpretation of the meaning of some of these key terms is taken from Sāyaṇa (14th century C.E.) who, even if attempting to be faithful to the original intention of the authors, must have been influenced by the Mīmāṃsā and Vedānta traditions of exegesis which preceded him. Hence, following Sāyaṇa's line of interpretation needs to be justified by more than an appeal to his authority. Consequently, whilst reference to Sāyaṇa's interpretation may yield fruitful results if it is taken as offering a possible line of enquiry, the fact that such an authority holds a particular view tells us little, in itself, about the meaning in the original context. Narahari's interpretation must therefore be supported by more than agreement with Sāyaṇa's view if it is to be persuasive. A further weakness in his interpretation is that he tends to regard any reference to an immortal essence in the human as indicating the presence of an Upaniṣad-like conception of ātman which, of course, is much too simplistic since the Vedic notion of ancestors living in heaven could also easily accommodate such a conception.

He divides the abovementioned terms into two types : those only implying an Upaniṣad-like conception and those referring directly to one. In the case of terms which Narahari regards as only implying the Upaniṣadic conception of ātman his interpretation of one, 'satya', rests solely on Sāyaṇa's authority whereas in the case of the other two, 'ajo bhāga' and 'suparṇa', additional argumentation is provided. With regard to 'satya' he points out that the term is mentioned fifty one times in the Ṛgveda and 'is once understood by Sāyaṇa to mean "Brahman, the true".'[93] This instance is found in Ṛg Veda 10.85.1. In Narahari's view, 'The word does not mean anything 'subtle'. But the context suggests the recognition of some 'subtle force' in the universe. This view appears to have been accepted by the Upaniṣadic seers when they speak of Brahman, the Supreme Principle, as being composed of 'Sat''.[94] However, the interpretations of Griffith and O'Flaherty both undermine such a view. Griffith's version reads :

> 'Truth [satya] is the base that bears the earth; by Sūrya are the heavens sustained. By law [kṛtena] the Ādityas stand secure and Soma holds his place in heaven.'[95]

O'Flaherty's translation is very similar:

> 'The earth is propped up by truth [satya]; the sky is propped up by the sun. Through the law the Ādityas stand firm and Soma is placed in the sky.'[96]

In both cases abstract principles, the truth and the law, are seen to have what might be regarded as a cosmic function and there is little to convince the reader that a meaning analogous to that given to 'brahman' in the Upaniṣads is intended.

The other two terms are more plausible candidates. When alone 'aja' can mean either 'goat' or 'unborn' though, according to Narahari, when found in the compound 'aja ekapad' it always means 'unborn'.[97] This is in conflict with Keith's view that 'goat' is the proper sense of 'aja'[98] but does have some support from Bergaigne, Grassman, Roth and Bohtlingk[99] and, with qualifications, Muir.[100] Yāska, in the Nirukta, also consistently interprets 'aja' as 'unborn'. Both Griffith and O'Flaherty are in agreement with Keith when they translate 'ajo bhāga' in Ṛg Veda 10.16.4 as 'thy portion is the goat' and 'the goat is your share' respectively. O'Flaherty, seemingly following Griffith, comments that making the goat Agni's share of the funeral rites 'refers to the practice of placing the limbs of a scapegoat over the dead man, so that Agni would consume them and not the corpse with his violent flames.[101] In his detailed comments on the disposal of the dead in Vedic India, Keith claims that the Ṛgveda, 'expressly refers to the burning of a goat which is the share of Agni and to the use of the flesh of a cow to protect the body against flame.'[102] His support for this is Ṛ.V. 10.16.4 and 7. Verse four, as we have noted, refers to 'ajo bhāga'; verse seven refers to a cow which, according to O'Flaherty, 'would be used in addition to or in place of the scapegoat.'[103] Keith goes on to state that the ritual texts give details about how the flesh of the cow is to be used. For some reason which he does not mention they omit to provide details of how the goat (?) is to be used. Such an omission is strange if the goat is the creature primarily used for such rituals. What seems to be happening here is that modern interpreters are understanding the term 'ajo bhāga' by associating it with the cow used in funery rites and then attaching what is said about the cow to 'ajo bhāga', a move which is only possible if one starts with assumption that this term means 'the goat part'. In the absence of such an assumption the 'scapegoat' interpretation of 'ajo bhāga' has little real foundation. In fact, given the uncertainty surrounding the terms 'aja' and 'ajo' bhāga the implication seems to be that in this particular instance–the only occurrence of 'ajo bhāga' in the Ṛgveda– something other than 'goat' is meant. The only other serious contender is 'unborn' which Narahari, in line with a number of other scholars and following Yāska and Sāyaṇa, suggests as the most accurate interpretation.

Even if we follow Narahari, however, the conception of 'self' along the lines of an Upaniṣadic ātman is far from being demonstrated as present in this hymn. The presence of an immortal element in man does not necessarily imply the existence of a self concept of the kind we find in the Upaniṣads since it is quite compatible, as was noted above, with the notion of continued existence in a heavenly realm as an ancestor (pitṛ). In fact, the Śatapatha Brāhmaṇa makes it clear in 10.4.3.9 that man only experiences immortality once the body has been shed at death. Only at this point can man take advantage of the immortality which is established in his innermost soul and which makes him like the gods.[104] Hence, though interesting and suggestive, the presence in the Ṛgveda of a term meaning 'unborn' or 'unborn part' or 'immortal element' does not allow the assumption that the Vedic thinkers had a conception of an essential part of man that approximated to the conception of ātman that we find in the Upaniṣads for that ātman is much more than an immortal essence, it is also the source of the world as well as of the individual vital and perceptual faculties.

Though appearing thirty five times in the Ṛgveda+ [105] the term 'suparṇa' is only once taken by Narahari to have a meaning analogous to the Upaniṣadic conception of ātman. On this occasion he again follows Sāyaṇa who, when commenting on Ṛ.V. 1.164.20 (a hymn which most scholars seem to regard as difficult to interpret), thinks 'suparṇa' is to be understood as an allegorical reference to the jīvātman. Nevertheless, despite its singularity, this passage constitutes an important component of Narahari's argument. The verse is most well known from the Śvetāśvatara Upaniṣad (4.6) and the Muṇḍaka Upaniṣad (3.1). O'Flaherty translates it as follows :

> 'Two birds, friends joined together, clutch the same tree. One of them eats the sweet fruit; the other looks on without eating.'[106]

In the Upaniṣadic context these birds have generally been taken to refer to the jīvātman and the paramātman and hence it is difficult to discount Narahari's view that the same interpretation should apply here and that, '... The Ṛgvedic seers were also aware of the fact that the individual soul reaps the benefit of its Karma, while the Supreme Soul is under no such compulsion.'[107] All one can really say in response to such a view is that since this interpretation puts the passage quite firmly in a thought world that appears to be generally at variance with what is usually taken to be the predominant Vedic view : individuals continuing existence as ancestors after death, it must be treated with caution. Furthermore, there is a significant body of scholarly opinion behind the view that the Upaniṣadic presentation actually inverts the relationship between the two birds that is required by the Ṛgvedic context (see above pp. 8-10 where some interpretations of Ṛ.V. 1.164 are discussed).

In sum, it seems reasonable to conclude that these terms which, according to Narahari, imply rather than directly refer to the

Upaniṣadic conception of ātman do appear to indicate a notion about the essential and immortal part of a person which, in some respects, is a move away from the traditional Vedic views of the ancestors (pitṛs) for although the pictures are similar in many respects the immortal element identified by Narahari seems to be impersonal, the same in all people, rather than characterised by individual personality features as is the case with the ancestor concept, based as it is on the continuity of an individual tanū accompanied by āyus and asu. If we add to this the fact that, in their descriptions of the relations between the individual and supreme selves, two Upaniṣads quote a Ṛgvedic verse to illustrate their teachings it suggest that in some Vedic circles at least there was a move to understand the human condition in a way that was developed in more detail during the Upaniṣadic period. More cannot be claimed unless the material which is taken to refer directly to Upaniṣadic conceptions of ātman can be demonstrated to do so.

The Vedic terms identified by Narahari as referring directly to an ātman-like concept similar to that found in the Upaniṣads are asu, jīva, manas, prāṇa, brahman and ātman. With regard to 'asu' he does little more than establish its meaning as 'life' or 'breath' which is separable from the physical body. Hence his claim that, 'it is but a step from such ideas to the Brahman in the Upaniṣads who is claimed to be the Pantheistic Absolute without a second'[108] can carry little weight since such notions can fit quite easily into the brahmanical cosmology where the ancestors exist in heaven and come down to earth in order to feast on the sacrifices offered by their descendants.[109] Again, though, where his observation does have some force is that the 'asu' concept, because of its generalizability, can be seen to be consistent with the Upaniṣadic teachings in a way that the notion of individual ancestors is not.

The term 'jīva' occurs twenty three times in the Ṛgveda, two of which, according to Sāyaṇa, mean 'individual soul'. These are 1.113.16 and 1.164.30. The first, part of a hymn to the dawn, reads as follows :

> 'Arise the breath [jīva], the life, again hath reached us : darkness hath passed away and light approacheth. She for the Sun hath left a path to travel : we have arrived where men prolong existence.'[110]

Here Griffith has translated 'jīva' as 'breath', and, given the context, a rendering of 'individual soul' would seem less plausible. Certainly Narahari's claim that here jīva must mean 'the "active and animating principle" of the individual in whose body it resides... [which is] ... nothing short of the Upaniṣadic idea that the Ātman is the inciter of the body into action'[111] would seem to be untenable. The second verse is :

> 'Life that breathes now lies still and yet moves fast, rushing but firmly fixed in the midst of the resting places. The life of the dead one wanders as his nature wills. The immortal comes from the same womb as the mortal.'[112]

Substituting 'individual soul' for 'life' here is more plausible but this is a hymn which, as has been noted, is extremely difficult to interpret with any degree of assurance. Even if 'individual soul' were allowed this would still not constitute a demonstration that the Ṛgvedic seers were operating with an Upaniṣadic-like concept of ātman.

The term 'manas', usually translated as 'mind' but also serving to indicate the intellect, occurs over two hundred times in the Ṛgveda.[113] Narahari, however, makes little of it. He offers no analysis of the passages where the term is employed and simply states that, 'It is possible that the Upaniṣadic seers, who speak of ātman as being "knowledge" (cit) in essence, must have been inspired to do so by the attitude of the Ṛgvedic seers who often take means in the sense of buddhi or prajñā.'[114] This is little more than wishful thinking. The later literature of the Vedānta, Sāṃkhya and Buddhist schools is almost unanimous in employing 'manas' as a term for the mental sense, the co-ordinator of the other five senses. Its similarity with ātman is also denied by Keith who, whilst acknowledging that manas 'never loses a place in the thought of India'[115] argues that it never achieves the rank of the ātman.[116] In fact, Keith points out that manas has always had a more specific meaning than ātman, even in the Ṛgveda where it is understood as, 'the means of knowledge of all internal events and a necessary link in the knowledge of external events en route from the senses,'[117] and he quotes Ṛ.V. 10.58 in support of this view. It seems, therefore, and this perhaps indicates a general flaw in Narahari's procedure, that 'manas' has been brought in to multiply the examples of instances where Ṛgvedic composers refer to some kind of consciousness principle in the hope that the main argument would be strengthened thereby. The actual effect, however, is simply to alert the reader to the looseness of the argumentation in general.

'Prāṇa', as we have noted above, is a term which had, in pre-Upaniṣadic times, connotations similar to those of the Upaniṣadic ātman. Narahari's treatment adds nothing to our understanding of this term. He puts more emphasis on the use of the terms 'brahman' and 'ātman'.

In summarizing his investigations of these two terms Narahari writes, 'Summing up then the views advanced above by scholars, both Indian and European, we have the following meanings of the words "Brahman" and "Ātman": the former in the masculine may mean the "brahmin singer", or "great", or "prayer", or "creator", or "Bṛhaspati", or the "Brahma priest"; it is also used sometimes to denote any "sacrificial priest" in general, or "Angirases or Maruts"; in the neuter, the word means "prayer", or "food" or "Rudra". According to some European scholars who attempt to derive "Brahman" etymologically, it means also the "latent electric power stirred up by such apparatus as sacred vessels, hymns, etc." or "fire", (internal in man or cosmic), or "speech or word". Ātman means "essence", or "body", or "intelligent principle", or "controller", or "one-self" or "breath", or "blissful", or "strength", or "multiplicity", or "offspring", or "years"; according to the majority of European scholars "breath" is the first meaning of "Ātman".'[118] However, his comments on the various uses of these two terms, which are undoubtedly employed frequently in the Upaniṣads, yield less that one might expect. He claims[119] that the Ṛgvedic seers were familiar with 'cit' and 'ānanda' as characteristics of brahman, but he provides no references. The case with regard to 'ātman' is better, though once again, exaggerated. His principal claims are that some Ṛgvedic passages suggest 'ātman' to have the characteristic of blissfulness, to be the 'essence' of the body and to be its inner controller.

With regard to 'blissfulness' he writes, 'In Ṛ.V. 1.73.2d, the seer exhorts that Agni is to be cherished for, like Soul, he is the source of happiness (ātmeva śevo didhiṣāyyo bhūt). We have here the later Upaniṣadic idea that 'blissfulness' (niratiśay-ānandasvarūpatva) is the nature of Ātman.'[120] However, his interpretation is not shared by either Griffith or Oldenberg whose translations give little support for such a view.[121] In fact, 'breath' would be an equally tenable rendering in this context.

In considering the 'essential' nature of ātman and its role as controller of the body Narahari points out that '... eight times at least the word Ātman denotes in the Ṛgveda that which is the essence (sarabhūtah or svarūpabhūtah), and is used once (7.87.2) to denote the "controller" (dhāraṇayitā). In this latter verse, the seer addressing Varuṇa says "Ātman te vātah", and Sāyaṇa interprets the line by saying that Wind (vāta) as directed by Varuṇa is the controller (Ātma) of all beings.'[122] The first point to make here is that if Sāyaṇa argues that vāta is the ātma of all beings he is more likely to be claiming that vāta is the Self or Essence of beings than their 'controller'. Furthermore, in 7.87.2 the notion of Varuṇa's breath being the controller of all is, at the most, only implicit. Griffith's version reads :

> 'The wind, thy breath, hath sounded through the region like a wild beast that seeks his food in pastures. Within these two, Exalted Earth and Heaven, O Varuṇa, are all the forms thou lovest.'[123]

Secondly, Narahari's claim that ātman means 'essence' at least eight times in the Ṛgveda goes against his earlier statement [124] that ātman denotes 'essence' only once: Ṛ.V. 10.92.13. Since the other seven references are not provided this stands as the only example of such usage. It reads :

> 'Dear to all gods, may Pūṣan guard the ways we go, the waters' child* and Vāyu help us to success. Sing lauds for your great bliss to Wind, the breath of all: ye Aśvins prompt to hear, hear this upon your way.'[125]

Such a state of affairs hardly inspires confidence in the reader and unless a more watertight case can be presented Narahari's interpretation of this material must be regarded as rather tenuous.

Overall, then, Narahari's case must be considered to be a weak one. In fact, scrutiny of his references would, on the whole, tend to support Ewing's view rather than his own, though there are one or two which do indicate Upaniṣadic-like conceptions. Thus, whilst a number of pre-Upaniṣadic terms may have meanings which are

* i.e. Agni, born as lightning from the storm clouds.

later incorporated into the ātman concept of the Upaniṣads none of them, except, perhaps, 'prāṇa', can be regarded as being anything like equivalent of it.

A.H.Ewing is reluctant to take any pre-Upaniṣadic references to ātman or to any other term as indicating anything like the Upaniṣadic concept of 'Self'. With regard to the Ṛgveda, he argues that '... the word "ātman" is to be translated by "breath" oftener than by any other single word ...'[126] and he cites a number of examples, including the following, to support his case :

Ṛ.V. 1.73.2–a hymn to Agni

'He who like Savitar the God, true minded, protecteth with his power all acts of vigour,

Truthful, like splendour, glorified by many, like breath [ātman] joy-giving, all must strive to win him.'[127]

Ṛ.V. 1.162.20–a hymn to the sacrificial horse

'Let not they dear soul [ātman] burn thee as thou comest, let not the hatchet linger in thy body.'[128]

Ṛ.V. 7.101.6–a hymn to Prajanya

'He is the bull of all, and their impregner : he holds the life [ātman] of all things fixed and moving.'[129]

Ṛ.V.8.3.24–a hymn to Indra

'Rainment is body, food is life [ātman], and healing ointment giveth strength.'[130]

Ṛ.V.10.16.3–a hymn to Agni at the time of a funeral

It is said to deceased :

'The sun receive thine eye, the wind [vāta] thy spirit [ātman]; go as thy merit, to earth or heaven.'[131]

Despite Griffith's varied translations of 'ātman' in these verses all can be seen to illustrate Ewing's point quite well. Reat (1980) refers to other hymns which echo the usage illustrated above :

Ṛ.V. 7.87.2 - a hymn to Varuṇa

'The wind [vāta] thy breath [ātman], hath sounded through the region like a wild beast that seeks his food in pastures.'[132]

Ṛ.V. 10.92.13 - a hymn to all the gods

> 'Dear to all gods, may Pūṣan guard the ways we go, the waters' child [Agni] and Vāyu help us to success. Sing lauds for your great bliss to wind [vāta] the breath of all [ātman]: ye Aśvins prompt to hear, hear this upon your way.'[133]

We may note that in these verses and in Ṛ.V. 10.16.3 (quoted above) there is a close link if not identity between ātman and vāta. Elsewhere we are told that Vāyu is the ātman of the gods.

> Ṛ.V.10.168.4–a hymn to Vāyu
>
> 'Germ of the world, the Deities' vital spirit [ātman], this God moves ever as his will inclines him.'[134]

Reat also draws attention to verses where other vitalistic terms are linked or identified, e.g.

> Ṛ.V.1.66.1–a hymn to Agni, who is said to be,
>
> 'Like the sun's glance, like wealth of varied sort, like breath [prāṇa] which is life [āyus], like one's own son.'[135]

He also points out that in the Ṛ.V. 'ātman', its shortened form 'tman' and 'tanū' are all used in a similar fashion as reflexive pronouns.[136] Ewing too, notes this similarity and refers to Bloomfield's work which 'shows that the instrumentals of "tanū" and "tman" are used synonymously– thus establishing the position that "ātman" has become "tman" by adapting itself to "tanū".'[137] 'Tanū', as Reat points out, is, for the Ṛgvedic thinkers, the core of individuality in both this life and the next, appropriating certain vital energies such as āyus (life/life force)[138] and asu (vitality) at death whilst other energies, like ātman, return to the wind or the universe at large. He concludes, therefore, that '... in the Ṛg Veda, the ātman is merely one of several vital faculties, standing on more or less equal footing with the others.'[139]

There does, however, seem to be a distinction between those vital forces which have a primarily universal location, such at ātman, vata and Vāyu and those, such as tanū, āyu and asu, which are more specifically associated with an individual. This division is, however, in conflict with Reat's claim that āyu, asu and ātman all have universal connotations.[140] Given the close connection between these terms and tanū and accepting Reat's own demonstration that tanū is the core of individuality in this life and the next and that it takes āyu and asu with it to the world of the ancestors it is nevertheless clear that in the Ṛ.V. at least all these words possess an individual dimension not shared by terms such as vāyu and vāta. However, it could be argued that ātman is an 'odd man out' here, for since it has close connections with vāta as well as with tanū it can be regarded as a kind of bridging term, combining both universal and particular dimensions. The same could be argued in the case of prāṇa which, by its identification with Vāyu in Ṛ.V. 10.90.13 and with ayus in Ṛ.V. 1.6.6.1, also links the universal dimension with the individual one.

Such ambiguities in the usage of 'ātman' can be seen to have persisted throughout the pre-Upaniṣadic period for in texts such as the Śatapatha Brāhmaṇa a frequent meaning of ātman is 'body'. Hence we read in Ś.B. 4.1.2.25,

> 'The sacrifice is fashioned like a bird: the Upāṃsu and Antaryāma (grahas) are its wings, and the Upamsusavana (stone) is its body [ātman].'[141]

Ś.B.4.2.2.5 requires a similar translation :

> 'And if the King (Soma) becomes exhausted, they extend him from out of that (bowl), make him issue therefrom; for the Āgrayaṇa is the body [ātman], and from the body [ātman] all these limbs issue.'[142]

There are also a number of instances where the reflexive use of ātman and its meaning of 'body' are difficult to separate, e.g. Ś.B. 4.2.2.1, 4.2.5.3, 4.4.1.5, 4.4.2.6 and 9.1.2.38. Hence, Eggeling uses the devices of 'body (self)' and 'self (body)' in his translations. In Ewing's view, the best way of dealing with this ambiguity is to translate 'ātman' in these contexts as 'animated organism' or simply 'organism',[143] a rendering which he regards as usefully combining the reflexive pronominal use and that of 'body'.

Despite these examples of what might be called a physicalist interpretation of 'ātman' it would be incorrect to think that other, more abstract uses were not being developed in post-Ṛgvedic texts. For example, in A.V. 10.8.43–44 we read,

> 'The lotus-flower of nine doors, covered with three strands (guṇa)–what soulful [ātmanvant] prodigy (yakṣa) is within it, that the brahman-knowers know.
>
> Free from desire [akāma], wise (dhira), immortal [amṛta], self-existent [svayambhū], satisfied with sap, not deficient in

any respect–knowing that wise, unaging young soul [ātman], one is not afraid of death.'[144]

Here we find an almost Vedāntic use of the term 'ātman' as Self. A similar meaning can be found in Ś.B. 10.6.3.2 :

'Let him meditate on the self [ātman], which is made up of intelligence [vijñāna] and endowed with a body of spirit ... which holds sway over all the regions and pervades this whole universe, which is speechless and indifferent ... it is greater than the sky, greater than the earth, greater than all existing things–that self of the spirit (breath) is myself: on passing away from hence I shall obtain that self.'[145]

Keith brings out a related meaning by reference to the adjective 'ātmanvant' which he translates as 'possessing existence'. Examples of such usage are found in A.V. 10.2.32 and 11.2.10. They read as follows :

'In that golden vessel, three spoked, having three supports–what soul possessing [ātmanvant] monster (yakṣa) there is in it, that verily the knowers or brahman know.'[146]

'Thine [O Rudra] are the four directions, thine the heaven, thine the earth, thine O formidable one, this wide atmosphere, thine is all this that has life [ātmanvant] ... that is breathing upon (anu) the earth.'[147]

Thus, the term 'ātman', which, like prāna, is derived from the root √an 'to breathe', developed a variety of meanings in pre-Upaniṣadic literature ranging from the very physical connotations of 'body' and 'trunk' through the more general, though still individualistic, relaxive uses of 'self' and 'oneself', to the much more metaphysical usage as 'Self' or 'immortal essence' of a person.

In a number of places prāṇa and ātman appear side by side. In at least one of these 'ātman' appears to mean something like 'spirit', in others a rendering of 'body' seems more appropriate. The clearest example of the former is A.V. 5.9.7:

'The sun my eye, the wind [vāta] my breath [prāṇa], the atmosphere [antarikṣa] my soul (ātman), earth my body [śarīra]; unquelled (astṛta) by name am I here; [as] such I deposit myself for heaven and earth to guard (gopītha).'[149]

The second kind of passage is far more numerous. Hence, we read in A.V.11.5.22,

> 'Individually do all that are of Prajāpati bear breaths [prāṇān] in their bodies [organisms-ātmasu] ...'[150]

Similar statements can be found in the Śatapatha Brāhmaṇa:

> '... there are ten vital airs [prāṇa], and the trunk (body) [ātman] is the eleventh...'[151]

The meaning of 'body' for ātman is not readily apparent in the following translations though a consideration of the context reveals that it is just as legitimate a rendering as 'soul' or 'self'.

> *V.S.6.30–31*
>
> 'Ye are Nigrābhyā waters (the technical name of the Vasatīvarī waters when poured into the Hotar's cup), heard by deities: make me content.
>
> Content my mind, content my speech, content my breath [prāṇa], content mine eye, content mine ear, content my soul [ātman] ...'[152]

> *V.S.14.17*
>
> 'Preserve my life. Preserve my breath [prāṇa]. Guard mind outbreath [apāna]. Preserve mine eyes. Preserve mine ears. Strengthen my voice. Quicken my mind. Preserve my self [ātman]. Vouchsafe me light.'[153]

> *V.S.18.29*
>
> 'May life succeed through sacrifice. May life-breath [prāṇa] thrive by sacrifice. May the eye thrive by sacrifice. May the ear thrive by sacrifice. May the voice thrive by sacrifice. May the mind thrive by sacrifice. May the self [ātman] thrive by sacrifice ...'[154]

> *A.V.19.51.1*
>
> 'Unrepelled (?ayuta) am I, unrepelled my soul [ātman], unrepelled my sight, unrepelled my hearing, unrepelled my breath [prāṇa] ...'[155]

> *Ś.B.3.8.1.3*
>
> '... here in man there are ten vital airs [prāṇāti], and the eleventh is the self [ātman], wherein those vital airs are contained...'[156]

With regard to these passages we may note that in the first, where ātman seems to mean something like 'soul', correspondences are established between cosmic (or universal) and individual spheres of existence. Also, ātman is specifically contrasted with body. In the remaining passages, however, both of these dimensions are lacking. In fact, it may not be insignificant that all the examples of the second type of passage put ātman alongside not just prāṇa but alongside prāṇa and the other individualized manifestations of the cosmic prāṇa, namely apāna etc. and the perceptual faculties, suggesting thereby that ātman too could have been regarded by authors of these verses as a diversified form of the cosmic prāṇa. What we witness in the Upaniṣads, however, it that ātman ceases to appear in the lists of prāṇic manifestations and becomes identified with the cosmic prāṇa itself. It is this move, I would suggest, which enabled the Upaniṣadic authors to make ātman into a concept which could operate comfortably as the source of all corporeal existence and as the immortal core of every individual.

The relationship between the concepts of prāṇa and ātman in the Upaniṣads and the process by which ātman came to occupy the role of the unitary prāṇa will be examined in the next chapter.

Conclusion

This chapter has focused on the relationship between the world view(s) found in pre-Upaniṣadic Vedic literature with those presented in the Upaniṣads. In particular, it has been argued that despite some significant differences the two perspectives should be regarded as essentially continuous, part of a pattern of development, the evolution of which extends without a significant break from the Ṛgveda through into the early Upaniṣadic period and beyond. On the basis of work by scholars such as Jeanine Miller and Maryla Falk, it has been suggested that the religious view of the Vedic period included a dimension that was much more mystical, much more introverted than many scholars have been prepared to concede.

One of the factors responsible for the reluctance of many scholars to accept this view has been growing awareness among investigators in this field of the influence on Vedic thought of non-Vedic ideas. That such influence existed can hardly be disputed. What has been suggested here is that it should not be understood as having the effect of turning a non-mystical tradition into a mystical one but rather of remoulding an existing mystical tradition and providing it with a new orientation. Within that new orientation many features from the earlier tradition were retained, though often in a somewhat modified form. At least this is how the arguments of Miller and Falk have been interpreted.

Such a view can be seen to be supported by an analysis of the prāṇa concept in pre-Upaniṣadic Vedic literature. The analysis offered here under the three headings of *Prāṇa and the Cosmos, Prāṇa and the Individual* and *Prāṇa and Ātman* demonstrates quite clearly that many of the fundamental teachings about the unity of the universe, its evolution from a single source and microcosmic representation in the individual that are found in the Upaniṣads were already present in the pre-Upaniṣadic literature.

More particularly, it has been argued that such features, can be seen to have developed most clearly in connection with the concept of prāṇa. Cosmically, prāṇa is one of the terms employed to refer to the masculine aspect of the primordial androgyne and synonymous with others such as puruṣa. It is also one of the terms used to designate the ultimate principle of existence, the source of all, the foundation of all. At the level of the individual, the unitary cosmic prāṇa exists as the inner controller, knowledge of which bestows immortality. When diversified it is distributed throughout the body in the form of the vital airs : prāṇa, apāna, vyāna, udāna and samāna, and as the sensory faculties. Speech and mentation are also seen to derive from prāṇa.

When the pre-Upaniṣadic concepts of prāṇa and ātman (both of which are derived from the same verbal root : √an, to breathe) are set side by side it becomes clear that in the pre-Upaniṣadic literature the term ātman had a much wider range of meanings than it did in the Upaniṣadic and post-Upaniṣadic periods. In some cases it seems to be presented as one of the derivatives or manifestations of the cosmic prāṇa; in others it is employed as a substitute for prāṇa in its role as fundamental principle of existence. What is not yet evident in this period, however, is the notion of ātman as the source and essence of the vital energies and sensory faculties. In this early period such phenomena were quite clearly tied to the concept of prāṇa. All this was to change, however, during the period when the principal Upaniṣads were being compiled.

REFERENCES

1. Miller (1974) and Falk (1) (1943) and (1943).
2. Feuerstein and Miller (1971) p. 102.
3. Miller (1974) p. 19.
4. Quoted in op. cit. p. 59..
5. Falk (1943) (2) p. 107.
6. Miller (1974) p. 96.
7. Conze (1971) p. 296.
8. Miller (1974) p. 37.
9. op. cit. p. 27.
10. op. cit. p. 180.
11. op. cit. p. 35.
12. op. cit. p. 87.
13. Ṛ.V. 2.24. 3-4 (Griffith's translation p. 146). For a discussion of the problems connected with the translation of the term 'brahman' see Miller op. cit. pp. 46–50.
14. Feuerstein and Miller (1971) p. 102; Brown (1968) p. 205.
15. Quoted in Miller (1974) p. 65.
16. loc. cit.
17. loc. cit.
18. op. cit. p. 53.
19. Whitney (1905) p. 389.
20. loc. cit.
21. Miller (1974) p. 96.
22. op. cit. p. 97.
23. op. cit. p. 81.
24. op. cit. p. 85.
25. op. cit. pp. 122-23.
26. Pande (1974); Zimmer (1967).
27. Miller (1974) p. 171.
28. op. cit. pp. 173–81.
29. B.A.U.6 2 15.
30. e.g. Maitrī 4.4 where the knower of brahman gains 'the state of supreme divinity above the gods.' (Hume (1931) p. 421).
31. O'Flaherty (1981) p. 71.
32. Johnson (1976) p. 253.
33. See notes 3–5 in op. cit. p. 248.
34. Brown (1968) p. 214.
35. Johnson (1976) p. 251.

36. op. cit. p. 250.
37. Brown (1968) p. 214.
38. Sastri (1957) p. 63.
39. Falk (1943 (1) pp. 10-14; idem (1943) (2) pp. 110-111; Miller (1974) pp. 63-67, 76-80, 153-154, 189 and 196.
40. Pande (1974) ch. 8; Reat 1980 passim.
41. Griffith (1973) p. 130.
42. op. cit. p. 146.
43. Brown (1968) p. 217.
44. op. cit. passim.
45. Miller (1974) pp. 214-215.
46. Like puruṣa-Virāj, Vāc was the first sacrifice Ṛ.V. 10.125.3), but only in her spoken form which is merely one quarter of her totality (Ṛ.V. 1.164.45). Thus, argues Falk, only a quarter of puruṣa-Virāj and of Vāc is manifest. Take both similarities together and we have a strong suggestion of identity.
47. Whitney (1905), in his notes on A.V. 4.1.2, writes, 'the queen is the divinity of speech–or else *this earth*' (vol. 1.p.142).
48. op. cit. p. 143.
49. Griffith (1973) p. 624. Falk (1) p. 21 provides the sanskṛt: yāvad brahma tiṣṭhati tāvatī vāk.
50. Keith (1906) p. 186.
51. Falk (1943) (1) p. 20.
52. See Miller (1974) pp. 94 ff.
53. Bhattacharji (1970) p. 164.
54. Monier-Williams (1899) p. 982.
55. Whitney (1905) p. 511.
56. op. cit. p. 633.
57. loc. cit.
58. Ewing (1903) p. 9.
59. Whitney (1905) pp. 632-33.
60. Griffith (1973) p. 233.
61. Keith (1969) p. 39 suggests that the terms Mahaitareya and Bahvṛca Upaniṣads sometimes refer to the whole of āraṇyakas two and three, as Müller states, but sometimes just to āraṇyaka two. Also, like Müller, he regards adhyāyas 1-3 of the second āraṇyaka as constituting an independent work which, he claims, is 'the oldest long Upaniṣad extant.' (p. 43).
62. Müller (1962) pp. xcii-xcvi.
63. Keith (1969) p. 205.
64. op. cit. p. 201.

65. op. cit. p. 206.
66. See loc. cit.
67. loc. cit.
68. loc. cit.
69. loc. cit. f.n.
70. op. cit. p. 208.
71. op. cit. p. 213.
72. op. cit. p. 220.
73. Ewing (1903) p.7.
74. loc. cit.
75. Eggeling (1882) (1) p. 121.
76. We may note, however, that 10.2.6.19 states, 'Some indeed, hold it (immortality) to be breath, saying, "the breath is fire, the breath is the immortal"; but let him not believe this, for something uncertain is breath.' Eggeling (1885) (4) p. 327.
77. idem (1895) (4) p.144.
78. idem (1900) (5) p. 3 c.f. 5.2.4.10 and 11.1.2.3.
79. 7.5.1.22.
80. 1.3.2.3, 8.3.4.5, 10.2.6.15, and 10.3.1.5.
81. 8.2.2.8.
82. 8.1.4.1, 8.7.2.14, 8.7.3.6.
83. idem (1894) (3) p. 331.
84. idem (1895) (4) p. 18.
85. op. cit. pp. 54-55.
86. op. cit. p. 337.
87. op. cit. p. 302.
88. loc. cit.
89. Ś.B. 6.3.1.13 and 15 Eggeling (1894) (3) p. 193).
90. Ś.B. 7.1.1.24, op. cit. p. 305.
91. Keith (1969) p. 220.
92. Narahari (1944) p. 47.
93. op. cit. p. 4.
94. op. cit. p. 5.
95. Griffith (1973) p. 593.
96. O'Flaherty (1981) p. 267.
97. Narahari (1944) p. 7.
98. Keith (1925) p. 137.
99. All quoted in Keith loc. cit.
100. Quoted in Narahari (1944) p.7. Miller, (1974) pp. 135–6, agrees with this but is not very rigorous in her refutation of the

alternative. c.f. Whitney, (1905) p. 601, who quotes Ludwig as translating 'aja' as 'the unborn one', a translation which he regards as being of equal worth as 'goat' in the context of A.V. 10.8.41. In my view, the context supports the 'unborn' rendering rather than the 'goat' one.

101. O'Flaherty (1981) p. 51.
102. Keith (1925) p. 419.
103. O'Flaherty (1981) p. 51.
104. See Ś.B. 2.2.2.14.
105. Narahari (1944) p. 12.
106. O'Flaherty (1981) p. 78.
107. Narahari (1944) p. 13.
108. op. cit. p.15.
109. Keith (1925) p. 405. For a more detailed discussion of this issue see Reat (1980) chap. 4.
110. Griffith (1973) p.75.
111. Narahari (1944) p. 10.
112. O'Flaherty (1981) p. 79.
113. Narahari (1944) p. 11.
114. op. cit. p. 12.
115. Keith (1925) p. 403.
116. loc. cit.
117. op. cit. p. 404
118. Narahari (1944) pp. 45-6.
119. op. cit. p. 46.
120. op. cit. pp. 46-7.
121. Griffith's version reads as follows:

    He who like the God, true minded, protecteth with his power all acts of vigour,

    Truthful like splendour, glorified by many, like breath joy giving,– all must strive to win him. (1977) pp. 48-9.

    Oldenberg's is:

    He who being truthful like the god Savitri protects by his power of mind all Settlements, praised by many like impetuous splendour, the truthful one has become dear like vital breath and worthy to be searched for. (1897) p. 88.
122. Narahari (1944) p. 47.
123. Griffith (1973) p. 377.
124. Narahari (1944) p. 44.
125. Griffith (1973) p. 605. 'Breath is his translation of ātman' here.
126. Ewing (1903) p. 12.

127. Griffith (1973) p. 48.
128. op. cit. p. 108.
129. op. cit. p. 384.
130. op. cit. p. 393.
131. op. cit. p. 540.
132. op. cit. p. 377.
133. op. cit. p. 605. Reat (1980) suggests that here Griffith is inaccurate 'rendering the single word ātman as "breath of all". p. 512 n. 140.
134. op. cit. p. 647.
135. op. cit. p.44.
136. Reat (1980) pp. 88-89.
137. Ewing (1903) p. 15.
138. For a discussion of the meaning of 'āyus' see Reat (1980) pp. 115-119.
139. op. cit. p. 128.
140. op. cit. p. 130.
141. Eggeling (1885) (2) p. 264.
142. op. cit. p. 289. For a discussion of this translation see op. cit. p. xxix and Ewing (1903) pp. 12-15.
143. Ewing (1903) p. 15.
144. Whitney (1905) p. 601.
145. Eggeling (1895) (4) p. 400.
146. Whitney (1905) p. 571. We may note here the very different translation which Whitney has employed to give a rendering of 'yakṣamātmanvant'. In A.V. 10.8.43 (see note 144) he offers 'soulful prodigy'; here this has become 'soul possessing monster'. There is obviously much work to be done on clarifying the meaning(s) of the term 'yakṣa' in the A.V.
147. op. cit. p. 621.
148. op. cit. p. 165.
149. op. cit. p. 235.
150. op. cit. p. 639.
151. Eggeling (1900) (5) p. 311. C.f. 8.4.3.8 and 11.2.1.2 for identical statements.
152. Griffith (1976) pp. 49-51. This is repeated in Ś.B. 3.4.4.7.
153. op. cit. p. 127.
154. op.cit. p. 165.
155. Whitney (1905) p. 985.
156. Eggeling (1885) (2) p. 185.

2

The concept of Prāṇa in Upaniṣadic literature

Rarely do the Upaniṣads[1] present a consistent teaching on any one subject. There are a number of reason for this. One is that they are a continuation of an already diverse tradition and consequently represent a variety of views. Secondly, the Upaniṣads themselves were composed over a considerable period of time and the later texts either attempt syntheses of earlier teachings or emphasise one view against others. We also witness in some of the verse and later prose Upaniṣads[2] the introduction of new ideas, many of which become influential in the post-Upaniṣadic period but are little represented in earlier Upaniṣads. All this makes it near impossible to provide an account of the 'Upaniṣadic teaching on ...' with regard to almost any subject. What can be provided, however, is an account of the material relevant to a particular teaching with the various contributory strands being separated and analyzed. This will be my approach in this chapter.

Before embarking on a study of the texts, though, a survey of earlier scholars' views on the use of the term 'prāṇa' in the Upaniṣads is in order, not least because it reveals the prevailing consensus of opinion on this subject. It also facilitates and appreciation of the methods by which this consensus has been arrived at and, hopefully, will illuminate the limitations and shortcomings of these earlier appraisals. Fortunately, such a survey can be quite brief for, despite scholarly investigation of the Upaniṣads for over a century, a comprehensive treatment, or anything approaching it, of the concept of prāṇa in this literature has not been forthcoming.

Deussen (1906) (1912), Keith (1925), Frauwallner (1973), Beidler (1975) and Ewing (1903) have all commented on the place of prāṇa in the Upaniṣadic world–picture. Apart from Ewing and, to some extent, Deussen, all these writers fail to acknowledge the centrality of the prāṇa concept in Upaniṣadic writings, arguing for a greater degree of subordination to the notions of brahman and ātman than is warranted by the texts. However, even Ewing, whilst recognising that 'prāṇa' has a key role in the cosmology and anthropology of many Upaniṣadic texts, provides little by way of analysis and argumentation, simply offering a list of relevant passages. The need for a more comprehensive treatment is thus, I would suggest, indisputable.

In *The Philosophy of the Upaniṣads* Paul Deussen offers an analysis of some, though by no means all, of the passages dealing with the disagreement among the perceptual/motor faculties (eye, ear etc.) about which of them is superior. Prāṇa, of course, comes out the victor. This, he suggests, is why in other places (e.g.Kauṣ. Up. 2.1-2) prāṇa is equated with brahman. In Deussen's view, however, such equations merely set the stage for a gradual subordination of prāṇa to brahman/ātman.[3]

In *The System of the Vedānta,* he goes much further. Having suggested that evidence for a polemic between different Upaniṣadic thinkers or schools can be found in a number of early Upaniṣads,[4] he offers some reflections, 'which can for the present only be presented as a hypothesis', about the reasons for the gradual subordination of the prāṇa principle to those of ātman and brahman. He suggests that during the Brāhmaṇa and Upaniṣadic period the question was asked, 'which part of our life is to be regarded as the clearest expression of the thing-in-itself–unconscious life which in waking and sleeping goes tireless on its way, or conscious life in whose preponderance consists the advantage of man over other beings?–As it seems to us, both these paths were taken... C.U. 7 [is]... a polemic of the younger school against the older and Kauṣ. 3 an attempt to reconcile the two; until finally the extreme intellectualism of the system of the Vedānta was reached, for which Brahman is pure intelligence (caitanyam), while the prāṇa in the shape of the mukhya prāṇa sinks to a mere upādhi of the soul.'[5]

The conclusions of the present study go a long way towards supporting this hypothesis though they differ on a number of points. As was seen in chapter one, prāṇa was a principal contender for the status of ultimate principle in the brahmanical world-view, though it was not the only one. The developing concept of ātman, whilst emerging from the same roots as the prāṇa concept, was seen in the Brāhmaṇas to be acquiring the characteristics of what Deussen calls 'conscious life'. That C.U.7 is an attempt by the proponents of the view that ātman is a more fundamental principle than prāṇa is certainly in line with my own analysis and I shall seek to demonstrate below exactly how this attempt was made.

However, I cannot agree with Deussen that Kauṣ. U.3 represents an attempt to reconcile the two views. In my opinion, and I will seek to substantiate this below, the Kauṣītakī Upaniṣad represents the best Upaniṣadic attempt to present the views of what Deussen calls 'the older school' in a clear and comprehensive fashion. The reason he regards it as an attempt at reconciliation is that his original distinction between conscious and unconscious life is probably overly influenced by Śaṅkara's claim in his commentary on B.S. 2.4.10 that prāṇa is 'non-intelligent'[6] or 'non-conscious'.[7] As was shown in chapter one, the thinkers of 'the older school' viewed prāṇa not only as the source of consciousness and mentation but also as the substance of these phenomena. This is exactly the view found in the Kauṣītakī Upaniṣad. Thus, in my opinion, the issue was not so much whether the essence of the universe and the self was best understood as being expressed through conscious principles or unconscious ones but more whether the mental arose out of the vital or the vital out of the mental. With regard to Deussen's last point, that the increasing emphasis on the fundamental nature of consciousness reduced prāṇa from being one of the terms employed to refer to the essence of the universe and the individual to that of a mere upādhi, I am entirely in agreement and will seek, in the next chapter, to indicate how this subordination was effected.

Keith also notes this process of subordination, regarding it as a simple development of Upaniṣadic insight towards a more and more accurate apprehension of the fundamental reality. He writes, 'We attain [through the positing of prāṇa as a kind of essence that persists after death]... the conception of the self as something which does not perish, which, therefore is without beginning and without end, and as the essential element in man we find all activities resolved ultimately into prāṇa on their cessation. On a *higher level of thought* we have the concept of prajñā, intelligence, substituted for the breath in recognition of the psychic side of man and the fact that it is consciousness or intelligence which is aware of breath and of all man's life, and in it also all else is resolved. The ātman is one more level of abstraction and ātman = brahman the ultimate step.'[8] Whilst having a certain logical appeal this account is patently inadequate as far as the texts are concerned. First of all, prajñā or prajñātman is often equated with prāṇa and not something separate lying behind it. Secondly, the developmental picture is much less in evidence in the texts than Keith seems to think. In fact, there are a number of instances where the equation ātman-brahman as the fundamental principle is found in texts considerably earlier than ones proposing prāṇa as fundamental.

Frauwallner too, presents us with a logical structure to facilitate an understanding of this material. In a somewhat less evolutionary appraisal than Keith's, he identifies in the Upaniṣads three general theories to account for the nature of existence. These he calls 'the water doctrine', 'the breath doctrine' and 'the fire doctrine'. The water doctrine, he argues, was derived from the observation of the water cycle and phases of the moon which, linked with an older idea about the moon being a gateway to the heavenly world,[10] provided an interesting account of the continued renewal of the world and a possible goal for human endeavour. The Upaniṣadic elaborations of this are to be found, he suggests, in the accounts of the soul's fate after death in B.A.U. 6.2 and C.U. 5.3-10. However, though the notions of different pathways after death continued to play a part in later Vedānta philosophy the cyclical notions of renewal underwent little further development. As Frauwallner himself puts it, 'It was a great non-recurring conception which created the doctrine and simultaneously gave its basic thoughts a final form. Beyond that, it neither developed itself further inwardly nor was able to give fruitful stimulation to other doctrines..'[11]

In his view, the breath doctrine was more promising. There is an obvious difference between a live and a dead body and it is breath (prāṇa) that seems to be the source of it. Thus, breath was presented as a fundamental principle of life or animate existence. The status of breath vis-a-vis the other faculties of a living being: eye, ear etc., was explored in stories where they are presented as disagreeing about which of them is superior (see below, p.p.67 f.f. for details). According to Frauwallner, the notion expounded in some of these passages, that in sleep only prāṇa is operational and the other faculties, including mind, absorbed into it, continued to be used as an explanatory principle in the later Vedānta, though the notion of prāṇa itself '... proved to be not suitable to unite itself with further reaching ideas.'[12] He continues, stating, '... the fact that it was not easy to make breath the bearer of the decisive processes of knowledge appears to have come in the way of the further formulation of the breath doctrine.'[13]

Here, of course, he fails to acknowledge that prāṇa had already been proposed as a fundamental principle and closely linked with, if not regarded as the source of, thought and knowledge in pre-Upaniṣadic literature. Neither does he mention that this link is preserved in much later literature as well.[14] Such observations do not, however, undermine the more philosophical point that there are conceptual difficulties involved in linking breath and thought and that an awareness of these could well have led to an emphasis on the mental rather than the vital principle.

The fire doctrine is the one identified by Frauwallner as having the greatest explanatory value and providing the principal foundation for later Vedānta philosophy. For his elucidation of this doctrine he takes as his starting point the universal fire that dwells in all men (agni vaiśvānara–B.A.U. 5.5.9) and links this with the account of the connection between man and the sun through rays of various colours that occurs in C.U. 8.6, pointing out that '... the sun is not only a heavenly world but also a door to heaven.'[15] He goes on to state that '... the light soul is defined as consisting of thought (manomaya) ... this idea... succeeded in explaining better the relation of the soul to the different life forces, than in the case of the Breath doctrine. Because in the Breath-doctrine, the connection of the independent life-forces with the Breath which, according to its nature, was entirely of a different sort, was rather forced or strained. Now, however, in the case of the Fire-doctrine it is assumed that the Fire-soul [= light soul?] enters, with its several parts, life-forces and thus lends them knowledge and efficiency.'[16] Again, although logically appealing, this interpretation of the Upaniṣadic teachings seems to be only precariously grounded in the texts. In fact, Frauwallner provides no references at all to illustrate his interpretation of the relationship between the fire/light soul and the life forces.

One thing all these scholars are agreed upon is that although the notion of prāṇa has some prominence in the Upaniṣads it is generally subordinated to ātman or brahman and, from an historical perspective, that prominence is abandoned as the Upaniṣadic world-picture develops. What thy fail to provide, however, is an adequate account (i.e. one well illustrated from the texts) of the reasons why such moves were made by the Upaniṣadic authors.[17] Deussen goes some way towards this but his account is much too sketchy. A close scrutiny of the texts reveals, on the one hand, that the subordination of the prāṇa concept is much less in evidence that these scholars seems to assume and, on the other, that the imposition of an historical-cum-evolutionary model on the texts is unwarranted in the case of this issue. It is clear that in the works of later systems which are grounded in or take inspiration from the Upaniṣads e.g. Vedānta and Sāṃkhya, the subordinate status of prāṇa is fairly clearly attested. It is not, however, legitimate to read such a situation back into the Upaniṣads themselves. In fact, I will seek to demonstrate below that in most Upaniṣadic texts which incorporate the prāṇa concept into their world picture its status is that of a supreme, primordial or fundamental principle.

One of the major reasons why these scholars have been inclined to read later views back into the Upaniṣadic material is that they all tended to place too much reliance on their interpretative models. They thus found what they expected to find. Frauwallner is less guilty of this than Keith. His recognition of the fact that different Upaniṣadic authors subscribed to different world-pictures alerts us to the fact that an historical-cum-evolutionary model is unlikely to facilitate an accurate exegesis of this material. His own scheme, however, is much too sketchy and poorly supported to do justice to the material.

A much more blatent example of distorting the facts to fit the theory is provided by William Beidler. This study requires comment here not only because it purports to be a comprehensive treatment of the concept of 'self' in the Upaniṣads[18] and thus needs to be taken into account by anyone working in this field but also because the concern of a substantial part of his work is to make sense of what is, by and large, the same material that provides the subject matter of this chapter. In addition, it demands consideration since it is based on a methodological premise which is fundamentally at variance with my own. For him, 'The first thing to realize about our texts, is their inherent wholeness : they may not be analyzable into parts when dealing with the concept of self except at the risk of losing their meaning.'[19] My own view, on the other hand, is that there are different schools of thought represented in the Upaniṣads and that on many points their teachings are not reducible to each other. Hence, I would suggest that the analysis of the texts and their division into component parts is more likely to yield an accurate account of Upaniṣadic views of the self than is Beidler's approach, which is based on the assumption of an 'inherent wholeness'. In fact, I shall seek to demonstrate that this assumption actually leads Beidler to misrepresent the material in order to make it fit with his scheme.

In the preface to *The Vision of Self in Early Vadānta* Beidler makes a number of remarks about his methodological procedure and how it avoids the errors of interpreters such as Śaṅkara who, he suggests, misinterpreted the texts in order to fit them into his own doctrinal scheme, and those of western scholars such as Garbe and Otto who assumed that the Upaniṣadic authors were purely rational philosophers. Hence, he expresses a concern not to impose a system of logic on the material '... since Western logic as the child of rational and empirical philosophy may not extract the whole meaning.'[20] Unfortunately, he fails on both these counts for his approach to the material is based upon his own framework which is dominated by western logical assumptions. He claims that his own procedure is based upon two methodological principles : 'coherence' and 'completeness'. About these he writes,'... one concept may be more complete than another when it can include the other with a satisfactory degree of coherence ... coherence and completeness taken together will enable us to evaluate internally and to classify the various concepts of self.'[21] 'Coherence' allows him to overlook interpolations into and redactions of the text and almost inevitably inclines him towards the kind of synthetic view subscribed to by the later Vadānta. 'Completeness' accords later, more comprehensive, schemata a higher status than earlier, more elementary ones. In fact, one could argue that such hermeneutic principles provide an exegetical licence to distort with impunity. Such sentiments would hardly be amiss in the writings of a modern western Śaṅkara.

In his treatment of Upaniṣadic material Beidler constantly wavers between identifying trends in the texts which point to an evolution of ideas and imposing a logical scheme onto the data in order to make sense of it. For example, on page 13 he argues that the beginnings of philosophical thought (an historical statement) are to be found 'in a search for the first principle, the essence of the cosmos and its source ... Interest is then focused on cosmology, how this first principle has created or projected the world... only then does man's interest focus on man, on psychology... Finally the thinker is led to consider problems of purpose and the ultimate destiny of the self, after he has some knowledge of the self as he immediately finds it.'[22] This would certainly be an interesting hypothesis to investigate in terms of the literature of the Veda. It is not, however, self-evidently true. Nevertheless, Beidler treats it as a kind of a priori assumption for he states that '... the above structure is a logical arrangement not necessarily a chronological one.'[23] This 'logical arrangement' is justified in turn by appeal to the principle of completeness. Each stage, he argues, is more 'complete' than the preceding one. Here then, the principle of completeness is employed in order to reinforce what can only be described as a 'sleight of hand': passing off a logical structure as an historical process.

An ambiguity similar to that outlined above underlies his entire approach to the Upaniṣadic material. He organizes the information relevant to the concept of self under three headings: puruṣa, ātman, and brahman, stating, 'Like the above logical order of completeness, these three terms will be seen to represent three different levels of considering self, each more complete in its coverage till with 'Brahman' we have a term for the ultimate reality.'[24] His procedure is thus not, as he claimed on page v., concerned with the elucidation of the various terms for 'self' in the Upaniṣads but, in fact, with employing these terms as headings under which a comprehensive treatment can be carried out. Not until the introduction to his treatment of ātman on page 44 is his method laid bare. Taking Deussen's three connotations of ātman as: 1) the corporeal self; 2) the individual soul; 3) the supreme soul,[25] as his starting point he reveals that he organizes material relevant to 1) under the heading of 'puruṣa'; material relevant to 2) under the heading of 'ātman' and material relevant to 3) under the heading of 'brahman'. In itself this is a reasonable procedure. However, it need not be linked with the three above mentioned terms. In fact, employing them in such a restricted way means that any attempt at elucidating their meanings as they are found in the texts must be sacrificed. Hence, when he tries to equate the meanings of the three terms as they are found in the Upaniṣads with the ideas associated with each of his three divisions the result is confusion. 'Puruṣa', for example, is definitely used in some contexts to refer to the highest reality and is equated with both ātman and brahman.[26] It is inaccurate, therefore, to suggest, as Beidler does, that the Upaniṣads '... limit "puruṣa" to the personal, individual sense of self.'[27]

In actuality then, Beidler's approach does not lead to an elucidation of the meanings of the various terms employed to mean 'self' in the Upaniṣads, as he claims in his introduction,[28] but to the construction of a synthetic view of 'self' in the Upaniṣads. The result is a more or less coherent account of 'self' as it exists at each of the three levels and a distorted picture of the meanings of a number of important terms in the Upaniṣads, including 'prāṇa'.

If his argument is examined in detail we see that with regard to the corporeal or personal sense of self he identifies a number of analyses in the Upaniṣads which, he claims, provide accounts of this level of existence. There are *two three-fold analyses,* one found in B.A.U. 1.5.3, the other C.U.6.4. In the first passage we are told that 'the self consists of speech [vāc], mind [manas] and breath [prāṇa].'[29] The second traces all existent forms back to three fundamental principles: food or earth (anna), water (apas) and heat (tejas). This latter analysis is not then strictly an analysis of the personal self but of the cosmos. He identifies *a fivefold analysis* in B.A.U. 1.3 where the constituent parts are speech (vāc), breath (prāṇa), eye (cakṣus), ear (śrotra), and mind (manas). In fact, the passage offers a sixfold analysis, the final element being the 'prāṇa-in-the-mouth' (āsanya prāṇa), though Beidler seems to overlook this. *An elevenfold analysis* is found in Kaṭh. U. 5.1 (2.2.1 in Radhakrishnan's arrangement) where the body is referred to as an eleven-gated citadel. The gates would seem to be the two eyes, the two ears, the two nostrills, the mouth, the two lower orifices (in the male)–all of which are listed as the bodily openings in Ś.U. 3.18 and Bhagavad Gītā 5.13–the navel (not listed as an opening or gate in other Upaniṣads but given as the tenth opening by Deussen, Hume and Radhakrishnan) and 'the door named 'the cleft' (vidṛti)'–following A.U. 3.12 (c.f. C.U. 8.6.6).

Two analyses of the personal self are identified by Beidler in the Praśna Upaniṣad. These are to be found at 4.8 and 6.4. The first presents the self as consisting of 19 or 38 parts (depending on how one does the calculation), the second dividing the self into 16 parts. However, like the Chāndogya analysis mentioned above, these are not really accounts of the personal self since they appear to enumerate all the basic principles of the whole creation. Praśna 4.8, certainly, relates all the principles to the supreme self (param ātman) which is mentioned in 4.7 and 4.9. The components in 4.8 are :

> 'Earth and the elements of earth, water and the elements of water, fire and the elements of fire, air and the elements of air, ether and the elements of ether, sight and what can be seen, hearing and what can be heard, smell and what can be smelled, taste and what can be tasted, the skin and what can

be touched, speech and what can be spoken, hands and what can be handled, the organ of generation and what can be enjoyed, the organ of excretion and what can be excreted, the feet and what can be walked, the mind and what can be perceived, the intellect and what can be conceived, the self-sense and what can be connected with the self, thought and what can be thought, radiance and what can be illumined, life-breath and what can be supported by it.'[30]

Those from 6.4 are life/breath (prāṇa), faith (śraddhā), space (kha), wind (vāyu), light (jyotis), water (apas), earth (pṛthivi), the sense organ (indriya), mind (manas), food (anna), virility (vīrya), austerity (tapas), hymns (mantra), works (karma), worlds (loka) and name (i.e. individuality) (nāma).

He also identifies *a sixteen-fold-analyses* of the self in C.U.7, 'The teachings of Sanatkumāra to Nārada'. Beidler lists the sixteen elements as name, speech, manas, saṅkalpa, citta, dhyāna, vijñāna, bala, anna, apas, tejas, ākāśā, memory, āśā, prāṇa and puruṣa/ātman.[31]

However, the text puts ten other elements between prāṇa and ātman. They are truth (satya), understanding (vijñāna), thought (mati), faith (śraddhā), steadfastness (nistiṣṭhati), activity (kṛta), happiness (sukha), the infinite (bhūma), the finite (alpa) and the self-sense (ahaṃkāra). I will return to the significance of this omission in my own treatment of this passage.

Beidler regards all these analyses as progressive attempts to explain the physical nature of man and the material creation,[32] and sees them as eventually culminating in the guṇa and tattva schemes of classical Sāṃkhya.[33] He fails, however, to provide any justification for such an interpretation. *The final analyses* of the personal self that he identifies is the one based on five sheaths (kośa) found in Taitt. U. 2.2, though we may note that the actual term 'kośa does not appear in this passage. The five components of this analysis are 'the person made of the essence of food' (puruṣo anna-rasa-maya), 'the self made of vitality' (ātmā prāṇa-maya), 'the self made of mind' (ātmā manomaya), 'the self made of consciousness' (ātmā vijñāna-maya) and 'the self made of bliss' (ātmā ānanda-maya).

Having established the existence of these various 'analyses' Beidler attempts to link together those which he regards as being most comprehensive : the two Praśna analyses, the Chāndogya 7 analysis and the Taittirīya analysis, summarizing the parallels by means of a table :

TABLE 3

Taitt. Kośa+ analyses	*Sanatkumāra and Praśna*	
1. Annakośa (Food sheath)	1. Anna, Apas, Tejas, Ākāśa of Sanatkumāra	
	2. 5 gross and subtle elements of Praśna analyses	
2. Prāṇakośa	1. Balam (Power) of Sanatkumāra	
	2. Vīryam (strength) of Praśna	
	Sanatkumāra	*Praśna*
	Name - speech as	Indriyas
3. Manaḥkosa	Manas	Manas
	Saṅkalpa	Buddhi
		ahaṃkāra
	Citta	Citta
	Dhyāna	
4. Vijñānakośa	Vijñāna	
5. Ānandakośa	Memory - hope and immensity[34]	(none)

One of the points to note about this table, besides its lack of clarity, is the absence of prāṇa and ātman from Sanatkumāra's list. Had these elements been included the neat parallelisms Beidler presents would have been significantly disrupted since prāṇa would have to be placed opposite the ānandakośa instead of the prāṇakośa. He subsequently tries to deal with the ambiguous status of prāṇa by embarking on a peculiar and unconvincing argument designed to demonstrate that the analyses where prāṇa is a fundamental or near-fundamental principle are compatible with the kośa analysis, where it is presented as a purely phenomenal or derivative one.[35]

The main thrust of this argument is that prāṇa is basic to bodily existence *and* to puruṣa's existence for, '... as the tree depends on its roots, the Puruṣa depends on its roots in prāṇa... those passages [where prāṇa is a fundamental principle] are not contrary to the conclusions of the Kośa analysis but supplement the concept and merely illustrate that the Puruṣa's expression is grounded in the two lowest Kośas, in the food and vital sheach [sic], without which

Puruṣa would not have bodily existence.'[36] Contrary to this assessment, I would suggest that here we have a clear example of two kinds of analysis that do *not* fit together in any coherent fashion. In each section of the Taittirīya analysis we find the statement that the form of any sheath is determined by the form of the one within it. In other words, the pattern is that the outer is determined by the inner. The puruṣo anna-rasa-maya is dependent on the ātmā prāṇa–maya, which is dependent on the ātmā manomaya, which is dependent on the ātmā vijñāna maya, which is dependent on the ātmā ānanda-maya. To claim that the puruṣa's expression (whatever that means) is grounded in the two lowest kośas is nonsense. The most appropriate thing to do when confronted with such a situation is to abandon the demand for compatibility and seek a theoretical framework that will do justice to the data. The kośa analysis is a powerful one because it links the individual with the cosmos through psychology. In doing so it subordinates prāṇa to the mentalistic faculties of manas and vijñāna. To pretend that prāṇa nevertheless retains a fundamental status is to distort the facts. The reason Beidler gets himself into this position is, I would suggest, because of the methods he employs to elucidate the teachings contained in the texts.

Compared to his treatment of the personal or phenomenal self (puruṣa) Beidler's analysis of the individual soul (ātman) and the supreme soul (brahman) are quite straightforward. For him the individual soul (what he calls ātman) is the link between the individual and the universe or ultimate reality. 'Ātman is the essence, the ultimate and true nature of puruṣa expressed on the highest, the ānanda level of its ontology.'[37] Ātman is '... the inner guide in the ether of the heart...'[38] and '... the fourth state of puruṣa as embodied yet not changing its status as puruṣa does in the waking state.'[39] Brahman, on the other hand, '... is the source, the underlying reality, as well as indefinable and unknowable,'[40] it is '... the ultimate reality, whether created or uncreated, personal or impersonal ... that which one would term the cosmic and supreme sense of being.'[41] Brahman is '... the most general sense of self to be found in the Upaniṣads. Its use seems to include both the microcosm and the macrocosm as well as the multiplicity and universality.'[42] However, whilst 'ātman and brahman' may have the meanings he ascribed to them such meanings are not restricted to these terms. Much of what has been said about brahman is true of ātman and puruṣa; much of what is said about both ātman and brahman, is, as I will proceed to demonstrate, equally true of prāṇa.

Before embarking on this enterprise though, it is worth noting the comments of one scholar whose assessment of the place of prāṇa in the Upaniṣads is based more on an appreciation of the texts that a commitment to some assumed model: those of A.H.Ewing. His two main points are that in the Upaniṣads we find '... a number of important references in which it (prāṇa) appears as the permanent factor in all life functions, and hence approximates in meaning to the Ego or Self'[43] and that the use of prāṇa as a term for the primeval principle 'is frequent in the Upaniṣads.'[44] In support of these claims he cites a number of examples. The use of 'prāṇa' for 'self' can be seen in C.U. 1.2.7, 1.2.9 and 1.5.3 (where it is called mukhya prāṇa, the prāṇa in the mouth); B.A.U. 1.4.21 and 2.21 (where it is called madhyama prāṇa, the middle prāṇa. These references should actually be 1.5.21 and 22 and 2.2.1. The ones in Ewing's text must be a misprint); B.A.U. 1.3.7 (where it is called āsanya prāṇa, the prāṇa in the mouth) and P.U. 2.3 (where it is called variṣṭha prāṇa, the chief prāṇa). The use of 'prāṇa' for 'primeval principle' can be seen in B.A.U. 3.9.9, 4.1.3 and 4.5.7; C.U. 4.10.5 and 7.15.1; Kauṣ.U. 2.1-2 and T.U. 2.3.1 (in all of which it 'is made synonymous with Brahman')[45] and in Maitrī.U. 6.8 (where it 'is made synonymous with The Supreme Ātman').[46] He also points out that 'In other passages, again, especially in Praśna Up, Prāṇa is used as in A.V. 11.4, without being linked up with Brahman or Ātman.'[47] Thus, Ewing, alone among the scholars discussed so far, recognizes that in the Upaniṣads prāṇa is often recognized as being identical with brahman or ātman and is also employed in its own right to refer to the primeval or ultimate principle of existence which is, at the same time, the core of individual existence. The case for such a view is actually far stronger than even Ewing recognizes, as I shall attempt to demonstrate below.

The Texts

An examination of all references to prāṇa in the Upaniṣads reveals that the prominent view is quite similar to that already outlined with regard to pre-Upaniṣadic literature : prāṇa is the primeval source of all and the immortal inner essence of individuals which manifests in the body as the various breaths (apāna etc.) and faculties. In a number of instances this is presented in an unambiguous manner, in others, however, close analysis is required to demonstrate their espousal of such a view. In yet other cases it can be seen that although the fundamental/

essential principle is called ātman or brahman the descriptions of its nature are modelled on accounts where prāṇa is the preferred term. Taken together, these passages suggest that in many Upaniṣadic circles something approaching a common conception of the fundamental/essential principle of existence was being promulgated. The terms used to refer to this principle varied but the descriptive content of the conception was modelled on earlier and contemporaneous conceptions of prāṇa.

However, this is not the only view of prāṇa to be found in the Upaniṣads. In a number of places it is presented as what I shall call a cosmic principle, i.e. one which is derived from the fundamental principle but which itself is the source of further manifestations at the level of phenomenal or individualised existence. In yet other places we find accounts of prāṇa only as it appears at the phenomenal level. In some other cases these could be taken to be statements about the phenomenal manifestation of a higher principle which is assumed but not referred to. In others, however, it is clear that the author(s) are operating with a different model of existence than that assumed in the passages referred to above and that, in these instances, prāṇa does not have the high status ascribed to it by the other accounts.

The bulk of this chapter will be given over to a demonstration of the accuracy of the interpretation outlined above. If it substantiates my claims it will require a reappraisal of earlier scholarly views about the place of prāṇa in the Upaniṣadic world-view and constitute a further refutation of the kind of methodology advocated by Beidler and a vindication of a more analytical approach.

Prāṇa as an ultimate or fundamental principle of existence

By far the most frequent way of presenting prāṇa in the Upanisads is as an ultimate principle. A number of these presentations occur in contexts where there is a competition amongst the various faculties about which of them is the greatest. These will be considered alongside all other accounts of such competitions at the end of this section. Straightforward passages presenting prāṇa as an ultimate principle are *B.A.U.* 1.6.1-3, 2.3.1-6, 3.9, 4.4.7 and 4.4.22; *C.U.* 3.15.4, 4.3.1-4, 4.10.4-5 and chapter 7; *P.U.*2; *Mund.U.* 3.1.4.

B.A.U. 1.6.1-3

> '...this world is a triad of name, shape and work... These three together are one, this self; the self, though one is this triad. This is the immortal (amṛta), veiled by the real [or true] (satya). Prāṇa, verily, is the immortal (amṛta), name and shape (nāmarūpa) are the real (satya). By them Prāṇa is veiled.'[48]

The three verses from which this extract is taken constitute a complete sub-section (brāhmaṇa), the last of chapter one. There is nothing in the preceding brāhmaṇa to suggest that the intention was not to convey the impression that prāṇa was the ultimate principle of existence, the essence of individuality. In fact, the final verses of 1.5 contain one of the many stories of the faculties competing. Prāṇa of course, is acknowledged as the greatest among them.

B.A.U. 2.3.1-6

> 'Verily, there are two forms of Brahman, the formed and the formless, the mortal and the immortal, the unmoving and the moving, the actual (existent) and the true (being).
>
> This is the formed Brahman, whatever is different from the air and the atmosphere. This is mortal. This is unmoving, this is actual. The essence of this formed, this mortal, this unmoving, this actual is the yonder sun which gives forth warmth, for that is the essence of the actual.
>
> Now the formless is the air (vāyu) and the atmosphere (antarikṣa). This is immortal, this is the moving and this is the true. The essence of this uniformed, this immortal, this moving, this true is this person who is in the region of the sun for he is the essence (of true). This, with reference to the divinities.
>
> Now with reference to the self; just this is the formed, what is different from the breath (prāṇa) and from the space which is within the self (antarātmann ākāśa). This is mortal, this is unmoving, this is actual (existent). The essence of this formed, this mortal, this unmoving, this actual is the eye, for it is the essence of the actual.
>
> Now the formless is the breath and the space which is within the self. This is immortal this is moving, this is the true. The

essence of this unformed, immortal, moving true is this person who is in the right eye, for he is the essence of the true. The form of this person is like a saffron-coloured robe, like white wool, like the Indragopa insect, like a flame of fire, like a white lotus, like a sudden flash of lightning. He who knows it thus attains splendour like a sudden flash of lightning. Now therefore there is the teaching, not this, not this for there is nothing higher than this, that he is not this. Now the designation for him is the truth. Verily, the vital breath (prāṇa) is truth and He is the truth of that (teṣām).'[49]

These passages constitute the whole of brāhmaṇa three and the end of Ajātaśatru's teaching (which began at 2.1.1). The final statement of 2.3.6 is 'prāṇā vai satyam teṣām eṣa satyam'. Radhakrishnan translates it in the singular despite the fact that prāṇā(ḥ) and teṣām are plurals. A more accurate rendering would be 'the prāṇas are truth and this (eṣa) is the truth of those (teṣām)'. Hume gives 'breathing creatures are the real. He is their real'[50] whilst Deussen offers 'the vital spirits are the reality and he (the puruṣa or Brahman) is its reality.'[51] 'Eṣa' is obviously the person in the right eye, whose identity here is uncertain. The most likely candidate, as far as the section itself is concerned, is the ātman mentioned in 2.1.20 for the person in the right eye is said by Ajātaśatru, in 2.3.5, to be the essence of the true' (tyasya hy eṣa rasaḥ)'[52] and ātman, in 2.1.20, is called 'the truth of truth' (satyasya satyam).[53] We also know from many other sources that the person in the right eye is Indra, who is prāṇa.[54] Thus, here we seem to have an equation of prāṇa and the ātman, in complete accord with B.A.U. 1.6.1-3.

B.A.U. 3.9

This is a brāhmaṇa dealing with Vidagdha Śākalya's questioning of Yajñavalkya about the number of gods. Interestingly, because this is the only place where Yajñavalkya makes such a claim, the one god (eka deva) is said to be prāṇa (3.9.9) and, in the same verse, prāṇa is also said to brahman and tyat (that)–possibly a reference to R.V. 10.129.2. The same account can be found at ŚB. 11.6.3.1-11, which ends with the statement that prāṇa is the one god. The B.A.U. version continues, however, informing us that the thirty three gods are but manifestations of that one god. In this scheme the eleven Rudras are the ten prāṇas and the ātman. For no apparent reason, Radhakrishnan translates 'ātman' in this context as 'mind'. This is peculiar because in these early accounts reference to the ten prāṇas usually means the five : prāṇa, apāna, vyāna, udāna and samāna, plus speech, eye, nose, ear and mind. Certainly this listing is not unfamiliar to the Śatapatha Brāhmana (of which this Upaniṣad is a continuation) where, as was shown above, when ātman is added as an eleventh the meaning is usually 'body'.

At the end of Śākalya's questions (3.9.36) Yajñavalkya is asked about the foundation of his personal existence (tvam cātma ca pratiṣṭhitan stha iti).[55] He replies that it is prāṇa, adding that prāṇa is based on apāna, apāna on vyāna, vyāna on samāna. Here the most logical translation of ātman is 'body' for later in the same verse we are told that the self (ātman) is none of these prāṇas. It is incomprehensible, indestructible, unattached, unfettered, free from suffering and injury. This incomprehensible ātman is clearly not the ātman that is just one of the eleven Rudras. Given the overall context this ātman would seem to be the one god, that one, the brahman, the unitary prāṇa which is the immortal element in all creatures and which divides itself up as the eleven Rudras when manifesting at the level of individuality.

B.A.U. 4.3 and 4

These two brāhmaṇas deal with Janaka's questions to Yajñavalkya. In 4.3.7 Yajñavalkya says that the ātman is the person who is the light within the heart, the one made of consciousness among the prāṇas (vijñānamaya prāṇeṣu hṛdyantarjyotiḥ puruṣa). This ātman is immortal (amṛta) (4.3.12). It abides in the space within the heart (antar hṛdayākāśa),it is brahman (4.4.5) and it is the controller of all, the lord of all, the ruler of all (sarvasya vaśī sarvasyeśānah sarvasyādhipati) (4.4.22). This ātman/brahman, who is the light within the heart, who is vijñānamaya prāṇeṣu, is prāṇa for as 4.4.7 informs us,

> '... this disembodied (aśarīra), immortal (amṛta) prāṇa is brahman only, is light indeed.'[56]

This ātman/brahman/prāṇa which abides in the space of the heart has, as its manifestations, vijñāna, manas, prāṇa, cakṣus, śrotra, pṛthivi, apas, vāyu, ākāśa, tejas, atejas, kāma, akāma, krodha, akrodha, dharma, adharma and everything (sarvamaya) (4.4.5). The five groups of five and space are established (pratiṣṭhita) on it. The gods worship it as the light of lights (jyotiṣām jyotiḥ) as life immortal (āyuramṛta).

When embodied this ātman/brahman/prāṇa becomes connected with evils (pāpa), at death these are left behind (4.3.8).

During sleep this immortal one leaves the body, guarding it, i.e. keeping it alive, with the phenomenal prāṇa (4.3.12). At death the prāṇas, which are described as particles of light (tejomātraḥ), gather around the immortal one, who takes them into himself and descends into the heart. He then quits the body by way of one of the bodily apertures and prāṇa (breath), followed by the other prāṇas, departs after him. He then becomes consciousness (sa vijñāno bhavati) and comes under the influence of former knowledge, action and experience (vidyā, karmani and prajñā; 4.3.38-4.4.2.). Those who know the immortal one who is the eye of the eye, the ear of the ear, the mind of the mind and the breath of the breath (4.4.17-18), who are without desire, themselves become immortal (4.4.6-7 and 17) and go by a narrow ancient path (4.4.8) to the heavenly world. The prāṇas of such a one do not depart to another body but go to brahman/prāṇa/ātman. However, those who still have desires and do not know the immortal one go from life to life like a caterpillar goes from one blade of grass to another (4.4.3).

In these brāhmaṇas then, we find a view of prāṇa which not only reinforces earlier views that it is the immortal source and foundation of all and the essence of individual existence, which manifests as the faculties and vital forces of the body and knowledge of which bestows immortality, it is also well integrated into the Upaniṣadic teaching about rebirth.

C.U. 3.15.4

'...prāṇa, verily, is everything here has come to be, whatsoever there is.'[57]

C.U. 3.15 appears to be separate from the preceding section, though possibly connected with the two subsequent ones. In all of 3.15, 3.16 and 3.17 there is no mention of brahman or ātman though they are central topics in the immediately preceding and following sections. These three khaṇḍas thus seem to constitute an independent section which is highly symbolic in nature and reminiscent of the brāhmaṇas. The quoted passage thus appears to be a reiteration of the earlier tradition of regarding prāṇa as the fundamental principle of existence.

C.U. 4.3.1-4

'Air (vāyu), verily, is the absorbent; for when fire goes out, it goes into the air. When the sun sets it goes into the air, and when the moon sets it goes into the air. When water dries up it goes into the air. For air indeed absorbs them all. This, with regard to the divinities. Now, with reference to the self : breath (prāṇa), indeed, is the absorbent. When one sleeps speech just goes into breath; sight goes into breath; hearing goes into breath; the mind goes into breath. For breath, indeed, absorbs all this. These two, verily, are the two absorbents, air among the gods, breath among the breaths.'[58]

This passage come is a short section on the story and teaching of Raikva. It begins at 4.1.1 and ends at 4.4.1. The teaching draws on the earlier equation of Vāyu and prāṇa. As cosmic phenomena such as sun, moon and water are all absorbed by Vāyu so individual faculties such as speech, sight, hearing and mind are all absorbed into prāṇa. These two are obviously two aspects of the same principle which is not only the greatest of the divinities/faculties (as in a number of the stories of the faculties competing) but also their source and ultimate destination. There is no mention of any principle which absorbs prāṇa/Vāyu.

This teaching continues in the form of a story, in the course of which we are informed that the one god (deva eka) is not seen by mortals though he abides in manifold forms. We are also told that it is through Virāj that the whole world becomes seen. Here are clear remeniscences of Falk's interpretation of the Vedic world picture where prāna is the puruṣa, the form (rūpa) and substance of all, whilst Vāc/Virāj is the apprehension or naming (nāma) of that and of Miller's Agni/Văc version of the same.

C.U. 4.10.4-5

'Then the fires said among themselves : This student of sacred wisdom has performed his penance and tended us well. Let us teach him then. They said to him, Prāṇa is Brahman, Joy (ka) is Brahman, Space (kha) is Brahman. Then he said, I understand that Prāṇa is Brahman, but joy and Space I do not understand. They said, Joy verily, that is the same as space, verily that is the same as joy. Then they explained to him prāṇa and space (ākāśa).'[59]

This passage comes from a section which commences at 4.10.1 and continues to 4.17.10 (the end of chapter four). It is the teaching given by Satyakāma to Upakosala, son of Kamala. The preceding section (4.4.1-4.9.3) is the teaching received by Satyakāma himself whilst the succeeding one (5.1.1-5.2.8) is the teaching given to Vyāghrapāda by Satyakāma. Hence, these three sections ought to constitute one coherent doctrine. Elsewhere in the section under consideration (i.e. at 4.15.1) we are told that

> 'The person who is seen in the eye, he is the self (ātman). This is the immortal, the fearless, this is Brahman.'[60]

Elsewhere, as was noted above in connection with B.A.U.2.3.1-6, that person is prāṇa. Ś.B. 10.5.2.9; B.A.U. 4.2.23 and Mait.U.7.11 make the person in the right eye Indra and the person in the left eye Virāj or Indranī Indra, here, seems to be identified with the cosmic puruṣa who, in Falk's scheme is prāṇa. Such equations are supported by Ś.B. 6.1.1.2-5, where prāṇa is declared to be Indra, puruṣa and Prajāpati, A.Ā. 2.2.3, where Indra declares that he, like all else in creation, is prāṇa and by Kauṣ.U. 3.2, where Indra states that he is prāṇa. C.U. 4.15.1, however, identifies the person in the eye with ātman-brahman. Since prāṇa is declared to be brahman in C.U. 4.10.4 the ātman referred to here must be prāṇa.

The statement in the preceding section, that prāṇa is one quarter of brahman (4.8.3), does not undermine this interpretation for it is clear that the reference is to the phenomenal prāṇa which is but one manifestation of the unitary prāṇa. The other quarters mentioned are eye, ear and mind, standard components in the various lists of the diversified forms of prāṇa.

C.U.7

This chapter does not, on the surface, present prāṇa as an ultimate principle for it distinguishes it from ātman and derives it from ātman. However, in my opinion this view has been redacted into an original account which presented prāṇa as the ultimate principle. The chapter deals with Sanatkumāra's instructions to Nārada on the progressive worship of brahman. The teaching begins with the statement that worshipping brahman as name (nāma) is quite legitimate. However, we are told that speech (vāc) is greater than name; in turn, mind (manas) is greater than speech; will (saṃkalpa) is greater than mind; thought (citta) is greater than will; contemplation (dhyāna) is greater than thought; understanding (vijñāna) is greater than contemplation; strength (bala) is greater than understanding; food (anna) is greater than strength; water (ap) is greater than food; heat (tejas) is greater than water; ether (ākāśa) is greater than heat; memory (smara) is greater than ether; hope (āśā) is greater than memory; breath/life (prāṇa) is greater than hope.

At this point the narrative changes. Whereas each of the preceding sections ended with the words 'Venerable Sir, is there anything greater than...? Yes, there is something greater than... Do, Venerable Sir, tell me that ...' section 15, where it is stated that prāṇa is greater than āśā, ends with 'Prāṇa is all this. Verily, he who sees this, thinks this, understands this, becomes an excellent speaker [ativādin]. Even if people should say to him, 'you are an excellent speaker', he should not deny it.'[61] The following section introduces a different kind of treatment, where concepts such as truth (satya), understanding (vijñāna) and faith (śraddhā) are described. It is clear that this set of verses forms part of a different analysis than that offered by the first set. Instead of commenting on the relative merits of the different concepts Sanatkumāra introduces them as being desirable to understand. Hence, each of the section from sixteen to twenty three, which introduces the concept of the infinite (bhūma), end with the words 'Venerable Sir, I desire to understand ...' The infinite is described in the following two verses, after which we read in 25.1, 'Now next, the instruction with regard to the self-sense (ahaṃkāra)'.[62] The following verse (25.2) introduces 'the instruction in regard to the self (ātman),' which is described as being 'this all'. Then, in 26.1, we are told that prāṇa springs from the ātman (ātmataḥ prāṇaḥ), hope (āśā) springs from the self, memory springs from the self and so on back down the list in 7.1.3-15.

What is peculiar about 26.1 is that none of the qualities listed between 16.1 and 25.1 are mentioned as springing from the self. This creates a distinct sense of discontinuity. The continuity can be restored however, by taking 7.25.2 and 7.26.1 and placing them immediately after 7.15.4. In fact, this is what Beidler does in his interpretation of this chapter though he does not indicate that he is doing so. The only problem with such a move is that 7.15.4 and 7.25.2 seem to contradict each other. The former states that prāṇa is everything (prāṇa hy evaitāni sarvāṇi bhavati); the latter makes an almost identical claim about ātman (ātmaivedaṃ sarvam iti) whilst, at the same time, in the next verse, stating that prāṇa is derived from the ātman. It is this incompatability which, I would suggest, explains why 7.16-25 was interpolated at this point. If the redactor wanted to subordinate prāṇa to ātman it would be foolish for him simply to add 7.25.2 and 7.26.1 onto 7.15.4 for the incompatibility just discussed would be readily apparent. What better way to disguise it than by creating a break between the statement exhalting prāṇa and that exhalting ātman? If the interpolation could have a style which created the impression of continuity all the better. This, I would suggest, is exactly what we have here: an original text presenting prāṇa as the ultimate principle which has been modified by two additions. One of these begins either halfway through 7.25.1, where ahaṃkāra is introduced, or at 7.25.2, where ātman is introduced. The purpose of this addition is to subordinate all the principles mentioned in 7.1-15 to the ātman. The second addition comprises 7.16 to 7.24.2 or 7.16 to 7.25. The purpose of this addition is to obscure the incompatibility of the statements in 7.15.4 and 7.25.2. C.U. 7.1-15 thus constitutes a complete unit in its own right and presents prāṇa as the ultimate principle.

Muṇḍ.U. 3.14

> 'Truly it is prāṇa that shines forth in all beings. Knowing him the wise man does not talk of anything else. Sporting in the self (ātman), delighting in the self, performing works, such a one is the greatest of the knowers of brahman.'[63]

In this verse prāṇa appears to be equated with ātman and, possibly, with brahman. This latter identification is, however, uncertain for the preceding verse makes the prāṇa/ātman the 'source of brahma' (brahmayoni). Deussen and Monier-Williams[64] opt for a neuter reading of 'brahma' in verse three and this makes the triple equation prāṇa/ātman/brahman difficult. Hume simply retains the masculine or neuter 'brahma' in his translation whilst Radhakrishnan opts for the masculine, which would mean that prāṇa/ātman/brahman is the source of the creator god, Brahmā. Whichever of these is the case it is clear that in this section prāṇa is being presented as one term for referring to the ultimate principle.

Kaṭh.U. 2.3.2

> 'The whole world, whatever here exists, springs from and moves in prāṇa.'[65]

The main theme of Kaṭh U. 2.3 is soteriology. We are first introduced to the fundamental reality. It is brahman; it is called immortal; in it all worlds rest; nothing goes beyond it (2.3.1). This supreme principle is prāṇa (2.3.2) and if one is not able to know this before the body falls away, one becomes fit for embodiment in the created world.[66] The order of principles in the created world, from lower to higher, is senses, mind, sattva, the great self (mahanātman), the unmanifest (avyakta) and, finally, the puruṣa which, given the context, can reasonably be taken as a synonym for prāṇa. If the puruṣa-prāṇa equation is accepted, 2.3.2 taken at face value and prāṇa accorded the status of ultimate principle the whole of 2.3 is intelligible; if not, 2.3.2 becomes an enigma. Hence, it seems likely that in this part of the Kaṭha Upanisad prāṇa is understood as a synonym for puruṣa and brahman.

If my interpretations of the foregoing passages are accepted then it can be seen that a number of Upaniṣadic teachers regarded prāṇa or, more accurately, the unitary prāṇa as the ultimate principle of existence even though some of them only do so implicitly rather than explicitly. That such a view was prominent in the Upaniṣadic period is attested, in addition to those passages examined above, in a number of Upaniṣadic versions of the contest of the faculties.

The contests of the faculties

These accounts are located at B.A.U. 1.3, 1.5.22, and 6.1.1–14; C.U. 1.2.1-14 and 5.1.1-15; Kauṣ.U. 2.14 and 3.3 and P.U. 2.1-13. Of these B.A.U. 1.3 and C.U. 1.2.1-14 are versions of the same account. The same is true for B.A.U. 6.1.1-14 and C.U. 5.1.1–15. Each of the others is an independent version. By and large, these accounts reiterate what has been said above about the nature of prāṇa in pre–Upaniṣadic and Upaniṣadic literature. They can thus be seen to support my interpretation of that material. In these stories prāṇa is presented as a major cosmic principle or as the one ultimate principle from which all else derives. At the material level of creation it diversifies itself to produce both the physical aspects of existence and the more subtle aspects which animate the physical ones. All these accounts describe the subtle manifestations in terms of the sensory faculties plus mind (manas), speech (vāc) and prāṇa (breath), the manifestation most directly derived from and closest in nature to the original cosmic prāṇa. Almost every account makes prāṇa an immortal principle and the Kauṣītakī accounts make it the intelligence self (prajñātman) and the self (ātman). Hence, as in the pre–Upaniṣadic accounts, prāṇa gives rise to mentation - through the manas–and, perhaps expressed more clearly here than in the earlier material, it is that reality which can be described as consciousness or intelligence (prajñā) or as self (ātman).

We may note, however, that there is a significant difference between the view of existence presented through these accounts and that which emerges from examination of pre-Upaniṣadic material. Here, the ultimate mutuality and bi-polarity of prāṇa and Vāc is not in evidence. In these accounts speech is simply derived from and dependent on prāṇa which exists on three levels. At the first level it is the ultimate principle of existence and often referred to by terms such as prajñātman, ātman and brahman. From it all other major cosmic principles such as the gods, derive. At the second level it manifests as the subtle animating principle and divides into the fivefold prāṇa, mind, speech and the sense faculties. These twelve constitute the subtle body. At the third level prāṇa manifests as the physical body (bana or śarīra) which is composed of ether (ākāśa), wind (vāyu), fire (agni), water (apa) and earth (pṛthivi).

B.A.U. 1.3 and C.U. 1.2.1-14

Both of these passages are variants of the same account. Deussen argues that the B.A.U. version is the oldest of the two.[67] Both passages inform us that the devas decided to overcome the asuras (the elder of the two parties according to the B.A.U.) by using the udgītha (the high chant of the Sāma Veda).[68] In the B.A.U. version the devas (speech, breath [in-the-nose], eye, ear, mind and breath-in-the-mouth) ask each other to chant (udgāya) for them; the C.U. version has the devas reverencing (upāsāṃcakrire) each other in turn as the udgītha. The order of introducing each deity (i.e. faculty) is also different in the two accounts. The B.A.U. version starts with speech and puts prāṇa second whereas the C.U. version starts with prāṇa-in-the-nose (nāsikya prāṇa) and puts speech second.[69] As in earlier versions of this story, prāṇa (here specified as prāṇa-in-the-mouth) emerges as supreme. In this version it is the only faculty able to defeat the asuras. Hence we are told in B.A.U. 1.3.7 that 'as a clod of earth would be scattered by striking against a rock, even so they (the asuras) were scattered in all directions and perished.'[70]

From B.A.U. 1.3.8 and C.U. 1.2.9 the two versions diverge considerably. The C.U. account is quite brief, with just a few verses on the nature of the breath-in-the-mouth. The B.A.U.version, however, adds a section on how the breath in the mouth carries each of the faculties beyond death (pareṇa mṛtyum), i.e. to immortality. In their descriptions of the breath-in-the-mouth both versions link it with Āṅgirasa[71] and Bṛhaspati. The B.A.U. also links it with Brahmaṇaspati by the statement 'Speech is brahman and this is its lord (vāg vai brahma tasyā eṣa patiḥ)' and states that it upholds all the world.[72]

Radhakrishnan[73] suggest that in this context Bṛhaspati and Brhmaṇaspati refer to the 'Lord of the Ṛgveda' and the 'Lord of the Sāmaveda' respectively, presumably because 1.3.22 states that 'this', i.e. prāṇa-in-the-mouth, is the Sāmaveda. However, there is a subtle change in the text at this point. Whereas 1.3.20 and 1.3.21 tell us that the prāṇa-in-the-mouth is the Lord of speech (Bṛhaspati) and the Lord of prayer (Brahmaṇaspati) 1.3.22 *identifies* the prāṇa in the mouth with the Sāma Veda. Exactly why this shift occurs is not clear, though at this point the concern of the whole brāhmaṇa (apart from verse 23, which states 'by vital breath (prāṇa) is this whole (world) upheld'.)[74] changes from a concern with the faculties to a discussion of the benefits to be derived from the sāman chant. Hence, 1.3.22-28 (possibly excluding verse 23) may well be a section that was originally independent of 1.3.1-21. If so, there is little justification for taking Bṛhati and Brahman in verses 20 and 21 as referring to the Ṛk and Yajur Vedas respectively.

Deussen has also noted this break in the text. In commenting on B.A.U. 1.3 he states that once the prāṇa had demonstrated its superiority over the other faculties '... it is then celebrated as Ayāsya Āṇgirasa, Bṛhaspati, Brahmaṇaspati–Now suddenly in the Bṛh 1.3.22, the situation is changed. The Prāṇa was previously the victorious singer of the Sāman, of Udgītha, now it is explained as the Sāman, as the Udgītha itself and the section ends with the glorification of the Sāman and an instruction regarding it to proceed with the chanting of the same by the Yajamāna (the performer of the sacrifice) and by the priests.

We believe that we discover here the joining point or the suture which binds together the two originally different pieces: (1) Bṛh (1.3.1–21) (akin to Talav[akāra] Up[aniṣad] Br[āhmaṇa] 2.1–2,2.10–11) describes in a legend the superiority of the Prāṇa conquering the demons, over to [sic] rest of the vital organs; (2) Bṛh. 1.3.22–28, on the other hand, appears to be originally devoted to the glorification of the Sāman (Udgītha) as Prāṇa ... on account of this, the original point of the narration gets lost.'[75]

However, Deussen offers no explanation as to why this disjunction should have occurred. From the perspective of the present analysis, the reason would be that the intention of the original author of the account found in the B.A.U. (i.e.1.3.1–21) was to extol the prāṇa as the supreme principle whereas that of the redactor of the Upaniṣad was to negate such a conclusion by a process of obfuscation. The same kind of device seems to have been employed in C.U.7 (see my analysis of this on pages 64–66 above).

If this analysis is accurate then, in the B.A.U. account at least, the prāṇa-in-the-mouth (mukhya prāṇa) possesses two qualities which suggest a status similar to that accorded to prāṇa in a number of earlier texts: being the foundation of the world and the source of immortality.[76]

B.A.U. 6.1.1-14 and C.U. 5.1.1–15

These two passages are, again, versions of the same account. The verses in the B.A.U. tend to be longer and extra verses are added concerning the 'faculty' of semen (vs. 6 and vs. 12). B.A.U. 6.1.7 = C.U. 5.1.6-7; B.A.U. 6.1.14 = C.U. 5.1.13–15. In the B.A.U. version the faculties go to Brahmā for ajudication about which is superior; in the C.U. account they go to Prajāpati. In both cases they are told that the most excellent faculty is that 'after whose departure this body is thought to be worse off'[77] As prāṇa starts to leave the other faculties start to be uprooted too; hence they declare prāṇa to be the most excellent. C.U. 5.1.15 rounds off the episode with a succinct statement about the ultimate identity of all these faculties: 'Verily, they do not call them speeches or eyes or ears or minds. They call them breaths for all these are breath (prāṇa).'[78] Here, there is nothing explicitly stating that prāṇa is the ultimate principle. This is, however, the only occasion in the Upaniṣads where this story does not contain such a statement. It would thus be reasonable, I suggest, to infer that the author was assuming that the recipients of the teaching would be aware that the prāṇa which is the true identity of all the faculties is, in fact, the primeval principle, source of all.

Kauṣ U. 2.1-14

> 'Prāṇa is Brahman, thus indeed Kausītakī used to say. Of this same prāṇa which is brahman, the mind, verily, is the messenger; the eye the protector, the ear the announcer, speech the housekeeper ... prāṇa is Brahman, thus indeed Paiṅga used to say. Of this same prāṇa as brahman behind the speech the eye is enclosed, behind the eye the ear is enclosed, behind the ear the mind is enclosed, behind the mind the prāṇa is enclosed'.[79]

The teaching in this part of the Upaniṣad is something of a patchwork of Kausītakī's views and those of Pratardana. Kausītakī commences by equating prāṇa and brahman. Then Pratardana equates the uktha (the high chant of the Ṛgveda–often used as a synonym for the highest principle) with the prāṇa that is brahman and, finally, we return to Kauṣītakī, who teaches that cosmic divinities such as sun, moon and lightning go to wind (vāyu) where 'though they die in the wind do not perish (altogether)'.[80] Similarly, he teaches that the faculties of the individual are all absorbed in prāṇa where 'though they all die in the prāṇa, do not perish (altogether). Therefrom, indeed, they come forth again'.[81]

The next verses deal with the controversy among the faculties. Here, instead of entering into conflict with asuras or taking turns at leaving the body, the faculties in this account try to animate the body. Only the prāṇa succeeds. Then we are told something that the other accounts do not provide; that the prāṇa is the prajñātman (intelligence self) and that when the faculties understood this they all went to the heavenly world (svar). Likewise, we are told that if a person has this realization they too will go to the heavenly world where dwell the gods 'Having reached that, he who knows this [that the prāṇa is the prajñātman] becomes immortal as the gods are immortal.'[82]

This passage provides one of the clearest statements about the nature and status of prāṇa : it is brahman, the uktha, the prajñātman. Cosmically, as Vāyu, it absorbs the other deities; individually, as prāṇa, it absorbs the other faculties. Knowing its true identity one becomes immortal. The passage to be considered next reinforces this and adds to it.

Kauṣ.U. 3.3

This account is part of a chapter extolling prāṇa as the highest principle. In the preceding verse Indra tells Pratardana that he is prāṇa, he is the prajñātman, he is life (āyus) and he is immortality (amṛta). He then offers to Pratardana (in Radhakrishnan's version) or, more likely, Pratardana presents to him (as in Deussen's and Hume's versions) the well known view that the prāṇas operate together as a unity (ekabhūyam gacchanti), none operates without the others. 'True', says Indra, 'but there is a most excellent one among the prāṇas.' This most excellent one is the prāṇa which seizes hold of or encompasses (parigṛhya) the body and animates (utthāpayati) it. That same prāṇa is the prajñātman and at death all the prāṇas merge with it and depart from the body. 3.8, the final verse of the chapter, informs us that this prāṇa, which is the prajñātman, which is bliss (ānanda), which is ageless (ajara) and immortal (amṛta) is 'the protector of the world ... the sovereign of the world ... the lord of all. He [says Indra] is my self (ātman) ...'[83]

P.U.2.1-13

Here the tale of the disagreement among the faculties is told to Bhārgava by Pippalāda. The actual account is abbreviated into two verses where prāṇa informs the other faculties (deva) that he alone, dividing himself fivefold, supports the body. They, however, do not believe him until he demonstrates that if he departs they will be pulled along with him and if he remains they too will remain. Once prāṇa has established his supremacy the other faculties praise him. Then we are told that prāṇa is Agni, Sūrya, Prajanya (the rain god), Vāyu, Pṛthivi, rayi (matter), god (deva), being and non-being (sadāsat), amṛta (immortality), Prajāpati, Indra and Rudra. 'As spokes in the centre of a wheel everything is established in prāṇa. All this is under the control of prāṇa, which is well established in the three worlds.'[84]

Prāṇa is thus, once again, presented as that power which diversifies and manifests as the various faculties of the individual and as the various cosmic principles. It is the immortal, the foundation and controller of all. However, prāṇa is not the only term described in this way. Similar descriptions can be found of brahman and ātman.

Model Accounts

These accounts are, I would suggest, modelled on existing descriptions of prāṇa which, in turn, provide the basic blueprint for Upaniṣadic conceptions of the inner essence of an individual and the fundamental principle of existence. There are a number of such 'model' accounts : B.A.U. 1.4.7, 2.1.17 and 4.1.2; Kauṣ.U. 4,20, A.U. 1.2, Mait.U. 6.1–3 and 8 and Kena U.1.

B.A.U. 1.4.7

The brāhmaṇa of which this verse is a part opens with the words 'ātmaivedam agra āsīt puruṣavidhaḥ' 'In the beginning this (world) was only the self (ātman), in the shape of a person.[86] The following verses then describe the process of creation through the bifurcation of the self into man and woman. These transform successively into all living forms. Verse five then informs us that 'he became the creation' (tataḥ srṣṭir abhavat) and verse seven that at the time 'this' was unmanifest (taddhedaṃ tarhy avyākṛtam āsīt), it became manifest through name and form (nāmarūpa). He (the ātman) entered that which had become manifest, 'even to the tips of the nails, as a razor is (hidden) in the razor case, or as fire in the fire source. Him they see not for (as seen) he is incomplete, when breathing he is called breath (prāṇa), when speaking voice (vāc), when seeing eye (cakṣus), when hearing ear (śrotra), when thinking mind (manas). These are merely the names of his acts ... The self is to be meditated upon for in it all those become one.'[86]

In verse ten, echoing verse one, we are told that in the beginning this (self? world?) was brahman (brahma vā idam agra āsīt). This brahman, like ātman in verse one, became the whole creation (tasmāt tat sarvam abhavat). These verses thus serve to equate ātman and brahman. The whole section, however, is highly reminiscent of statements about prāṇa who, as seen, is incomplete, who manifests as prāṇa, vāc, cakṣus, śrotra and manas and who is ultimately the unitary immortal source of all. In other words, the pattern employed in this text to establish ātman-brahman as the fundamental principle is one which is modelled on earlier accounts of the nature of prāṇa. The accuracy of this interpretation is reinforced by Kauṣ.U. 4.20 (discussed below).

B.A.U. 2.1.17

This verse describes how the vijñāna-maya-puruṣa (the person made of consciousness) takes the consciousness (vijñānam) of the prāṇas, here referring to the various faculties, into itself and resides in the space within the heart (antar-hṛdaya-ākāśa) during sleep. The verse ends with the statement 'when the breath (prāṇa) is restrained, speech (vāc) is restrained, the eye (cakṣus) is restrained, the ear (śrotra) is restrained, the mind (manas) is restrained.'[87] Verse twenty indicates that this vijñāna-maya-puruṣa is, in fact, the ātman, from which come all prāṇas, all worlds (loka), all deities (deva) and all beings (bhūta). The verse ends with the statement 'prāṇas are the truth (satya) and their truth is this (ātman).'[88]

Here again we have the connection between the prāṇas (faculties/vital breaths) and the self (ātman). The relationship between the two is identical to that which in other contexts operates between the unitary prāṇa and the diversified prāṇas. Again, Kauṣ.U. 4.20 supports such an interpretation.

B.A.U. 4.1-2

There are seven verses in the first brāhmaṇa of this chapter, for which Radhakrishnan provides the sub-heading 'Inadequate definitions of brahman'.[89] It is part of Yajñavalkya's teaching. Here he asks King Janaka of Videha what other teachers have said about the highest brahman (parama brahman). Upon receiving this request Janaka states that Jītvan Śailini says 'speech (vāc) is the highest brahman', Udaṅka Śaulbāyana says 'breath (prāṇa) is the highest brahman', Barka Vārṣṇa says 'the eye (cakṣus) is the highest brahman', Gardhabhīvipīta Bhāradvāja says 'the ear (śrotra) is the highest brahman', Satyakāma, Jabāla says 'the mind (manas) is the highest brahman', Vidagdha Śākalya says 'the heart (hṛdaya) is [the highest] brahman'. To all these claims Yajñavalkya has just one reply : 'This brahman is only one–footed, Your Majesty', i.e.it is incomplete or inadequate.

However, Yajñavalkya himself makes no statements about the nature of the highest brahman. Rather, in 4.2 he asks Janaka where he will go after death. Janaka admits his ignorance and asks Yajñavalkya to enlighten him. Yajñavalkya points out that the person in the right eye is Indra (Indha) and the person in the left eye is his wife Virāj. These two are united in the space within the heart and move in that channel (nāḍī) which goes upward from the heart. Nourishment flows to them through the channels (hitāḥ) of the heart. 'Therefore that (self composed of Indha and Virāj) is, as it were, an eater of finer food than the bodily self (śarīra ātman).'[90] The next verse (v.4) then states that his (the self's) western side are the western breaths, the eastern side the eastern breaths etc. but the self (ātman) is not this, not this (neti neti); (see C.U. 3.13.1-6 for a correlation between individual breaths and each of the five directions). The ātman is then described in exactly the same words that are found in the description of the ātman in B.A.U. 3.9.29: it is incomprehensible, indestructible, unattached, unfettered, free from suffering and injury.

These two brāhmaṇas constitute what is obviously a version of the competition of the faculties. Vāc, prāṇa, cakṣus, śrotra, manas and, here, hṛdaya are all deemed to be incomplete expressions of brahman. The complete expression appears to be ātman, who is said to be none of the prāṇas (here linked with the various directions; in 3.9 stated to be prāṇa, apāna etc.) and to be incomprehensible etc. The ātman in this passage is Indra, who inhabits the right eye, along with his wife, who inhabits the left. They are united in the heart (echoes of the puruṣa sūkta?). As was pointed out above, in connection with B.A.U. 2.3.1-6, the Indra in the right eye is frequently identified with prāṇa. Also the treatment of the faculties differs from other versions of their competition.

Nevertheless, it is clear that the manner of introducing and describing the ātman is modelled on other accounts where the unitary prāṇa occupies the place of the ātman. Here, however, instead of the ātman which is prāṇa occupying the body completely like a razor in a razor case, as in Kauṣ. U. 4.20, it abides in the heart.

Kauṣ.U. 4.20

Here Ajātaśatru teaches Dṛpta Bālāki of the Gargya clan, as he did in B.A.U. 2.1.17. The teaching is that during sleep speech (vāc) together with all names, eye (cakṣus) together with all forms, ear (śrotra) together with all sounds and mind (manas) together with all thoughts enter the prāṇa. On waking the prāṇas proceed from the self (ātman = prāṇa), the gods (deva) from the prāṇas and the worlds (loka) from the gods. We are then told that the prāṇa, the intelligence-self (prajñātman) enters the bodily self (śarīrātman) upto the hairs and nails like a razor in a razor case 'on that self these other selves depend as upon a chief his own men.'[91]

This passage is only a 'model' account in terms of its form for it clearly presents prāṇa as the ātman. It is included here, however, since it can be employed as a kind of 'key' for interpreting other 'model' passages. It is clear that there is much in common between this passage and B.A.U. 1.4.7. It seems likely that one borrowed from the other or that they both drew on a common source. The Kausītakī account is more detailed and makes it clear that the ātman/brahman of B.A.U. 1.4.7. and 10 is the prāṇa/prajñātman, this last term being used to indicate the supreme self in A.U. 3. Similarly, the context in which these equations occur is also found at B.A.U. 2.17 where the term vijñāna-maya–puruṣa is employed to refer to the ātman. It would appear then, that the terms prāṇa, ātman, prajñātman, vijñāna-maya–puruṣa and brahman were regarded as being synonymous in meaning by a number of Upaniṣadic teachers. This Kausītakī account, because it draws the various elements from other places together, thus gives substance to what elsewhere was simply inference. It is an ideal 'model'.

A.U. 1.2.

This is a complex text which is difficult to interpret but, given the foregoing analysis of other Upaniṣadic passages and the argument set out below, its status as an account of the nature of ātman which is 'modelled' on similar accounts of the nature of prāṇa is not difficult to appreciate. The story line is that of the ātman creating the universe. First he creates the worlds (loka), which are water (ambhas), light space or light rays (marīci), death (mara) and water (apas).

Water (ambhas) is above heaven or sky (dyaus), which is its support. The light space (marīci) is the atmosphere; death (mara) is the earth (pṛthivi) and beneath that are the waters (apas). Many translators take the following verses to teach that puruṣa was then created out of the waters by the self. The text reads 'so 'dbhya eva puruṣam samuddhṛtyāmūrchayat',[92] and this could legitimately be rendered as something like, 'From out of these (udbhya–ablative plural) he took and gave form to the puruṣa'. In other words, the puruṣa was derived from all the worlds created by the self and not just from the waters. Then the ātman broods over (abhyatapa)[93] the puruṣa and 'hatches' (nirabhidyata) the world guardians (lokapāla), which are the various faculties and phenomena, from the parts of the puruṣa's body. The pattern of derivation can be set out as follows :

TABLE 4

mouth (mukha) →	speech (vāc)→	fire (agni)
nostrils (nāsike)	breath (prāṇa)	wind (vāyu)
eyes (akṣinī)	sight (cakṣus)	the sun (āditya)
ears (karṇau)	hearing (śrotra)	directions (diśa)
skin (tvac)	hairs (loma)	plants and trees (oṣadhivanaspatya)
heart (hṛd)	mind (manas)	moon (candra)
navel (nabhi)	digestive faculty (apāna)	death (mṛtya)
phallus (śiśna)	seman (reta)	waters (āpa)

Once created, these divinities (devata): speech, fire breath, wind, sight, sun hearing directions, hairs, plants and trees, mind, moon, digestive faculty, death semen and waters, all fall into (prāpatan) the great ocean (mahatyarṇava) where they experience hunger and thirst. They then ask the ātman to find them somewhere to become established (pratiṣṭhita) and eat food. They are offered a cow and then a horse but both are deemed to be inadequate. Then the/a puruṣa is offered and this is found to be an acceptable home. Each of the principles/deities in the right hand column enters the one from which it was derived and these, in turn, enter into the parts of puruṣa's body from whence they came. Hunger and thirst, however, are then left without an abode, so the ātman allows them to enter the puruṣa along with the other principles/deities. Finally, the ātman produces material[95] form (mūrti) from the water (s) (a/āpa) and this acts as food.

We are then presented with a version of the contest of the faculties. Food tries to escape being consumed by the puruṣa who tries to seize it with each of his faculties in turn: speech, breath, sight, hearing, skin, mind, generative organ and digestive faculty (apāna).[96] It is the digestive faculty alone that is able to seize the food. Then comes a peculiar statement: (Vāyu is the grasper of food, 'Vāyu is the one who lives on food.' Vāyu, of course, is derived from prāṇa in the first list so why it is introduced at this point is unclear.[97]

So constituted, the individual puruṣa seems to be complete. It is a macrocosm of the macrocosm and has the ability, indicated by the list of derivations, to apprehend phenomena and satisfy the needs of hunger and thirst. The ātman wonders how (or whether) the puruṣa, as it is constituted, can live without him. He then considers the means by which he could enter this being and dismisses each of the routes listed in columns one and two since he does not identify himself (solely?) with any faculty or part of the body. He thus decides to enter through the door called 'the cleft' (vidṛti), located at the crown of the head (sīman).[98] Once inside, he perceives 'this very person–'etam eva puruṣa' (i.e. himself?) as brahma tataman' (just that supreme one)[99] The following verse tells us that this perceiver (the ātman) is Indra.

The purpose of the whole chapter seems to be the presentation of a view wich not only makes the self the source of all existence but also makes external phenomena derive from the puruṣa. The facts that the ātman is the ultimate identity of all the worlds, faculties and phenomena, that he enters the body through the top of the head and that he is identified with Indra all remind one of prāṇa, which in other contexts does all these things and has all these characteristics.

The final chapter of this Upaniṣad, just four verses long, supports this connection. It provides information about the nature of the ātman. The sanskṛt is not clear, however, and verse one could be either a series of questions and answers or just a series of questions.

Hume points out that all the published texts of this Upaniṣad open with the words 'ko 'yam' though Müller, Bohtlingk and Deussen amend it to 'ko yam'. Given the context, I would favour the amendation for the issue would then be cast in familiar mould: that of the faculties competing. Hence, verse one would read 'Who is he whom we worship as the ātman? Which one is the ātman? [Is it he] by whom one sees, or [he] by whom one hears, or [he] by whom one smells odours, or [he] by whom one speaks speech, or [he] by whom one distinguishes between the sweet and the unsweet?' The implied answer is 'None of these', and this would certainly fit with the conclusions of all other similar competitions. However, instead of straightforward answers, verse two provides a list of mental phenomena, all of which are stated to be names of intelligence (prajñāna). Verse three then informs us that this prajñāna is everything. It is brahman, Indra, Prajāpati and all the gods. It is the five elements, the foundation (pratiṣṭhita) of all things, the guide or eye (netra) of all things. The final verse tells us that 'he'[100] by means of the intelligence-self (prajñātman), left this world and, having obtained all his desires in the world of heaven, became immortal (svarge loke sarvān kāmān aptvāmṛtaḥ samabhavat).[101]

The prajñātman thus seems to be the self referred to in verse one. Such a conclusion would put this text in agreement with the other Upaniṣad of the Ṛgveda, the Kauṣitakī, in employing the term prajñātman to refer to the supreme self. There, of course, the prajñātman is explicitly equated with prāṇa and such an equation would not be out of character here. If so, we see, once again, that the concept of prāṇa has been employed as a kind of blueprint for the presentation of ātman as the supreme principle.

Mait.U. 6.1-3 and 8

> 'He (the self) bears himself in two ways, as he who is breath (prāṇa) and he who is the sun (āditya). Yonder sun, verily is the outer self; the inner self is breath... There are, assuredly, two forms of Brahman, the formed and the formless. Now that which is formed is unreal (asatya); that which is the formless is the real (satya); that is the Brahman, that is the light. That which is the light is the sun... The self (ātman) is the lord (īśāna), the beneficent (śambhu), the real (bhava), the terrible (rudra), the lord of creation (prajāpati), the creator of all (viśvasṛk), the golden germ, truth (satya), life (prāṇa), spirit (haṃsa), the ordainer (śāstā), the pervader

(viṣṇu), Nārāyaṇa [abode of man], the shining (arka) [the] vivifier (savita), the upholder (dhātā), the maker (vidhātā), sovereign (samrad) Indra, the moon (indur)... He who has all forms, the golden one, who is all-knowing, the final goal, the only light, who gives heat, the thousand rayed, abiding in a hundred places, the life (prāṇa), of creatures, the yonder sun, rises.'[102]

In this passage it is not self-evident that prāṇa is being presented as the ultimate principle. However, if we examine the concept of self (ātman) as it is presented in this material it appears to be being employed as a synonym for the unitary prāṇa. In the Śatapatha Brāhmaṇa Agni is often put in the same role as the unitary prāṇa.

Hence, in Ś.B. 10.3.3 1-8 we are told that Agni manifests in the body as speech, eye (sight), mind (mentation), ear (hearing) and 'the agni who is everything here': prāṇa. This is exactly the kind of statement which, elsewhere, describes the manifestation of the unitary prāṇa in the body. The first four pass into prāṇa during sleep and emerge again on waking. Cosmically, fire corresponds to speech, the sun to the eye, the moon to the mind, the ear to the quarters and Vāyu to prāṇa. Similar correspondences are found throughout the Śatapatha Brāhmaṇa. Numerous references make Agni, Vāyu (or prāṇa) and Āditya the three principal manifestations of Agni[103] and in other places there are statements about Agni which exactly parallel thoses made about the ātman in the above quoted Upaniṣadic text, namely that Agni is the sun (āditya) in the cosmos and breath (prāṇa) in the individual.

In this Upaniṣadic passage the sun (āditya) is the formless (amūrta) and real or true (satya) aspect (rūpa) of brahman. In B.A.U. 2.3.1-6 we have a similar account. Here the formless (amūrta) and real or true (sat) aspects (rūpa) of brahman are prāṇa. Another similar account but with Vāyu replacing Āditya can be found at C.U.4.3 1-4, discussed above (p. 62-63). Taking all this information together it is clear that although it is not explicit in the text the author is drawing on a range of established associations and equivalences where the unitary Agni, the unitary prāṇa and the ātman can all be equated. This Agni/prāṇa/ātman is the real, unformed brahman, the supreme principle which manifests as a variety of cosmic and individualized phenomena. In the final analysis, however, all these manifestations are unreal (asat or asatya).

Kena Up. 1

Brahman is described as the ear of the ear, the mind of the mind, the speech of the speech, the eye of the eye and the prāṇa of the prāṇa (1.2). Brahman is not expressed through speech but is that by which speech is expressed; is not thought by the mind but is that by which the mind thinks; is not seen by the eye but is that by which the eye sees; is not heard by the ear but is that by which the ear hears; is not breathed by the breath (prāṇa) but is that by which the breath breathes. A later verse of the same Upaniṣad (3.1) tells us that Brahman once conquered for the devas and they gloried in his conquest (a reference to B.A.U. 1.3 and C.U. 1.2. 1-14 where prāṇa defeats the asuras?) It would appear, therefore, that here again we have an example of the prāṇa concept being employed as a 'model' for the description of brahman.

Overall, I think the foregoing analyses demonstrate that, in some Upaniṣadic circles at least, the concepts of ātman and brahman were developed on the basis of already existing conceptions of prāṇa. I am not claiming, however, that Upaniṣadic accounts of ātman and brahman are always to be understood in this way. Some Upaniṣads, such as the Iśā and the Māṇḍūkya, do not mention prāṇa at all and it could hardly be argued that their presentation of ātman and brahman are derived from descriptions of prāṇa. The same applies to the Śvetāśvatara Upaniṣad which mentions prāṇa only once.[104] Other texts clearly subordinate prāṇa to ātman and/or brahman and it is to these that I now turn.

Prāṇa as a purely derivative principle

There are a number of passages in the Upaniṣads which make prāṇa a derivative of the ultimate principle. Such references, found in early, middle and late Upaniṣads, point to a tradition of teaching which does not acknowledge prāṇa as the ultimate principle and does not equate it with ātman or brahman. The Taittirīya Upaniṣad is perhaps the best example of such a view though parts of the Praśna and Maitrī Upaniṣads also unambiguously subordinate prāṇa to the ātman. Other references such as those in the fourth and fifth vallis of the Kaṭha Upaniṣad are not so clear but because of their ambiguity they are included here. When these are taken together with what I have called the 'model' accounts the process by which prāṇa came to be subordinated to ātman and brahman becomes clear. On the one hand, some teachers employed existing doctrines about prāṇa to introduce their own teachings about ātman and brahman; on the other hand, some teachers developed a world-view in which the concepts of ātman and brahman were quite different from earlier versions of the prāṇa concept whilst, nevertheless incorporating some of its characteristics. It is with these teachings that this section is concerned. The material to be examined is B.A.U. 1.2; C.U. 1.1, 3.12–18 and 6; Taittirīya Upaniṣad 1-3; Kaṭha Upaniṣad 4 and 5; Praśna Upaniṣad 3 and Maitrī Upaniṣad 2. 6–7.

B.A.U. 1.2.

This brāhmaṇa begins with a creation account. In the beginning 'He' (death/hunger) created a self (ātman). He divided himself threefold: as fire (agni), as the sun (āditya) and as wind (vāyu). He is also prāṇa divided threefold and the cosmos in his body. Through the union (mīthuna) of mind (manas) and speech (vāc) the year was produced. Death was initially inclined to eat the offspring of this union, which cried out 'bhāṇ' and became speech (vāc) so he desisted.

> 'With that speech, with that self he brought forth all this whatsoever exists here, the Ṛgveda, the Yajurveda and the Sāmaveda, the metres, the sacrifices, men and cattle. Whatsoever he brought forth that he resolved to eat.'[105]

Wanting to perform a further sacrifice he sent out from himself the prāṇas. As they left, his body (śarīra) began to swell.

This material is not easy to interpret. The threefold division of the ātman into fire sun and wind is paralleled by the threefold division of prāṇa and hence prāṇa and ātman must be complementary principles or identical with each other. The threefold manifestation of Agni as Agni, Āditya and Vāyu is common is the Ś.B. and, as was noted in chapter one, prāṇa sometimes replaces Vayu or can be identified with Agni. Here then, prāṇa is presented as a penultimate or antepenultimate principle. The prāṇas referred to in 1.2.6 are, presumably, the three forms of prāṇa which arise from the threefold division mentioned in 1.2.3.

C.U. 1.1

This is the first section in a chapter which deals in a number of different ways, with the nature and symbolism of the udgītha. It tells us that the udgītha is the syllable 'aum' that it is the quintessence of the essences (rasa), the supreme (parama), the highest place (parārdhya), the eighth (aṣṭama). With regard to the relationship between prāṇa and the udgītha, 1.1.5–6 informs us that

> 'Speech (vāc), indeed, is Ṛk; breath (prāṇa) is Sāman, the syllable aum is the udgītha. Now this is a pair namely speech and breath, and also the Ṛk and the Sāman. This pair is joined together in the syllable 'aum'.[106]

Here we have clear echoes of the prāṇa/Vāc (=puruṣa/Virāj) co-ultimacy. In this context, however, they are not two aspects of the ultimate principle but two penultimate principles which are merged into a higher one, the syllable aum. In the A.Ā. prāṇa alone was identified with the uktha (the Ṛgvedic equivalent of the udgītha) but here it occupies a subordinate position. Of course, the entire discussion may not have any ontological import at all, being imply a series of comments on the nature of various chants which, naturally, require combination of vocalization and breathing for their manifestation. If there is any ontological import, however, it is clear that prāṇa is not being treated as the ultimate principle.

C.U. 3.12-18

Section twelve of this chapter informs us that the gāyatrī is everything that exists. This gāyatrī is then equated with speech, which is equated with the earth, which is equated with the body of man, which is equated with the heart within man, a kind of macro-microcosmic equation. The prāṇas (called brahma-persons (brahma-puruṣāh) in 3.13.6) are said to be established (pratiṣṭhita) in/on the heart. They are, in fact, the five openings of the heart. Knowledge of any one brings benefits such as wisdom, health or fame; knowledge of them all bestows heaven. The penultimate verse of section 13 than states,

> 'Now the light which shines above this heaven, above all, above everything in the highest worlds beyond which there are no higher, verily, that is the same as this light which is here within the person.'[107]

The text is unclear about the identity of the 'light which shines above' but if it is taken to be the sun then the light within the person is most likely prāṇa. B.A.U. 4.4.7 and C.U. 4.15.1 both describe prāṇa as 'light' and Mait.U. 6 links the sun and the prāṇa within an individual.

The next section states that everything is brahman (14.1) and that the self within the heart (ātmāntar hṛdaye) is brahman (14.4). This self is described as being made of mind, as having prāṇa for its body, light for its form, truth for its will/conception (saṃkalpa) and space for its self (ātman). It is extremely small yet greater than everything.[108] 15.4 describes prāṇa in the same way that 14.1 described brahman; as 'everything here that has come to be, whatsoever there is'. [109] Later, in 3.18.2-6 we are told that at the individual (adhyātma) level brahman has four quarters : vāc, prāṇa, cakṣus and śrotra; at the cosmic (adhidaivita) level these are agni, vāyu, āditya and diśa (the directions).

The prāṇas are obviously of considerable significance in this scheme since knowledge of them enables the knower to reach heaven (svarga). There are also features of this material which give it the characteristics of 'model' answer. Certainly, the almost identical descriptions of prāṇa and brahman and the equation of brahman with the innermost self suggest a view of prāṇa akin to that outlined in both earlier and later texts. However, the descriptions of the self do not have parallels in the literature concerned more explicitly with prāṇa. This is thus a different kind of model answer from those commented on above. It seems that the author/redactor of this material has sought to present a new view of self but has incorporated elements of the prāṇa concept into it rather than simply substituting the term ātman for prāṇa. In particular, the location of the self in the heart and its description as being extremely small are not found in passages where it can be clearly demonstrated that the ātman referred to is prāṇa. Also, the fact that prāṇa is said to be the body of the self rather than equated with it serves to underline that here prāṇa is being subordinated to the ātman within the heart.

C.U.6

This chapter is concerned with Uddālaka Āruṇi's teaching to his son Śvetaketu. This teaching is based on a view of existence not found in other early Upaniṣads. Ultimately all existence is being (sat), which is one only, without a second (ekam evādvītyam). This being initially manifests itself in three forms: tejas (heat), āpa (water) and anna (matter or food). All modifications of these three forms have no reality in themselves, 'the modifications being only a name arising from speech while the truth is that it is only the three forms.' In this scheme prāṇa is simply a modification of water. Here then is a view of prāṇa quite different from that in other early

Upaniṣads. In this context it is just a derivative principle manifesting at the level of the individual human being. It has neither cosmic nor ultimate status.

Taittirīya Upaniṣad 1–3

This Upaniṣad consists of three sections (valli). Deussen[110] notes that the relationship between them is a matter of some dispute. In his own presentation he follows Śankara, who took all three together and regarded them as comprising one Upaniṣad, but he does note that the second two sections are particularly closely connected. Certainly, the first section appears to have much in common with other Upaniṣads in its treatment of the self and the cosmos, whilst the second and third present a quite distinctive view.

In 1.1 and 1.12 Vāyu is called the 'perceptible brahman' (pratyakṣa brahman), which is the right (ṛta) and the true (satya), a statement which echoes B.A.U. 2.3.1-6 and Mait.U. 6.3. In these passages the real (sat) and formless (amūrta) aspect (rūpa) of brahman is distinguished from the false (asat) and formed (mūrta) aspect. At the cosmic (adhidaivata) level this real brahman is equated with Vāyu and the atmosphere (antariksa); at the individual (adhyātma) level the real brahman is prāṇa and the space within the self (antar-ātmann ākāśa). This division into adhidaivata and adhyātma levels of existence is paralleled in T.U. 1.7 where we find a distinction between elemental (adhibhūta) and individual (adhyātma) existence. The components listed under each of these two can be seen to have much in common with A.U. 1.2. Both sets of components in the Taittirīya account are arranged into three groups of five.

The adhibhūta components are :

earth (pṛthivī), atmosphere (antarikṣa), heaven (dyaus), the quarters (diśa) and the intermediate quarters (avāntaradiśa);

fire (agni), wind (vāyu), the sun (āditya), the moon (candra) and the stars (nakṣatra);

water (āpa), plants (oṣadhi), trees (vanaspati) ether (ākāśa) and body (?) (ātman).

The adhyātma components are:

prāṇa, vyāna, apāna, udāna, and samāna;

eye/sight (cakṣus) ear/hearing (śrotra), mind/mentation (manas), speech/voice (vāc) and skin/touch (tvac);

skin (carma), flesh (māṃsa), muscle (snāva), bone (asthi) and marrow (majja).

Other resonances with the B.A.U and A.U. can be found in the two verses of T.U. 1.6 where there is mention of the space within the heart (antarhṛdayākāśa)–space within the self in B.A.U. 2.3.5–wherein a person (puruṣa) abides. Here he is made of mind (manomaya), there he is 'the essence of the true' (tyasya hy esa rasaḥ); here he is immortal (amṛta) and made of gold (hiraṇyamaya), there he is immortal (amṛta) and is 'like a saffrom–coloured robe, like white wool, like the Indragopa insect, like a flame of fire, like a white lotus, like a sudden flash of lightning'[112] Similarly, the mention of the self's exit from the body by way of the top of the skull (śirsa kapāla) to autonomy, bliss and immortality is reminiscent of A.U. 1.3.12 where the self enters the body by the opening at the top of the head known as viḍṛti.

Thus, in this first section of the Taittirīya Upaniṣad we find an account of the cosmos and the individual which parallels those found in a number of other Upaniṣads. Where it differs is that here we have no suggestion, apart from the reference to Vāyu as pratyakṣa brahman, that prāṇa is anything other than just one manifestation of brahman at the adhyātma level. The other two sections of this Upaniṣad also share this feature.

At the beginning of the second section, in verse two, we read that

> 'He who knows Brahma, attains the highest. As to that this [verse] has been declared : He who knows Brahma as the real (satya), as knowledge (jñāna), as the infinite (ananta), set down in the secret place [of the heart] (guha) and in the highest heaven (parame vyoman), he obtains all desires, together with the intelligent (vipaścit) Brahma.'[113]

The verse goes on to inform us that from this self (ātman), which is the brahman referred to above, all things, including the person/individual (puruṣa) arise.

Then we have what are, perhaps, the most famous verses of this Upaniṣad: those describing this puruṣa as existing on five levels. Outermost is the anna-rasa-maya-ātman (the self made of the essence of food, i.e. the physical form of a person). Next is the prāṇa-maya-ātman (the self made of prāṇa). This is different from and within the outermost self. It fills and determines the form of the anna-rasa-maya-ātman and it is composed of prāṇa, vyāna, apāna, ākāśa and pṛthivī. Then comes the mano-maya-ātman (the self made of mind), which relates to the preceding one as that did to its own predecessor. It is composed of the Yajur, Ṛk and Sāma Vedas, teaching (ādeśa) and the hymns of the Atharvans and Aṅgirasas. Then comes the vijñāna-maya-ātman (the self made of consciousness), which relates to the mano-maya-ātman as that did to the prāṇa-maya-ātman. It is composed of faith (śraddhā), the right (ṛta), the truth (satya), contemplation (yoga) and the great one (mahas). Finally, within the vijñāna-maya-ātman is the ānanda-maya-ātman. It relates to the vijñāna-maya-ātman as that did to its predecessor.

T.U. 2.6 returns to the theme of the fruit of knowledge. We are told that those who know brahman as non-being (asat) become non-being; those who know that brahman exists (asti) know it as existent. The latter is the bodily self (śarira-ātman) of the former. 'He', presumably the latter of the two, became everything here and then entered what had been created. The following verse offers a different, though similar in many respects, account of creation. Here non-being (asat) creates being (sat), which creates for itself (svayam) a self (ātman) which in turn, is described as the essence (rasa) of existence. On attaining that essence one becomes blissful (ānandī). The last two verses, eight and nine, deal with the different kinds of bliss and the benefits of knowing the highest of them. This highest bliss is the bliss of brahman and those who experience it know no fear. The person who obtains it appears to be, though the text is not explicit on this point, one who knows that 'he who abides in a person' and 'he who abides in the sun (āditya)' are one. Such a knower experiences all the five selves referred to earlier.

This view is quite radical in the early Upaniṣads though it is taken up later by the Maitrī Upaniṣad. There, in 6.1-3 and 8, discussed above, the inner person and the person in the sun is the unitary prāṇa. Here, however, there is nothing to suggest that prāṇa is anything other than the next to outermost of the five selves.

In T.U. 3.1, Varuṇa explains to his son Bhṛgu that brahman is

> 'food (anna), breath (prāṇa), eye (cakṣus), ear (śrotra), mind (manas) and speech (vāc).'

Brahman is also that

> 'from which these components (anna etc.) are born... by which when born, they live [and]... into which, when departing they enter.'[114]

Bhṛgu meditates on each of anna, prāṇa manas, vijñāna and ānanda, not the five constituents of brahman described by Varuṇa, and discovers that each is the source, support and ultimate destination of beings (bhūtāni). This links with the view presented in section two and, once again, there is no suggestion that prāṇa is anything more than one constituent of the ultimate brahman, though 3.1 does have many of the characteristics of a model answer. With regard to this Upaniṣad in particular it is easy for the reader to conclude that the author(s) had deliberately set out to construct a cosmology which explicitly ran counter to a number of contemporary views on the nature and status of prāṇa.

Katha Upaniṣad 4 and 5

The fourth and fifth sections (valli) of the Kaṭha Upaniṣad contain one reference to 'prāṇa' and two to 'prāṇa and apāna'. The latter references are located at 5.3 and 5.5. 5.3 tells us that prāṇa and apāna (here appearing to mean in and out breathing) are controlled by a dwarf (vāmana) who is seated in the middle (madhye āsīnam) [of the body]. 5.5 adds that mortals do not live by prāṇa and apāna but by that on which they depend, which is, presumably, the dwarf.

This dwarf would appear to be the same entity as the 'person the measure of a thumb' (aṅguṣṭha-mātrah puruṣo), who also resides in the middle of the body (madhye ātmani tiṣṭhati), mentioned in 4.12 and 13. This person is lord of the past and the future and is like a light without a smoke. He is declared to be 'that' (i.e. the ātman referred to it 4.1). This puruṣa/ātman is called the inner self (antarātman) in 5.9-12. It looks outward through the senses (4.1) and is pure (4.15). It is resplendent (śukra), it is brahman, it is immortal (amṛta) and all the worlds rest within it (5.8).

In the middle of the body, according to Taittirīya Brāhmaṇa 1.2.1.3, [115] is the secret place (guha). There, according to Kaṭh.U. 2.20, abides the ātman who is smaller than the small, greater than the great. Two verses, six and seven, from section four also mention this secret place. However, Hume points out that both are probably corrupt and that the first 'contains an ungrammatical form and impossible constructions.'[116] Hence their interpretation is difficult. They read as follows:

> 'He who was born of old from austerity (tapas), was born of old from the waters, who stands entered into the secret place

> (guha) [of the heart], who looked forth through beings–this, verily, is that [i.e. the ātman].
>
> She who arises with prāṇa, āditi (infinity), maker of divinity, who stands entered into the secret place (guha) [of the heart], who was born forth through beings–this, verily, is that.'[117]

Hume takes the masculine subject in verse six to be puruṣa and the feminine one in verse seven to be prakṛti. Whether they inhabit the secret place along with the ātman/puurṣa or are to be identified with him is not clear. My own inclination is to favour the latter view. This would align the above account with that found at B.A.U. 4.2.2-3, where the ātman is composed of Indra and his wife Virāj who reside separately in the right and left eyes respectively and unite in the space within the heart (antar-hṛdaya-ākāśa). This androgynous conception of ātman, of course, echoes the puruṣa sūkta and the other versions of ultimate bi-polarity identified in chapter one. The two subjects of these Kaṭha verses would then be the two principles which constitute the ātman, its two faces. The most likely identity of the prāṇa which arises with the 'she' of verse seven would then be the 'he' of verse six. Such an interpretation would make these sections much more consonant with my exegesis of 2.3.2. than would its alternative. However, prāṇa might not be equitable with the subject of verse six and may be just an incedental reference, in which case it would clearly be a derivative rather than the ultimate principle. Because of this ambiguity Kaṭh.U. 4 and 5 has been included in this section rather than alongside my comments on 2.3.2 above.

P.U. 3

In the third question of the Praśna Upaniṣad Kauśalya Aśvalāyana asks Pippalāda,

> 'Venerable Sir, whence is this prāṇa born? How does it come into the body ? And how does it distribute itself and establish itself? In what way, does it depart ? How does it support what is external and what relates to the self ?'[118]

Pippalāda's response is to state that such questions are highly transcendental (atipraśnān). Nevertheless, Kauśalya is told that prāṇa is born of the ātman. It relates to the ātman as does a shadow to a person and enters the body through the activity of the mind (manas).[119]

This prāṇa is the ruler (samrāj) of the other prāṇas and directs them to their respective places in the body. Apāna is located in the organs of excretion and generation; prāṇa is located in the eyes, ears, mouth and nose; samāna is located in the middle of the body and deals with digestion. Vyāna is located in the 727,200,000 nāḍī which has 100 branches. Each of these branches has 72,000 sub-branches. The udāna moves through one of these (seemingly at death) and leads (nayati) them all/the ātman (?) to a good or evil world according to the nature of the deeds performed in life.

The final verse of the section informs us that one who knows the birth, the entrance, the abode, the fivefold overlordship and the relation to the ātman of prāṇa obtains immortality. This is the kind of statement found frequently in earlier literature. The main difference is that where as before was knowledge of prāṇa and how it functioned in the body that bestowed immortality now there is the addition of knowing how it is related to the ātman. In some respects P.U. 3 exhibits the characteristics of a 'model' answer. However, since it clearly subordinates prāṇa to the ātman rather than substituting the latter for the former it is more appropriately included in this section.

Mait.U. 2.6-7

This passage, part of Śākāyanya's instruction to Bṛhadratha, tells of how Prajāpati divided himself fivefold into prāṇa, apāna, samāna, udāna and vyāna in order to animate his lifeless creation. Prajāpati thus occupies the position taken by prāṇa in other versions of this fivefold dividing. Śākāyanya goes on to explain that prāṇa rises upwards, apāna moves downwards; vyāna supports (sthaviṣṭha) prāṇa and apāna; samāna, which is a higher form of vyāna (uttaram vyānasya rūpam), distributes the essential ingredients (dhātu), of food to the limbs whilst udāna 'belches forth and swallows down that which has been drunk and eaten.'[120] This Prajāpati, who is made of mind, whose body is prāṇa, whose form is light (bhā), whose conception or will (saṃkalpa) is truth (satya), whose ātman is space (ākāśa), having divided himself fivefold is hidden in the secret place (guha), is the controller of the body, is the ātman.

Here we have two references to prāṇa. The first is the phenomenal breath, one of the five prāṇas; the second is the prāṇa as the body (śarīra) of Prajāpati/ātman. The first reference presents no significant interpretative problems though it does reveal that when Upaniṣadic teachers explained the nature and function of these prāṇas they did so in various ways. Compare, for example, this passage with P.U. 3. The second reference is more problematic, though intelligible in the light of my overall analysis. In earlier texts it is prāṇa that divides into the five prāṇas. Here it is Prajāpati who is the ātman. Hence, once again, this passage exhibits some of the characteristics of a 'model' account. However, like P.U. 3 it clearly subordinates prāṇa to Prajāpati/ātman by making it his body. In this context it is clear that the prāṇa which is the body of Prajāpati is not the prāṇa of the fivefold list. It is, presumably, the unitary prāṇa which, here, is being presented as just one component of Prajāpati/ātman.

In summing up the material from the preceding sections of this chapter it can be said that throughout the period of composition of the principal Upaniṣads the concept of prāṇa played a prominent role in the world-view accounts of many teachers. In the majority of instances where prāṇa figures in Upaniṣadic accounts it is presented either explicitly or implicitly as a primal, ultimate or supreme principle of existence. It is the controller of all, the foundation of all, the true essence of the individual, the self (ātman). Knowledge of prāṇa bestows immortality, for prāṇa itself is immortal. However, in a number of places prāṇa is clearly subordinated to other principles, most frequently ātman and/or brahman, and presented as just one component of them. In other places these principles can be seen to have assimilated most of the characteristics of prāṇa, displacing the term itself as they did so. In the pre-Upaniṣadic period a number of different contenders for the status of ultimate principle can be identified. In the Upaniṣadic period some of these, such as Vāc, were no longer considered to be worthy of that status. Others, however, such as puruṣa, prāṇa, ātman and brahman retained that status in the eyes of various teachers. Increasingly, they each came to take on the characteristics of the others and be identified with each other. Throughout the Upaniṣadic period it is clear that ātman and brahman, perhaps because they received less detailed definition in the pre-Upaniṣadic period, were the favoured pair. This flexibility must have been a significant factor in the process which led to their assimilation and subordination of the concepts of prāṇa and puruṣa. Hence, in the later Upaniṣads, although prāṇa occasionally fills the role of ultimate principle it more frequently figures but little in the cosmology, is often subordinated to other principles or is not mentioned at all. Before considering the role it played in later thought, however, it behoves us to be clear about the Upaniṣadic views on the nature and functions of the five prāṇas and their relationship with the interior channels called hitā or nāḍī.

The channels in the body, the prāṇas and their adhyātma and adhidaivata parallels

In chapter one the possibility that once in the body prāṇa moved through a system of connected pathways was noted. The pre-Upaniṣadic evidence was, however, ambiguous. The Upaniṣads likewise, are unclear on this matter. Only one text, P.U. 3.6, explicitly states that one of the prāṇas: vyāna, moves along a system of pathways. Some other references, C.U. 3.13.1–6 for example, are suggestive. Here the five prāṇas are equated with five openings in the heart and most of the references to channels (hitā, nāḍī) in the body have them originating in the heart. Overall, however, I would suggest that in the Upaniṣads no clear links are established between the movements of the prāṇas and the various channels in the body. In fact, the same P.U. text appears to locate prāṇa, apāna, udāna and samāna *outside* of these channels.

The B.A.U. employs the term 'hitā' for the channels in the body. There are 72,000 of these, connecting the heart and the pericardium and they are as fine as a hair divided 1,000-fold.[122] They are filled with five colours : white (śukla), blue (nīla), golden/tawny (piṅgala), *green* (harita) and red (lohita). The C.U. favours the term 'nadī' when referring to these channels. In 8.6.1-6 we are told that they originate in the heart, are 101 in number and are connected with the sun. They consist of a fine substance (a/ā(?)nimnas tiṣṭhanti) which is variously coloured: white (śukla), blue (nīla), *yellow* (pīta), golden/tawny (piṅgala) and red (lohita). The sun too, displays these colours. Kauṣītakī Upaniṣad 4.19 follows the B.A.U. in calling these channels 'hitā' and describing them as being as fine as a hair divided 1,000 fold. However, the colours of these 'hitā' are said to be golden/tawny (piṅgala), white (śukla), *black* (kṛṣṇa) and red (lohita). In P.U. 3.6 the number of these channels (nāḍi) is said to be 101 × 100 × 72,000 = 727,200,000. Here however, instead of being told the colours of within them we are informed that vyāna moves inside them. The Maitrī Upaniṣad lists six colours of the rays/strings (raśmayaḥ) of the one who dwells in the heart like a lamp. They are white and black (sitāsitaḥ), brown and blue (kadrunīlāḥ), tawny and pale red (kapilamṛdulohitāḥ). As was noted above, the ātman abides in the secret place of the heart. Muṇḍ.U. calls this the place where the nāḍīs come together like the spokes of a wheel.

There are sufficient differences between these accounts to satisfy the reader that they are not simply reiterations of some authoritative tradition though the later texts do suggest that their authors were aware of earlier descriptions. Despite this diversity, the level of comformity in these passages is quite high, given that the descriptions are based on information not accessible to sensory perception and hence presumably derived from the spiritual experiences of various individuals. Furthermore, they all agree in claiming that one channel leads upwards to immortality, heaven (svarga) or emancipation (apavarga). In Mait.U. 6.21 this nādī is called 'suṣumnā'. It serves as a passage for the prāṇa and is divided within the palate. In sleep or at death the prāṇas merge with prāṇa and enter the channels by way of the heart.[123] If at death, desire has been conquered and knowledge of prāṇa and/or ātman has been gained the prāṇas depart by the channel which leads upwards to immortality. If, however, this attainment and knowledge is lacking they depart by the other channels to either the worlds of the gods or to other births where the fruit of karma is experienced.[124]

Within the body the five prāṇas are said to have symbolic correspondences or, perhaps, actual connections with a number of cosmic and individual phenomena. Prāṇa is identified with the eastern direction,[125] the eye[126] and either the sun[127] or fire.[128] It is also linked with heaven and what is under heaven,[129] and with the āhvanīya fire.[130] It is supported by apāna.[131] Apāna is identified with the western direction,[132] speech[133] and either fire[134] or the sun.[135] It is also linked with the earth and what is under the earth,[136] and with the gārhapatya fire.[137] It is supported by vyāna[138] Vyāna is identified with the southern direction,[139] the ear[140] and the moon.[141] It is also linked with the directions and what is within the directions,[142] and with the anvahārya pacana (the southern sacrificial fire).[143] It is supported by samāna.[144] Samāna is identified with the northern direction,[145] the mind[146] and the rain god.[147] It is also linked with lightning and what is under lightning,[148] and is said to equalise (saman nayati) the in and out breathing (ucchvāsa-niḥśvāsa).[149] It is a higher form of vyāna[150] and its support would appear to be ātman, though the text is not clear on this.[151] Udāna is identified with the upward direction,[152] the wind[153] and space.[154] It is also linked with the skin and what is under space[155] and with fruit of the sacrifice.[156] It is not mentioned in B.A.U. 3.9.26 where the sequence of supports in listed.

Two Upaniṣadic passages P.U. 3 and Mait.U. 2.6 (both commented upon above) provide information about the locations and functions of the five prāṇas. According to P.U.3, prāṇa is located in the eye, ear, mouth and nose, and it is supported (anugṛhnāna) by the sun. Mait.U. 2.6 states that it 'rises upwards'. They are thus in general agreement though the P.U. claims are in tension with the symbolic correlations identified above where prāṇa is linked with just one of the sensory faculties, the eye. With regard to apāna, P.U. 3 informs us that it is located in the organs of excretion and generation (pāyūpasthe) and is supported by the earth deity. This is in agreement with Mait.U. 2.6 where it is said that apāna moves downwards though again, not very compatible with its associations with speech. Vyāna, according to P.U. 3, moves in the nāḍīs thereby, presumably, supporting, as Mait.U.2.6 and B.A.U. 3.9.26 inform us, prāṇa and apāna. Again, this data is not compatible with the abovementioned associations with the ear. P.U.3 locates samāna in the middle of the body, from where, according to Mait.U. 2.6, it distributes the essential ingredients (dhātu) of food to the various limbs, a function carried out by the more general term 'prāṇa' in the Ś.B. and B.A.U. Udāna is identified with tejas (heat/light) in P.U.3. It is said to lead that which departs at death through one of the nādīs to either a good, bad or a human world, depending on a person's merit or demerit. In Mait.U. 2.6 it has a very different function: belching forth and swallowing down that which has been drunk and eaten.

Thus, with regard to the manifestation of prāṇa as the five prāṇas in the body, the Upaniṣads retain the kinds of symbolic associations found frequently in the Brāhmaṇas. Here, as in the Brāhmaṇas, the system of correspondences is not haphazard but, with few exceptions, quiet precise and consistent from text to text. But the Upaniṣads also go beyond the Brāhmaṇas in their accounts of the functions of the prāṇas. These accounts present a different picture than one might expect from a study of the symbolic connections and also make it clear that whilst prāṇa, in the form of vyāna, moves through the channels during life and that udāna leads the prāṇas and the ātman out of the body by one of them at death the activities of the prāṇas are not confined to the channels. Overall then, the Upaniṣadic view of the nature and functioning of prāṇa is quite close to that found in pre-Upaniṣadic leterature, sharing the same general picture and similar sorts of ambiguities. In later literature, attempts are made to make the accounts of how the prāṇas function and where they are located more precise and consistent, and to subordinate prāṇa to other principles; although, as will be seen, its high status is also preserved in some quite interesting ways.

Conclusion

In this chapter the views of various scholars on the Upaniṣādic concept of prāṇa have been reveiwed and all passages where prāṇa is mentioned analysed. Overall, the review revealed that none of the scholars whose work was considered had carried out a detailed analysis of the prāṇa concept in Upaniṣadic literature. All were agreed, however, on the fact that a general trend can be identified in Upaniṣadic attitudes towards prāṇa, a trend which made it a principle which is subordinate to or derived from brahman or ātman. A variety of reasons were offered to account for this trend though all were deemed to be inadequately grounded in the actual texts to be fully convincing. On the other hand, an observation by Deussen (who translated sixty of the most well known Upaniṣads) was particularly noted since, in terms of its general thrust, it pointed to a process of world-view adjustment which appears to lie behind the actual contents of the texts.

In essence, Deussen's argument was that whilst the compilers of the Upaniṣds continued the earlier trend of tracing the whole of existence back to a single source which, after creation, continued to support the universe and control it from within, a dispute arose about how to characterize the nature of that source. Although he explains the two main views rather differently, the conclusion suggested by this study is that the disagreement centred on the issue of whether the first principle should be understood vitalistically or mentalistically. Those associating themselves with the first of these options, Deussen calls the older school; those associating with the second he dubs the newer school. Whether the notion of a school, a group of teachers having some kind of affiliation with each other and subscribing to more or less identical views, is appropriate here is a moot point. The analysis of Upaniṣadic texts presented in this chapter does not fit such an interpretation very well. Rather, the situation seems to be more that there were two general orientations among those who were concerned with these issues. One of these was that which sought to maintain the vitalistic character of the ultimate principle whilst also giving full recognition to its consciousness dimension. The other sought to emphasise the consciousness aspect and subordinate the vital. Many of the teachers can be seen to have presented their views in terms which can be seen to be steering a course for some kind of middle ground. Texts exemplifying the ends of the spectrum would be the Kauṣītakī Upaniṣad for the older perspective and Chāndogya Upaniṣad for the newer.

This view of Deussen's was implicitly challenged by Willam Beidler, whose own thesis is based on the notion that the teachings of the Upaniṣads should be understood in terms of their 'inherent wholeness', that is, they are to be understood as conveying a unified view of the self and cannot, without a potential loss of meaning, be analysable into parts. Beidler's reconstruction of the Upaniṣadic conception of the self was shown to be fundamentally flawed. The essence of the flaw was seen to lie in Beidler's attempt to fit all the passages he considers into his own pre-determined framework, a tendency exhibited by most of the other scholars who have written on this subject. By contrast it was argued that the methodological premise of the present study : that of taking each teacher's views as independent unless evidence from the texts was forthcoming to demonstrate that two or more teachers had exactly or more or less the same conception, would actually produce a more accurate account of the views about the self to be found in the Upaniṣadic texts.

The bulk of the chapter was given over to a consideration of all passages in the principal Upaniṣads mentioning prāṇa. There it was observed that some Upaniṣads do not mention prāṇa at all. Some subsections within the other Upaniṣads do not mention it either and thus, since such subsections are taken as independent works as far as this study is concerned, prāṇa can be seen to have been at best a peripheral concept for many Upaniṣadic thinkers. On the other hand, when the concept of prāṇa does find a place in the texts it can generally be seen to have had the status of ultimate principle in the minds of the teachers who first formulated the doctrines found in any particular section. On occasions the fact that such a presentation was intended could only be determined by careful analysis. Sometimes this was required because the text in question was ambiguous or unclear. At other times, however, it appeared that an original text had been redacted with the result that its original import had been changed. Deussen identified B.A.U. 1.3 as one such text; the present author identified C.U.7 as another. The full extent of meaning–changing redactions in the Upaniṣads has not been pursued here but it seems likely that an accurate reconstruction of the doctrinal milieu in which the

Upaniṣads were formulated and compiled will be dependent on just such an investigation.

In some instances, fewer than those presenting prāṇa as the source, foundation and controller of all, the vital principle is presented as being derived from something more fundamental. In these cases prāṇa is viewed either as a major cosmic principle, from which other phenomena evolve, or as phenomenal only. Thus, the concept of prāṇa can be seen to fit into the world views of Upaniṣadic teachers in at least four different ways :

1) as a fundamental principle from which the whole universe springs but which has, at the same time phenomenal manifestations which reflect its nature in various ways. Most important of such manifestations are the vital energies: prāṇa, apāna, vyāna, udāna and samāna, and the sensory faculties;
2) as a cosmic principle;
3) as a purely phenomenal principle;
4) not at all.

In the final part of this chapter it was shown that whilst different Upaniṣadic teachers understood the vital energies (prāṇa, apāna etc.) to be distributed throughout the body in various ways there was little by way of consensus on the details. Likewise, even though the vyāna energy is specifically stated to circulate through channels (hitā/nāḍī) during a person's lifetime and the udāna energy to lead the others along one of them at death there is no reason to think that the activity of these energies is confined to the channels nor that there is a particularly strong connection between the vital energies and the various channels. The symbolic correspondences between the vital energies and other phenomena which are set out in some Upaniṣads are reminiscent of the Brāhmaṇas and seem to have been taken up by very few Upaniṣadic teachers. Like the Brāhmaṇas, the Upaniṣads remain ambiguous on the relationship between the vital energies and the bodily channels.

REFERENCES

1. The Upaniṣads consulted for this section are those designated as 'Principal Upaniṣads' by R.E. Hume (1931) plus the Mahānārāyaṇa Upaniṣad, though this contains little on the topic of prāṇa. Hume's list is Īśā, Aitareya, Kaṭha, Kena, Kauṣītakī, Chāndogya, Taittirīya, Praśna, Bṛhadāraṇyaka, Māṇḍūkya, Muṇḍaka, Maitrī (or Maitrāyaṇīya) and Śvetāsvatara. Śaṅkara comments on or refers to all of these except the Maitrī. He also refers to the Jabala and Paiṅgala Upaniṣads. I have included the Maitrī because, as Deussen observes, 'It appears as a universal compendium of Upaniṣadic thought vis-a-vis the heretical view ... [and] ... renews the old Upaniṣadic doctrines with a mixture of the elements of the Sāṃkhya doctrine and of Buddhism' (1980, p. 329). On the other hand, I have omitted the Jabala and Paiṅgala for both of them seem to be late (i.e. post Bādarāyaṇa). It is true that Vedānta Sūtra 1.2.32 may refer to the Jabala but the reference is uncertain and since this text has nothing of significance to say on the topic of prāṇa it is justifiable to omit it from consideration here. As far as the Paiṅgala Upaniṣad is concerned, it is definitely late. Ideas which seem to indicate a stage of development that is post-Bādarāyaṇa are prominent and the material is highly structured in its arrangement. Neither Deussen nor Hume include it in their lists of older Upaniṣads.
2. For details of this division and terminology see Deussen P. (1906) pp. 22-26.
3. op. cit. pp. 101-111.
4. Deussen (1912) pp. 146-7.
5. op. cit. p. 339.
6. Thibaut (2) (1896) p. 88.
7. Radhakrishnan (1960) p. 427.
8. Keith (1925) 567, emphasis mine.
9. Compare, for example, C.U.8.7.4 and Kaṭh U. 2.32.
10. See Ś.B. 11.1.1 and Jaiminiya Brāhmaṇa 1.18 and 1.49.
11. Frauwallner (1973) p. 41.
12. op. cit. p.45.
13. loc. cit.
14. e.g. Haṭhayogapradīpikā and Lakṣmī Tantra.
15. op. cit. p. 46.
16. op. cit. p. 47.
17. Radhakrishnan (1953) p. 637 exemplifies this deficiency well. He notes that prāṇa was 'originally' a term used to denote the supreme being but he offers no explanation as to why it ceased to do so.

18. Beidler (1975) pp. ii-iv.
19. op. cit. p. vii.
20. loc. cit.
21. op. cit. p. ix.
22. op. cit. p. 13.
23. loc cit.
24. op. cit. p. 14.
25. Deussen (1906) p. 94.
26. Muṇḍaka Upaniṣad 2.
27. Beidler (1975) p. 16.
28. op. cit. pp. 4-5.
29. Radhakrishnan (1953) p. 175.
30. op. cit. p. 663.
31. Beidler (1975) p. 21. Why he gives the sanskṛt in some places and the English in others is not explained.
32. op. cit. p. 19.
33. op. cit. p. 22.
34. Taken from op. cit. p. 23.
35. op. cit. p. 25.
36. loc. cit.
37. op. cit. p. 46.
38. op. cit. p. 47.
39. loc. cit.
40. op. cit. p. 66.
41. loc. cit.
42. op. cit. p. 97.
43. Ewing (1903) p. 5.
44. op. cit. p. 9.
45. op. cit. pp. 9-10.
46. loc. cit.
47. op. cit. p. 10.
48. Radhakrishnan (1953) p. 183. In commenting on this passage, Hume (1931, p.34) states that prāṇa is a 'designation of the Ātman'. Presumably he means that such is the case in this particular passage rather than generally.
49. op. cit. pp. 192-194.
50. Hume (1931) p. 97.

51. Deussen (1980) p. 433.
52. Radhakrishnan (1953) p. 193.
53. op. cit. p. 190.
54. Ś.B. 10.5.2.9; B.A.U. 4.2.23. and Mait.U.7.11.
55. op. cit. p. 242. We may note that here Radhakrishnan translates 'tvam' by 'body' and 'ātman' by 'heart'. Hume offers 'you' and 'soul' respectively.
56. op. cit. p. 273.
57. op. cit. p. 393.
58. op. cit. pp.404-405.
59. op. cit. p. 413 (slightly modified).
60. op. cit. p. 416.
61. op. cit. pp. 468-483.
62. op. cit. p. 487.
63. op. cit. p. 687.
64. Monier-Williams (1899) p. 739.
65. Radhakrishnan (1953) p. 642.
66. op. cit. p. 642 f.n.
67. Deussen (1980) p. 70.
68. The devas are the faculties: speech (vāc), breath (prāṇa), the eye (cakṣus), the ear (śrotra), the mind (manas) and the breath in the mouth (āsanya prāṇa). The asuras, according to Śaṅkara (see Radhakrishnan (1953) p. 155), are the negative aspects or tendencies of the faculties. 'These very organs become demons when influenced by their natural thoughts and actions based (only) on perception and inference [i.e. not influenced by scripture] and directed to visible (secular) ends' (loc.cit.). This explanation, however, does not fit very well with the statement in B.A.U. 1.3.10-11 which suggests that the asuras are the afflictions (the worst of which is death) of the faculties nor with the fact that the asuras are said to be older than the devas.
69. Radhakrishnan (1953) informs the reader in his notes (p. 156) that 'prāṇa' in B.A.U. 1.3.3 is used for 'ghrānam' (the organ of smelling, the nose), presumably because the nose is not included in the list of faculties and because the C.U. version offers the more explicit 'nāsikya prāṇa'.
70. op. cit. pp. 157-158.
71. It is Āṅgirasa because it is the essence (rasa) of the limbs (aṅga) and we are informed, as we were by the Śatapatha Brāhmaṇa, that 'from whatever limbs prāṇa departs, that indeed, dries up ..'. op. cit. p. 160.

72. loc. cit.
73. loc. cit.
73. op. cit. p. 161.
74. op. cit. p. 161.
75. Deussen (1980) pp. 403-405.
76. The C.U. 1.2.1-14 account makes the prāṇa-in-the-mouth the source of life and does not link it with any of the Vedas. It also lacks the additional piece on the Sāma Veda, except to mention that Baka Dālbhya, an udgatṛ priest (i.e. a chanter of the Sāma Veda) knew the prāṇa-in-the-mouth and this enabled him to perform a service to the people of Naimiṣa. What the service was is unclear. Radhakrishnan (1953) renders 'sa ha smaibhyaḥ kāmān āgāyati' as 'he sang out for them their desires' (p. 341). Hume's version (1931) reads, 'He used to sing to them what they desired' 'p.180), whilst Deussen (1980) offers '... he used to sing to them what they desired' (p. 71). It is difficult not to infer that he was doing more than simply reiterating to the people what they wanted and in some way contributing to the realization of those desires. Just how this contribution worked is not, however, very clear.
77. Radhakrishnan (1953) p. 306.
78. op. cit. p. 423.
79. op. cit. pp. 761-762.
80. op. cit. pp. 769-770.
81. op. cit. p. 770.
82. op. cit. p. 771.
83. op. cti. p. 782.
84. op. cit. pp. 657-658. We may note, however that in the following section prāṇa, after being described in such exhalted terms, is said to be derived from the ātman and related to it as a shadow is related to a body.
85. op. cit. p. 163.
86. op. cit. p. 166 (slightly amended).
87. op. cit. p. 189.
88. My translation.
89. Radhakrishnan (1953) p. 246.
90. op. cit. p. 253.
91. Radhakrishnan (1953) p. 791. Something worth noting about this passage is the way it makes the existence of the worlds (loka) dependent on the gods (deva = faculties?) which, in turn, are dependent on the prāṇas (prāṇa, apna etc.?) which, in turn, are dependent on prāṇa/prajñātman. This reverses the common

Upaniṣadic pattern of emphasising cosmology over psychology by making the cosmos dependent on the individual perceiver.

92. op. cit. p. 515.

93. In their translations, Deussen, Hume and Radhakrishnan all seem to be influenced by the watery connotations of 'ud' and 'samuddhṛti', c.f. note 91.

94. 'oṣadhivanaspatya'–an interesting term. Besides meaning 'plant' 'oṣadhi' often refers to medicinal herbs. Its literal meaning is possibly 'light-containing' and this would link with one meaning of the derivative term 'oṣadhipati', 'lord of herbs', i.e. soma. Similarly, whilst 'vana' alone means plant, tree or forest, 'vanaspati' can mean 'lord of plants, i.e. soma. Hence, translators who render 'oṣadhivanaspatya' simply as 'plants and trees' without explanatory annotation ignore the 'pati' part of the compound and, perhaps, thereby significantly misrepresent the meaning.

95. It may be that because water(s) (a/āpa) are here specifically stated to be the source of food, the various translators felt it reasonable to derive puruṣa from the waters alone, even though the text itself makes no such specific statement in the case of puruṣa's creation.

96. We may note here that whilst speech, breath, etc., all come from column two, skin and generative organ come from column one. Furthermore, the order of digestive faculty and generative organ are reversed in the 'seizing' list. Exactly why skin replaces hairs here is not clear. Radhakrishnan suggests that 'touch' is what is implied. The reason why touch, which would have been the most logical entry in column two, was initially displaced by hairs was probably that the author (or redactor) wanted to get 'oṣadhivanaspatya' into column three and this would seem to be a peculiar derivation from touch. The reason for the reversal of śiśna and apāna is more obvious. The writer wanted to end the list with the only successful faculty. The reason for the original order would seem to be the simple physical progression from higher to lower: heart, navel and phallus.

97. Deussen (1980) p. 17, suggests that presenting vāyu as the grasper of food is a play on the terms 'āvayat' and 'vāyu'. Presenting vāyu as the one who lives on food is, similarly, a play on the terms 'vāyu' and 'annāyu'.

98. Note here that this term had already been used in texts like A.V.4.1; V.S.13.3 and S.V.4.1.3.
Translations can be found in Griffith (1976) p. 114 vs. 3 and (1963) p. 64 vs. 9; Keith (1914) vol 2, p. 231 and Vimalānanda (1957) pp. 71-72 (where it is vs. 45, not 42 as Whitney notes it). Falk thinks that A.V. 4 is a yogic work and equates 'sīmatas' with the brahmarandhra of later yogic texts.

99. Deussen gives 'the most penetrating brahman', Hume offers 'veriest brahman' whilst Radhakrishnan renders the phrase as 'all-pervading brahman'.

100. Deussen, Hume and Radhakrishnan all suggest that 'he' is Vāmadeva. Only Deussen offers a reason for this and it is a weak one: 'deliverance is painted out as the end of the cycle of births, which is envisaged as an immortal continuance in the heavens for him who (supposedly like Vāmadeva, Ṛ.V. 4.27.1) sees through or has a clear understanding of this cyclic course of births.' (1980) p. 14. In terms of the Upaniṣad itself, the principal contenders would be puruṣa and ātman.

101. Radhakrishnan (1953) p. 524.

102. op. cit. pp. 816-817 and 821–822.

103. e.g. 6.3.3.16; 6.7.4.4; 7.1.1.22-23; 8.5.2.8.9.1.1.23.9.2.1.21 and 10.6.2.1-11.

104. 2.9 'Repressing (*prapīḍya)* his breathings (breaths–prāṇān) here (in the body), let him who has controlled all movements, breathe through his nostrils with diminished breath; let the wise man restrain his mind vigilantly as (he would) a chariot yoked with vicious horses'. Radhakrishnan (1953) p. 721.

105. op. cit. p. 153.

106. op. cit. p. 338.

107. op. cit. p. 390.

108. Compare this with Mait.U. 2.6-7.

109. Radhakrishnan (1953) p. 393.

110. op. cit. pp. 451-452.

111. Deussen (1980) p. 219.

112. Radhakrishnan (1953) p. 194.

113. Hume (1931) p. 283.

114. Radhakrishnan (1953) p. 553.

115. op. cit. p. 601.

116. Hume (1931) p. 354.

117. loc. cit.

118. Radhakrishnan (1953) p. 658, slightly amended.

119. Here we find a reaffirmation of the connection between manas and prāṇa that was so clearly expressed in C.U. 6.8.2.

120. Hume (1931) p. 416.

121. B.A.U.2.1.19.

122. B.A.U.4.3.20.

123. See, for example, B.A.U. 2.1.7; 4.4.1; C.U. 4.3.1 4 6.8.6; Kauṣ. U. 2.1-2; 3.3; 4.20.
124. Mait.U.6.30.
125. C.U. 3.13.1-6 and Mait.U.7.1-5.
126. C.U. 3.13.1-6 and 5.19.
127. C.U. 3.13.1-6 and 5.19.
128. Mait.U. 7.1-5.
129. C.U. 5.19.
130. P.U.4.3-4.
131. B.A.U.3.9.26.
132. C.U. 3.13 1-6; Mait.U. 7.1-5.
133. C.U. 3.13. 1-6; 5.21.
134. C.U.3.13. 1-6; 5.21.
135. Mait.U. 7.1-5.
136. C.U.5.21.
137. P.U. 4.3-4.
138. B.A.U. 3.9.26.
139. C.U. 3.13.1-6; Mait.U.7.1-5.
140. C.U. 3.13.1-6; 5.20
141. C.U. 3.13.1-6; 5.20; Mait.U. 7.1-5.
142. C.U. 5.20.
143. P.U. 4.3-4.
144. B.A.U. 3.9.26.
145. C.U. 3.13.1-6; Mait.U. 7.1-5.
146. C.U. 3.13.1-6; 5.22.
147. C.U. 3.13.1-6; 5.22.
148. C.U. 5.22.
149. C.U. 3.13.1-6; Mait.U.7.1-5.
150. Mait.U. 2.6.
151. B.A.U. 3.9.26.
152. C.U. 3.13.1-6; Mait.U. 7.1-5.
153. C.U. 3.13.1-6; 5.23.
154. C.U. 3.13.1-6; 5.23.
155. C.U. 5.23.
156. P.U. 4.3-4.

123. See for example, B.A.U. 2.1.7; 4.4.1; C.U. 1.3.1; 4.3.3; Kaus. U. 2.5; 3.2; 4.20.
124. Mai.U.6.30
125. C.U. 3.13.1-5 and Mai.U.2.1-6.
126. C.U. 3.13.1-6 and 5.19.
127. C.U. 3.13.1-6 and 5.19.
128. Mai.U. 2.6.
129. C.U. 5.19.
130. P.U. 4.3-4.
131. B.A.U. 3.9.26.
132. C.U. 3.13.1-6; Mai.U. 2.6.
133. C.U. 3.13.1-6; 5.21.
134. C.U. 3.13.1-6; 5.21.
135. Mai.U. 2.6.
136. C.U. 5.21.
137. C.U. 5.24.
138. B.A.U. 3.9.26.
139. C.U. 3.13.1-6; Mai.U. 2.6.
140. C.U. 3.13.1-6; 5.20.
141. C.U. 3.13.1-6; 5.20; Mai.U. 2.6.
142. Ibid.
143. C.U. 5.20.
144. B.A.U. 3.9.26.
145. C.U. 3.13.1-6; Mai.U. 2.1-6.
146. C.U. 3.13.1-6; 5.22.
147. C.U. 3.13.1-6; 5.22.
148. C.U. 5.22.
149. C.U. 3.13.1-6; Mai.U. 2.6.
150. Mai.U. 2.6.
151. B.A.U. 3.9.26.
152. C.U. 3.13.1-6; Mai.U. 2.6.
153. C.U. 3.13.1-6; 5.23.
154. C.U. 3.13.1-6; 5.23.
155. C.U. 5.23.
156. P.U. 4.4.

3

PART ONE: The Concept of Prāṇa in the Vedānta Tradition

The Vedānta tradition is primarily concerned with constructing an interpretation of the Upaniṣads, which, as noted in chapter two, constitute the end portion of the Veda (Veda-anta). By the time when newly compiled Upaniṣads could be clearly linked with one or other of the Vedic śākhās (schools),[1] which was probably sometime during the period when the great epics were being composed,[2] it became evident that there was considerable disagreement among Vedāntins about both central issues and technical details of Upaniṣadic teaching.[3] As Thibaut surmizes, 'The followers of the different Vedic śākhās no doubt recognized already at an early period the truth that, while conflicting statements regarding the details of sacrifice can be got over by the assumption of a vikalpa, i.e. an optional proceeding, it is not so with regard to such topics as the nature of brahman, the relation to it of the human soul, the origin of the physical universe, and the like.'[4]

As a consequence of this recognition the adherents of the Vedānta tradition, who regarded the Upaniṣads as revelation (śruti) and hence divinely inspired and inerrant, began to formulate interpretations of Upaniṣadic teachings which would demonstrate that they offered a single coherent doctrine. The oldest surviving example of such a work is the Brahmasūtra attributed to Bādarāyaṇa.[5] There are many different views about the authorship and composition of this text. Some scholars, such as Dasgupta[6] and Pandey[7] assume a single author whose name was Bādarāyaṇa. Others, such as Radhakrishnan,[8] avoid any definitive statement on the matter whilst yet others argue that the work was compiled by a later editor[9] or team of editors.[10] Similar attitudes can be discerned with regard to the unity of the text. Dasgupta and Pandey[11] regard it as unitary whereas Nakamura[12] and Mayeda[13] regard it as composite, having been expanded over some 700 years.

By far the most detailed and convincing studies of these is that of Nakamura. In addition to demonstrating the composite nature of the Brahmasūtra and its compilation over a considerable period of time[14] he shows that it was probably a product of schools of the Sāmaveda which had a particular association with the Chāndogya Upaniṣad. He suggests that in the first phase of their activities synopses of Upaniṣadic teaching were attempted which centred on the Chāndogya Upaniṣad and followed its arrangement of topics. Next came a process of enlargement which incorporated other schools' first phase activities and, thirdly, came a final revision which included refutations of the views of schools other than the Vedānta. Thus, whilst in the later period the Brahmasūtra was a text subscribed to by Vedāntins from all Vedic schools it emerged out of a partisan activity which is still evident in the final recension. Despite this, there can be little doubt that the Brahmasūtra as we have it is the text which indicates most clearly the general tendency of Vedānta thought during the epic period.

What that tendency was is not easy to determine, however, for whilst the sūtras of other schools such as Nyāya, Vaiśeṣika and Yoga are simply difficult to understand without a commentary those of the Mīmāṃsā and Vedānta are unintelligible without one.[15] As Thibaut explains, 'The most essential words are habitually dispensed with; nothing is, for instance, more common than the simple omission of the subject or predicate of a sentence. And where here and there a Sūtra occurs whose words construe without anything having to be supplied, the phraseology is so eminently vague and obscure that without the help derived from a commentary we should be unable to make out to what subject the Sūtra refers.'[16] Hence, an essential item for the would-be interpreter of the Brahmasūtra is a reliable commentary. The main problems with this for the modern student are that on the one hand, the traditional commentaries all assume the unity and coherence of Upaniṣadic teaching and yet, on the other, few of them agree about the overall purport of the text.

The two most influential of the traditional commentators are Śaṅkara[17] and Rāmānuja.[18] At the time Thibaut wrote his introduction to his S.B.E. translation of Śaṅkara's and Rāmānuja's commentaries on the Brahmasūtra these two works were the oldest interpretations of the text available to western scholarship. Subsequently, however, the commentary of Bhāskara has been discovered and published in the Chowkhamba Sanskrit Series, Benares. Bhāskara interpreted the Brahmasūtra from a bhedābheda (difference-non-difference) position, a kind of half-way stage between Śaṅkara's full-blown advaita or māyāvāda and Rāmānuja's viśiṣṭādvaita, though tending to be philosophically more akin to the latter.[19]

With regard to the division of the text, however Bhāskara follows Śaṅkara on all but three occasions (3.3.29-30 and 32; 4.2.12 and 4.3.7-16).[20] Rāmānuja's arrangement, on the other hand, differs from Śaṅkara's in a considerable number of cases, though when set against the total number of sutras (555 in all) even these do not constitute what might be called a sizeable proportion. As Thibaut points out, '... in spite of very numerous discrepancies ... the two commentators [Śaṅkara and Rāmānuja] are at one as to the general drift of the Sūtras and the arrangement of topics. As a rule, the adhikaraṇas [divisions into topics] discuss one or several Vedic passages bearing upon a certain point of the system, and in the vast majority of cases the two commentators agree as to which are the special texts referred to.'[21] The same appears to be true of Bhāskara's commentary,[22] which Nakamura regards as most accurately interpreting the view of the sūtras.

What is of interest, as far as the present investigation is concerned, is that many of the Upaniṣadic passages deemed problematic by the compilers of the Brahmasūtra are ones where prāṇa is a prominent feature. What is more, there is very little difference between Śaṅkara, Rāmānuja and, as far as I can tell, Bhāskara about how these passages are to be understood. That the understanding of the place of prāṇa in the teachings of the Upaniṣads should have been a controversial issue for the compilers of the sūtras yet a matter of general agreement between the most influential later commentators indicates that in the period between the sūtras taking their final form and the time of Rāmānuja a consensus about the nature and function of prāṇa had been arrived at by the representatives of the mainstream Vedānta tradition.

This does not mean that the nature and role of prāṇa in the teachings of the Upaniṣads ceased to be an issue or a problem for interpreters of the Vedānta, far from it. What it does mean, rather, is that after the compilation of the Brahmasūtra Vedāntins were more agreed on how to deal with it. By and large their approach was to marginalize the prāṇa concept as much as the texts would allow. Hence, whenever possible, writers like Śaṅkara and Rāmānuja avoid any discussion of the nature or role of prāṇa and, as far as they are able, omit it from their teachings altogether.

That this is the case can be ascertained from an examination of their writings. In an effort to identify the authentic works of Śaṅkara Mayeda has proposed that Śaṅkara should be understood as the author of the Brahmasūtra commentary which goes under his name. This commentary can then be employed 'as the yardstick against which to measure the authenticity of other works ascribed to him.'[23] On this basis he accepts the following works as authentic writings of Śaṅkara : the commentaries on the Bṛhadāraṇyaka, Chāndogya, Aitareya, Taittirīya, Kena, Īśā, Kaṭha, Muṇḍaka, Praśna and Māṇḍūkya Upaniṣads, the commentaries on the Gaudapādīyakārikā and the Adhyātmapaṭala of Āpastamba-Dharmasūtra and, finally, the Upadeśasāhasrī which he suggests 'is the only non-commentarial work whose authenticity has been conclusively demonstrated.[24]

Given the greater degree of freedom for the author in a non-commentarial text it is here we should look for evidence of matters that were of central interest for him and omissions of those which were not. The Upadeśasāhasrī has two main parts, a metrical one and a prose one. Śaṅkara mentions prāṇa four times in the metrical portion and not at all in the prose portion. In two of these references: 17.27 and 17.57, he appears to be using the term prāṇa to refer to states of waking and sleeping.[25] One, (13.2), makes prāṇa nothing but an upādhi and thus, in only one verse: 14.15, is there any intimation that 'prāṇa' could have any cosmic connotations at all.[26] However nothing is made of this reference and a reader of the Upadeśasāhasrī would conclude, rightly, that prāṇa was a very minor principle in the Vedāntic world-view as understood by Śaṅkara.

This attitude to prāṇa, on the part of Śaṅkara, goes a long way, I would suggest, towards explaining why he did not write a commentary on the Kauṣītakī Upaniṣad, the only early prose Upaniṣad to escape such attention. Deussen finds this omission remarkable,[27] but if one accepts that the Kauṣītakī offers the most articulate presentation of the views of what he calls 'the older school' and does not take it, as he himself does, as a kind of compromise document then the reason is easy to discern. The Kauṣītakī Upanisad represented for Śaṅkara the most lucid statement to be found in śruti of a position he wanted to reject. To interpret it consistently from his own standpoint would have been an extremely difficult task and hence better left alone, a solution to which he seems to have been quite enamoured.

The situation is extremely similar in the case of Rāmānuja. In his long lifetime he composed only nine works,[28] all in Sanskrit. They are : three commentaries on the Brahmasūtra: Śrībhāṣya, Vedāntadīpa and Vedāntasāra; one commentary on the Bhagavadgītā, the Bhagavadgītābhāṣya; three prose hymns (gadya): Śaraṇāgatigadya, Śrīrangagadya and Vaikuṇṭhagadya; one manual for daily worship, the Nityagrantha, and the Vedārthasaṃgraha. There is some controversy over the authenticity of the three gadyas and the Nityagrantha and hence they cannot with certainty be attributed to Rāmānuja. Of the remaining works only the Vedārthasaṃgraha is not a commentary on an existing text. It is Rāmānuja's summary of the teaching of the Upaniṣads. The Vedārthasaṃgraha could be said to be to Rāmānuja what the Upadeśasāhasrī is to Śaṅkara. Not only is it his only non-commentarial work but, like the Upadeśasāhasrī, it gives more space to a discussion of C.U. 6 (Uddālaka's instruction to Śvetaketu, which contains the mahāvākya 'tat tvam asi') than to any other topic.

He mentions prāṇa or one of its derivatives on only six occasions in the Vedārthasaṃgraha and five of these are found in quotations employed to make a particular point rather than as explanations of prāṇa's place in the Upaniṣadic world-view. Hence, in paragraph 43 he quotes B.A.U. 4.3.6 as stating that brahman '... is "The real of the reals", for life principles (prāṇa) are real and this is more real than life principles' in order to demonstrate that brahman is the supreme and ultimate reality.[29] In two places, paragraphs 98 and 235, he quotes the Manusmṛti. 12.123 ('... some say he is Agni, others say he is Prajāpati, others again say that he is Indra, while some others say that he is Prāṇa. Others say that he is the eternal Brahman'[30]) in order to establish that terms such as Agni etc., when referring to the ultimate principle, do not have their normal meanings but should be understood as indicating brahman. The same point is made in paragraph 144 where he informs the reader that it is a well-established practice to take scriptural passages suggesting that entities like prāṇa or ākāśa are the ultimate principle of existence as really referring to brahman.

The final two references both occur in quotations. Paragraph 137 quotes a phrase from the Atharvaśikha Upaniṣad: 'prāṇaṃ manaṣi saha karaṇaiḥ'[31] in order to encourage meditation on the highest Self, which is to be understood as the cause or source of prāṇa and manas. The last passage, a verse from Āpastamba (22.4), is quoted to establish that the ātman is the animator, controller but also prisoner of the body.[32] For Rāmānuja then, the prāṇas are simply the life functions of living beings, who are animated by the ātman; where 'prāṇa' seems to mean something like 'supreme principle' what is to be understood is not prāṇa but brahman.

Thus, when we examine the independent works of Śaṅkara and Rāmānuja we find that, by and large, the term prāṇa is employed to mean either a 'life principle', an instrument of the ātman, one or more states of waking or sleeping or is regarded as a term employed by some writers, who did not mean what they wrote, to refer to brahman. When we come to the texts interpreted by both Śaṅkara and Rāmānuja : the Bhagavadgītā and the Brahmasūtra, we find that the former has very little to say on the topic of prāṇa whilst the latter regards it as a controversial subject, which is, of course, why it was chosen for comment.

The term 'prāṇa' is used eight times in the Bhagavadgītā, six of which are noted by Jacob.[33] The references are 1.33; 4.27 and 29-30; 5.27; 8.10 and 12; 18.33. Little in these passages offers anything additional to what can be found in the Upaniṣads on the topic of prāṇa. The exceptions to this are 8.10 and 12. These passages are reminiscent of Mait.U. 6.20-21 though the Gītā explicitly states that the processes described occur at the time of death (prayāṇa-kāle) whereas the Maitrī account suggests that they occur during life.

Mait.U. 6.20-21 reads as follows :

> '... By pressing the tip of his tongue against the palate, by restraining voice (vāc), mind (manas), and breath (prāṇa), one sees Brahma through contemplation ... There is a channel (nāḍī) called the suṣumnā, leading upward, conveying the breath, piercing through the palate. Through it, by joining the breath (prāṇa), the syllable Oṃ, and the mind (manas) one may go aloft ... Thence he goes to selflessness. Because of selflessness, one becomes a non-

experiencer of pleasure and pain; he obtains the absolute unity (kevalatva).'[34]

The Gītā passages are:

> 'With mind unmoving at the time of passing on, by love-and-devotion integrated (bhaktyā yukto) and by the power of spiritual exercises too (yoga-balena c'aiva), forcing (āveśya) the breath between the eyebrows duly, so will that man draw nigh to that divine exhalted Person.
>
> Let a man close up all [the body's] gates, stem his mind within the heart, fix his breath within the head, exposed in yogic concentration.[25]

First of all, it may be noted that 'fixing the prāṇa between the eyebrows' is not present in the Upaniṣadic account and, in fact, is a technique not found in any of the principal Upaniṣads. Both Śaṅkara and Rāmānuja, however, accept this innovation without comment. In his interpretation of this Gītā verse Śaṅkara appears to combine the information from the Maitrī account and from elsewhere in the Upaniṣads to provide a more complete picture of the process to which the Gītā refers. He writes in his comments on both 8.10 and 8.12, that

> 'At first the mind (citta) is subdued in the lotus of the heart (hṛdayapuṇḍarika); then, by means of the up-going nādī (suṣmnā), after gradually obtaining control over the several stages of matter (earth and the other four rudimentary elements), the life breath of the heart is drawn up and carefully fixed betwixt the eye-brows. By this means the wise man, the yogin, reaches the Supreme Puruṣa, who is resplendent.
>
> Having closed all the avenues of knowledge and having concentrated thought in the lotus of the heart, and with thought thus controlled, he ascends by the nāḍī which passes upwards from the heart, and then fixing the life breath in the head he utters the syllable 'Oṃ', the appelation of the Brahman, and meditates on Me.[36]

It is perhaps noteworthy that nowhere does Śaṅkara refer to the fact that these processes take place at death. Rather, following the Maitrī Upaniṣad, the implication is that they can take place during one's lifetime.

Rāmānuja, on the other hand, is at pains to emphasize, perhaps as a counterbalance to Śaṅkara, that the attainment mentioned in the text is only secured after death. He writes,

> 'While representing God to himself with his mind which *in his dying hours* remains fixed on God as the result of daily practice and yoga, the aspirant to aiśvarya will *after his death* attain a form equal to God's because of the eminent aiśvarya which will be his. He will attain the aiśvarya which God himself possesses, when he has concentrated his prāṇa between the brows and then ... represents God to himself as etc., etc. ...'[37]

An exponent of Deussen's 'older school' could make much of this material, arguing that here the importance of prāṇa in the soteriology of the Gītā is most apparent for in both these verses the concentration of the prāṇas in the head/between the eyebrows is necessary if one is to retreive the experience of that immortal, unitary state which is the experience of the primeval prāṇa which created the cosmos and enters human beings by way of the head. Śaṅkara and Rāmānuja, however, make nothing of it, simply repeating, with a little expansion on Śaṅkara's part, what the text itself says.

The same kind of procedure is adopted by both writers in their commentaries on the Brahmasūtra. Bādarāyaṇa, the sūtrakāra (= the compilers of the Brahmasūtra), is clearly an adherent of Deussen's 'younger school' and his approach to the interpretation of the nature of 'prāṇa' in the Upaniṣads is very similar to that adopted by Śaṅkara in the Upadeśasāhasrī and by Rāmānuja in the Vedārthasaṃgraha : whenever it is presented as the ultimate principle of existence it is taken to be a reference to Brahman; on other occasions its meaning is adapted to fit with the opinion of the author (the siddhānta statement as distinct from the pūrvapakṣa–prima facie or opponent's view–which, in fact, is often closer to the purport of the Upaniṣadic text though still committed to the overall coherence of Upaniṣadic doctrine).

The treatment of prāṇa in the Brahmasūtra

An examination of the way in which the Brahmasūtra along with its two principal commentators, Śaṅkara and Rāmānuja, deal with Upaniṣadic references to prāṇa reveals the process by which a concept so central and important to many Upaniṣadic texts becomes, for the interpreters of those texts, a peripheral notion that contributes hardly at all to the world-view of the Vedānta tradition. Such an examination also reveals the fact that although the Vedānta is described as an exegetical system (mīmāṃsā), the most influential Vedānta teachers blatantly distort the teachings of the Upaniṣadic texts in order to develop their own positions, which often incorporate non-Upaniṣadic concepts at the expense of Upaniṣadic ones.

Śaṅkara and Rāmānuja employ a number of hermeneutical devices to marginalize the concept of prāṇa in Upaniṣadic teaching. One of them is the simple denial of the fact that prāṇa ever means ultimate principle. Whenever passages are quoted where prāṇa appears as the ultimate principle it is simply stated that what the writer really meant by the term 'prāṇa' was 'brahman'. This is not, however, an argument for synonymity, for both Śaṅkara and Rāmānuja are clear that prāṇa is not a synonym of brahman. In addition, both commentators deny prāṇa any involvement with the processes of awareness or mentation. This is achieved through simple, unsupported denials that prāṇa has anything to do with sentience and by the separation of prāṇa from what in Vedic literature are some of its principal manifestations : the faculties. In the Brahmasūtra these are designated as 'indriyas' and are declared to be different in nature from prāṇa.

As was pointed out above, the sūtrakāra, Śaṅkara, Rāmānuja and, often, the pūrvapakṣin are representatives of the 'younger school' of Vedānta thought. Hence, arguments supporting the view of prāṇa set out in the first two chapters of this study are never really presented in the Brahmasūtra. As often as not the purvapakṣin merely acts as a 'straw man', whose views are mentioned so that they can be rejected rather than as genuine alternative interpretations of the material under consideration. Also evident, and this goes counter to Thibaut's claim that, overall, Rāmānuja is more faithful to the sūtrakāra than is Śaṅkara, is that as far as the sūtras dealing with prāṇa are concerned Śaṅkara's interpretation is probably closer to the intention of the sūtrakāra and more alert to the issues with which he has to deal than is Rāmānuja's. In only a small number of cases are his interpretations less convincing than Rāmānuja's. Moreover, in his comments on these sūtras the distinctive features of Śaṅkara's own philosophical position are much less in evidence than are those of Rāmānuja, who rarely misses an opportunity to emphasize the difference between brahman, the individual soul (jīva) and the world. The material substantiating these conclusions will be presented under four headings: Prāṇa and Brahman; Prāṇa and the Prāṇas; Prāṇa and the process of death; Prāṇa in C.U. 7.

Prāṇa and Brahman

The first adhyāya of the Brahmasūtra is concerned with the topic of brahman, its nature, its activities and the range of terms denoting it that are found in the Upaniṣads. The second half of pāda one is given over to a consideration of the terms space or ether (ākāśa), breath (prāṇa) and light (jyotis). Two topic divisions (adhikaraṇa) (sūtras 1.1.23 and 1.1.28-31 in Śaṅkara's version) deal with the question of whether references to prāṇa in some Upaniṣadic passages, primarily C.U. 1.10-11 and Kauṣ.U. 3, should be taken as genuine references to prāṇa or whether they should be taken as references to brahman. In discussing this material Śaṅkara and Rāmānuja agree about which sūtras go into which topic divisions, though the number of sūtras in the first pāda of adhyāya one is different in Śaṅkara's and Rāmānuja's versions of the text. Rāmānuja adds an extra sūtra after sūtra eight and hence his text has 32 sūtras whilst Śaṅkara's has only 31. Consequently, sūtra 23 in Śaṅkara's version is sutra 24 in Rāmānuja's and so on.

Sūtra 22 (23 in Rāmānuja) seeks to establish that when, in C.U. 1.9, ākāśa (ether or space) is said to be the origin of the world the term 'ākāśa' is not be be understood in its ordinary sense but as a substitute for 'brahman'. Hence it states 'ākāśas talliṅgāt'[38] (ākāśa (is brahman) as brahman's characteristic marks (are mentioned)). Linking with this, sūtra 23 (24 in Rāmānuja) states 'ata eva prāṇaḥ'[39] (prāṇa (is brahman) for the same reason). Śaṅkara is by far the most detailed in his comments on this sūtra. First he deals with the pūrvapakṣin (the opponent offering the prima facie interpretation of the text), who

> 'maintains that the word (prāṇa) must be held to denote the fivefold vital breath, which is a peculiar modification of wind (or air) [vāyu]; because, as has been remarked already, that sense of the word prāṇa is the better established one.'[40]

Śatapatha Brāhmaṇa 10.3.3.6, which states that all the faculties merge into prāṇa during sleep, is quoted by the pūrvapakṣin as scriptural support for this interpretation.

Śaṅkara, however, whilst agreeing that the mukhya prāṇa, the fivefold prāṇa, is the primary meaning of the term 'prāṇa' and that the Ś.B. account can be understood as a reference to this principle the same cannot be claimed for C.U. 1.10-11 since there it is not just the faculties but 'all beings' which merge into prāṇa. Rāmānuja elaborates stating,

> '... breath is not present in things such as stones and wood, nor in intelligence itself and that hence of breath in the ordinary sense it cannot be said that 'all beings enter into it', etc. We therefore conclude that Brahman is here called 'breath' in so far as he bestows the breath of life on all beings'.[41]

It is clear from this sūtra and the elaborations of both commentators that the sūtrakāra, Śaṅkara and Rāmānuja are all adherents of what Deussen calls 'the younger school'. The pūrvapakṣin must also be placed in this category since one of the distinguishing characteristics of this school is that its members refuse to admit the multivalence of the term 'prāṇa'. It was demonstrated in chapter one that for many Saṃhitā, Brāhmaṇa and Āraṇyaka teachers 'prāṇa' could mean that which is the source and substance of all existence as well as cosmic and individualized manifestations of the same. Here, however, this view is not even referred to by the pūrvapakṣin. As was argued in the preceding chapters, 'prāṇa' can be understood to mean 'ultimate principle of existence' more or less as often as it can be understood to mean 'the fivefold prāṇa'. Furthermore, the arguments of both Śaṅkara and Rāmānuja that 'all beings' cannot enter into prāṇa' is at variance with scripture itself for there are frequent scriptural statements that everything is established (pratiṣṭhita) in prāṇa and, as was noted in chapter two, Kauṣ.U. 4.20 has the worlds (loka) entering into and emerging out from the senses (deva), the senses to and from the prāṇas and the prāṇas to and from ātman (= the unitary prāṇa).

The unbiased exegete would have to conclude from this material that 'prāṇa' was, for some Upaniṣadic teachers, a synonym of brahman/ātman and that the characteristics of prāṇa were thus the same as those of brahman/ātman. For the sūtrakāra and commentators, however, prāṇa is not a synonym of ātman/brahman; when it appears to be used as such the intention of the writer is taken to be the emphasis of some aspect of ātman/brahman. As Rāmānuja puts it,

> '... the words 'ether' and 'breath' denote something other than what is ordinarily denoted by those terms, viz. the highest Brahman, the sole cause of this entire world, free from all evil, etc. etc.'[42]

Sūtras 28-31 (29-32 in Rāmānuja) develop this interpretation of the sūtrakāra by an exegesis of Kauṣītakī Upaniṣad 3. They run as follows :

> 'Prāṇa is Brahman on account of connexion (28). If it be said that (Brahman is) not denoted on account of the speaker denoting himself; (we say, not so), because the multitude of connexions with the inner self (is possible only) in that (speaker if viewed as Brahman) (29). The instruction (given by Indra about himself) (is possible) through insight based on scripture, as in the case of Vāmadeva (30). If it be said (that Brahman is not meant) on account of the characteristic marks of the individual soul and the chief vital air; we say no, on account of (such threefold meditation) being appropriate here (also) (31)'[43]

Once again, Śaṅkara offers the more detailed comments and Rāmānuja concurs with his interpretation almost entirely. Following sūtra 28, Śaṅkara quotes a number of passages from Kauṣītakī Upaniṣad 3 and sets up the problem which is tackled in the remaining sūtras of the first pāda. He writes,

> 'Here the doubt presents itself whether the word prāṇa denotes merely breath, the modification of air [vāyu] [option one], or the Self of some divinity [option two], or the individual soul [option three], or the highest Brahman [option four].'[44]

The sūtras deal with each of these options in turn and, of course, only the last is deemed to be satisfactory. But why, says the objector, is this necessary since 1.1.23 has already established that where the characteristic marks of brahman are mentioned in connection with prāṇas the reference is to brahman and not to prāṇa as ordinarily understood. Śaṅkara's answer is that in these Kauṣītakī passages we find references to the characteristics of being the intelligent self (prajñātman), of being bliss (ānanda), of being ageless or imperishable (ajara) and of being immortal (amṛta); these are different from the characteristic mentioned under 1.23, of being the source and foundation of all beings.

He then turns his attention to each of the options in turn. First of all he argues that prāṇa cannot here be understood as a modification of air for air is non-intelligent and prāṇa is equated with the intelligent self (prajñātman).[45] The second possibility is that Indra, the speaker in these Kauṣītakī passages is describing himself and not brahman. This cannot be the case, says Śaṅkara, because, as sūtra 30 points out, in these passages Indra is simply expressing his awareness that he is one with brahman just as the sage Vāmadeva had done.[46] The third possibility, that prāṇa refers to the individual soul (jīva), is more difficult to refute, not least because in the Kauṣitaki Upaniṣad there is no clear distinction made between individual self and univesal self. But the sūtrakāra is in a strong position to deny the possibility that the reference is to the individual self for, having already established to his satisfaction that when characteristics attributed to brahman are connected with another term that term is to be understood as a reference to brahman, he simply has to affirm the obvious unity of the text in order to reach the desired conclusion. Śaṅkara puts it as follows :

> 'Your [the purvapakṣin] interpretation would involve the assumption of devout meditation of three different kinds, viz. on the individual soul, on the chief vital air, and on Brahman. But it is inappropriate to assume that a single sentence should enjoin three kinds of devout meditation; and that all the passages about the prāṇa really constitute one single sentence (one syntactical whole) appears from the beginning and the concluding part. In the beginning we have the clause 'know me only' followed by 'I am prāṇa, the intelligent Self, meditate on me as Life (prāṇa), as Immortality (amṛta)'; and in the end we read, 'And that prāṇa indeed is the intelligent Self, blessed, imperishable, immortal.' The beginning and the concluding part are thus seen to be similar, and we therefore must conclude that they refer to one and the same matter ... Thus we see that the one meditation on Brahman is here represented as threefold, according as Brahman is viewed either with reference to two limiting conditions (upādhi) or in itself.'[47]

Throughout his comments on these sūtras Śaṅkara seems to be aware of the problems to which the sūtrakāra is addressing himself and his exposition of the sūtrakāra's views appears to be a legitimate one.

Rāmānuja, however, although commenting in much less detail than Śaṅkara, uses the opportunity to make his commentary serve his own theological position and in the process offers a highly untenable interpretation. He writes

> 'The highest Self is called by these different terms [i.e. prāṇa and Indra] in order to teach threefoldness of devout

meditation; viz. meditation on Brahman in itself as the course of the entire world; on Brahman as having for its body the totality of enjoying (individual) souls [= Indra]; and on Brahman as having for its body the objects and means of enjoyment [= prāṇa].'[48]

Two other passages deal with the problem of prāṇa being described as possessing characteristics of brahman. They are 1.3.39 (40 and 41 in Rāmānuja)[49] and 1.4.16-18. 1.3.39 reads 'kampanāt' '(The prāṇa is Brahman), on account of the trembling (predicated of the whole world)'[50] Both Śaṅkara and Rāmānuja are agreed that this sūtra refers to Kaṭh.U. 6.2:

> 'Whatever there is, the whole world when gone forth trembles in the prāṇa. It (the prāṇa) is a great terror a raised thunderbolt. Those who know it become immortal.'[51]

Once again, Śaṅkara and Rāmānuja argue that here the term 'prāṇa' is being used to refer to the highest brahman, though they do so in rather different ways.

Śaṅkara starts his commentary by presenting the pūrvapakṣa view (which was obviously more of an issue in his day than at the time of Rāmānuja, who quotes the purvapakṣin much less frequently than does his predecessor). It is that the subject of this sūtra is ordinary air (vāyu) for

> '... this whole world trembles, abiding within air with its five forms – which is here called prāṇa – and the terrible thunderbolts also spring from air ... Through the knowledge of that air immortality also can be obtained; for another scriptural passage says, 'Air is everything by itself, and air is all things together. He who knows this conquers death.'[52]

Once again we see that the pūrvapakṣin cannot be regarded as a representative of 'the older school' for here is another example of a situation where the multivalence of the term 'prāṇa' could be emphasized but the purvapaksin persists in reducing statements about prāṇa as the ground, source and immortal essence of all to a statement about the element air. As presented then, the purvapakṣa view is something of a 'straw man', offered only because it is easy to refute.

Śaṅkara's own line is essentially the 'characteristics of brahman' argument with some elaboration related to the passage in question. In support of his claim that in this passage too, 'prāṇa' really means 'brahman' and not 'prāṇa' he draws attention to the verse immediately preceding the one in question. There it says,

> 'That only is called the Bright, that is called Brahman, that alone is called the immortal. All worlds are contained in it, and no one goes beyond it.'[53]

With this as foundation he goes on to launch a two-pronged attack on the pūrvapakṣin. He writes,

> 'That the brahman there spoken of forms the topic of our passage also, we conclude, firstly, from proximity; and secondly, from the circumstance that the clause, 'The whole world trembles in 'prāṇa', we recognise a quality of Brahman viz. its constituting the abode of the whole world.'[54]

With slightly different elaborations, such as contextualising the Kaṭha Upaniṣad passage in question into a wider framework of a discussion about the 'person the size of a thumb' who abides in the heart, Rāmānuja presents the same argument. He writes,

> 'This text declares that the whole world and Agni, Sūrya, and so on, abiding within that person the size of a thumb, who is here designated by the term 'breath', and going forth from him tremble from their great fear of him ... what is described here is the nature of the highest Brahman; for that such power belongs to Brahman only we know from other texts ...'[55]

Of course the other texts do not claim that such power belongs to brahman only but just that it belongs to brahman, which a member of 'the older school' would declare to be prāṇa. Once again we witness an example of one of the central deceptions perpetrated by the later Vedāntins: the appropriation of all accounts of the ultimate principle by their ātman/brahman concept, accompanied by a denial that the Upaniṣadic teachers meant what they said when they employed other terms to denote such a principle.

B.S. 1.4.16-18 discusses the subject of Kauṣ.U. 4, the dialogue between Bālāki and Ajātaśatru. The specific reference of the sūtra is to Kauṣ.U. 4.19, where Ajātaśatru says,

> 'O Bālāki, he who is the maker of these persons, he of whom this is the work, he alone is to be known.'[56]

The problem, as Śaṅkara understands it, is whether the object of knowledge in this passage is the individual soul (jīva), the chief vital breath (mukhya prāṇa) or the brahman. The pūrvapakṣin argues that it must be one of the first two whilst the sūtrakāra, Śaṅkara and Rāmānuja all maintain that the object of knowledge must be brahman. As Śaṅkara points out, reiterating the 'characteristics' argument, 'None ... but the highest Lord is capable of being the maker of all these persons as he only is absolutely independent.'[57] In support of this conclusion the next sūtra (1.4.17) refers back to B.S. 1.1.31 (1.1.32 in Rāmānuja) where a threefold meditation on Brahman is declared to be the object of the text under discussion. The same is said to apply here. In commenting on 1.4.17 Rāmānuja writes,

> '... we must understand the mention of prāṇa to be made with a view to meditation on Brahman in so far as having the prāṇa for its body'.[58]

That the individual soul is also to be understood in this way is demonstrated by the next sūtra, which quotes the opinion of the teacher Jaimini. He thinks, and the sūtrakāra, Śaṅkara and Rāmānuja are in agreement iwth him, that the individual soul is mentioned in this text to point to what is different from it: the highest brahman. This opinion is based on the contents of a question and answer sequence in the abovementioned dialogue :

> 'Bālāki, where did this person here sleep? Where was he? Whence came he thus back? ... When sleeping he sees no dream, then he becomes one with that prāṇa alone ... From that Self all prāṇas proceed each towards its place, from the prāṇas the gods, from the gods the worlds.'[59]

In Rāmānuja's view,

> '... this reply, no less than the questions, clearly refers to the highest Self as something different from the individual Self. For that entering into which the soul, in the state of deep sleep, attains its true nature and enjoys complete serenity, being free from the disturbing experiences of pleasure and pain that accompany the states of waking and dream; and that from which it again returns to the fruition of pleasure and pain; that is nothing else but the highest self.'[60]

He adds, moreover,

> 'We ... also reject the Pūrvapakṣin's contention that question and answer refer to the individual soul, that the veins called

hitā are the abode of deep sleep, and that the well-known clause as to the prāṇa must be taken to mean that the aggregate of the organs becomes one in the individual soul called prāṇa. For the veins are the abode, not of deep sleep, but of dream, and ... Brahman only is the abode of deep sleep; and the text declares that the individual soul, together with all its ministering organs, becomes one with, and again proceeds from, Brahman only–which the text designates as prāṇa'[61]

These interpretations of the commentators highlight clearly the extremes to which they will go to develop their own position; in particular, the extent to which they are prepared to distort the obvious sentiments of the Upaniṣad to advance their own standpoint. In the Kauṣītakī passage under discussion there is no distinction made between the chief vital air, the individual self and the highest self. In fact, this classification is alien to the text. The terminology of the text is 'prāṇa', 'prajñātman' and 'śarīrātman'. The first two are explicitly equated and the entity which is prāṇa/ prajñātman is said to enter the śarīrātman, filling it up to the hairs and nails: sa eṣa prāṇa eva prajñātmedaṃ śarīram ātmanam anupraviṣṭa ālomabhyā ānakhebhyaḥ/ 'This very prāṇa, this prajñātman, has entered this bodily self (śarīrātman) up to the very hairs and nails.'[62] In this Kauṣītakī account prāṇa, individual self and highest self are all the same. The prāṇa/prajñātman is brahman.

The same kind of textual misrepresentation is evident in Rāmānuja's claim that the veins (hitā) which extend from the heart to the pericardium are not the abode of a person (puruṣa) in deep sleep but only during dreaming. Kauṣ.U. 4 19, on the other hand, explicitly states that the puruṣa abides in the hitā during deep sleep. The same view can be found in B.A.U. 2.1.19, where the ātman is said to rest in the pericardium during deep sleep. No wonder Rāmānuja never wrote commentaries on individual Upaniṣads, being content to regard the Brahmasūtra as a synthetic interpretation ... the key to the meaning of all the Upaniṣads.'[63] Not only did this enable him to claim concurrence with an authoritative interpretation of śruti (and one which was so terse it enabled him to develop his own doctrinal predelictions as the views of an established authority) it also gave him much more freedom to quote out of context and misrepresent Upaniṣadic teachings than would be the case with detailed commentaries on individual texts.

Overall, it is clear from an examination of these texts on prāṇa and brahman that the exegetical technique of Śaṅkara and Rāmānuja is, in this context, little more than the dogmatic imposition of their own predelictions. With regard to their interpretations of C.U. 1.10-11, Kauṣ.U. 3 and Kaṭh.U. 2.6.2-3 their views rest on just one argument which amounts to this : when terms which we do not accept as referring to the supreme principle appear to do so they are not to be accepted as synonyms for that principle but as phenomena which point to it. The truth of such an assertion is clearly not self evident yet neither Śaṅkara nor Rāmānuja seek to justify it. In fact, as has been pointed out, there are a number of scriptural statements which present the opposite point of view.

A supplementary technique employed by both writers is to misrepresent the content of the text under consideration. In the case of Kauṣ.U. 3, Śaṅkara's four possible interpretations of the text are not really genuine options at all. It is clear that the term prāṇa is being employed to refer to the highest principle and not in the ways suggested by the other three options. Similarly, a distinction between the individual soul and the highest principle is not present in the text, whilst Rāmānuja's claim that 'Indra' means 'the totality of enjoying (individual) souls' is a blatant fabrication. This is no more than obfuscation and has little or no exegetical validity simply serving as it does to 'soften up' the reader's mind so that it will accept the crude dogmatism of 'the only synonyms of brahman are the ones that we allow'.

Prāṇa and Prāṇas

All but three sūtras of B.S. 2.4 are devoted to the topic of prāṇa and the prāṇas. The exceptions are 20-22. In Rāmānuja's version, sūtras two and three, 14 and 15, 18 and 19 of Śaṅkara's text are conflated into sūtras two, 13 and 16 respectively. Overall, what we witness in these sūtras is a continuation of the attempt to organise Upaniṣadic teaching into a coherent doctrine. As Śaṅkara points out in his comments on B.S. 2.4.1, from the standpoint of the Vedānta, although scripture may seem to contradict itself on various issues this is not, in fact, the case. The sūtras of B.S. 2.4 contribute to the demonstration of this position by clarifying what is meant by the terms 'prāṇa' and 'prāṇas', their nature, function and relation to each other. Six topics are discussed : the origin of the prāṇas, their number, their size, the mukhya prāṇa, the autonomy of the prāṇas and the relationship between the prāṇas and the mukhya prāṇa.

Sūtras 1-4 (1-3 in Rāmānuja) deal with the origin of the prāṇas. Both commentators discuss three kinds of scriptural passage deemed relevant to this question :

(1) those where the prāṇas are stated *not* to have been produced, e.g. Ś.B. 6.1.1.1;

(2) those where the prāṇas *are* stated to have been produced, e.g. B.A.U. 2.1.20; Muṇḍ.U. 2.1.3 and 8; P.U. 6.4;

(3) those creation accounts where the prāṇas are not mentioned at all, e.g. C.U. 6.2.3.

In Śaṅkara's commentary the pūrvapakṣin is presented as holding either that no opinion can be formed about the origin of the prāṇas or that texts indicating an origin for the prāṇas should be taken metaphorically. Rāmānuja has the pūrvapakṣin hold only the second of these alternatives. The view of the sūtrakāra, Śaṅkara and Rāmānuja is that the prāṇas *do* have an origin. The 'no opinion' position is obviously dealt with by the presentation of the sūtrakāra's own 'well substantiated' argument; the other alternative, however, has to be refuted. With regard to the texts which do not mention the prāṇas in their creation accounts, Śaṅkara points out that they can have no weight in the discussion.

> 'For the circumstances of a thing not being stated in some places has no power to invalidate what is stated about it in other places.'[54]

With regard to the notion that passages describing the origin of the prāṇas should be taken in a secondary or metaphorial sense Śaṅkara argues, in his comments on B.S. 2.4.2-3, that it is not acceptable since such exegesis emphasis appropriate where, as is the case with the texts in question, there are clear assertions made about the matter under discussion.

Both of Śaṅkara's arguments are faulty, though the first less so than the second. For the modern exegete the absence of some term from an account *can* be as significant as its presence. The significance of absence depends on the term itself, the texts where it is present and absent and the overall context in which the materials under consideration are to be placed. The second argument is a double-edged sword, for where some texts make clear statements denying that something has an origin whilst others make similar statements to the opposite effect there is a contradiction and neither view can be deemed more accurate or true than the other. Seemingly alert to this situation, Rāmānuja, in his commentary on 2.4.1, presents the pūrvapakṣin engaging in some rather unskillful exegesis. In Rāmānuja's text the pūrvapakṣin equates the poets (kavi) of R.V. 10.129, who,

> '... searching in their heart's wisdom, discovered the kinship of the created with the uncreate,'[65]

with the non-being (asat) mentioned in verse one. These poets are then equated with the seers (ṛṣi) who are the prāṇas in Ś.B. 6.1.1.1. This tenuous list of identifications is hardly likely to persuade anyone but the converted and since this is what is contrasted with clear statements about the origin of the prāṇas in some Upaniṣadic texts the case for taking the pūrvapakṣin's passages in a secondary sense is extremely convincing. Here, then, is a good example of a commentator using the pūrvapakṣin's argument to enhance his own view.

Śaṅkara's solution is to make the prāṇas near–ultimate principles from which others in turn evolve. He writes,

> 'We must ... view the statement about the existence of the prāṇas before the creation as having for its object a subordinate causal substance, and being made with reference to the latter only. For it is known from śruti and smṛti that even in the universe of evolved things many states of being may stand to each other in the relation of causal substance and effect.'[66]

The weakness of such a view lies, of course, in its arbitrariness. There is no compelling argument here to make anyone understand the prāṇas as subordinate causal substances. Rāmānuja's exegesis of the next sūtra is rather convoluted and unconvincing. Instead of understanding 2.4.2 to be saying that the statement about the non-origination of the prāṇas cannot be taken in a secondary sense since statements about their origin are unambiguous, he regards it as referring to the texts quoted in the discussion of sūtra one: Ṛ.V. 10.129 and Ś.B. 6.1.1. For him, it is the use of the plural form 'prāṇās' that is to be taken in a secondary sense because it is impossible for plurality to have existed before creation. Interestingly, he states that,

> 'In the text quoted by the pūrvapakṣin, "Non-being indeed was this in the beginning." etc., the word prāṇa can denote the highest Self only ...'[67]

for the word 'prāṇa' does not appear in Ṛ.V. 10.129. Hence, his statement under 2.4.3 (2.4.4 in Ś.) that, '... the word 'prāṇa' in the text quoted, can denote brahman only'[68] seems odd to say the least. Once again, it seems that, whatever its faults, Śaṅkara's exegesis of the sūtras appears to be more in tune with the context in which the sūtrakāra was writing than does Rāmānuja's.

B.S. 2.4.5 and 6 (4 and 5 in Rāmānuja) deal with the number of the prāṇas. 2.4.5 appears to be a provisional or pūrvapakṣa opinion which is rectified by 2.4.6. They read as follows :

> '(The prāṇas are) seven, on account of this being understood (from scriptural passages) and of the specification (of those seven) (5). But (there are also, in addition to the seven prāṇas mentioned,) the hands and so on. This being a settled matter, therefore (we must) not (conclude) thus (viz. that there are seven prāṇas only) (6).'

We may note that the sūtras never actually specify that it is 'prāṇas' which are seven in number, though both Śaṅkara and Rāmānuja take 'prāṇas' to be the subject of the sūtras.

After quoting examples of various scriptural passages where different numbers of prāṇas are mentioned Śaṅkara presents the pūrvapakṣa view as being that there are seven. The argument supporting this view is that although different numbers of prāṇas are listed in scripture only one of them can be definitive.

> '... hence we [the pūrvapakṣins] decide in favour of the number seven, in deference to the (simpler) assumption of a low number, and consider the statements of other numbers to refer to the difference of modifications (of the fundamental seven prāṇas).'[70]

This is an exegetical principle unacceptable to Śaṅkara for he quickly counters it, in his comments on the next sūtra, with the opposite view :

> '... wherever there is a conflict between a higher and a lower number, the higher number has to be accepted because the lower one is contained within it ...'[71]

However, instead of taking the highest number from all the scriptural statements Śaṅkara, seemingly following sūtra six, maintains that eleven is the correct number. In justification of this he writes,

> 'Should it be objected that scripture also mentions numbers higher than eleven, viz. twelve and thirteen, we admit that, but remark that there are no objective effects in addition to the eleven (well-known) objective effects on account of which additional organs would have to be assumed. There are five distinctions of buddhi having for their respective objects sound, touch, colour, taste and smell, and on their account there are the five intellectual organs [= prāṇa]; again there are five classes of action, viz. speaking, taking, going, evacuation and begetting, and on their account there are the five organs of action; finally there is the manas...'[72]

Here it is clear that Śaṅkara, and Rāmānuja follows him in this, takes the term 'prāṇa' to mean 'indriya' (organ or faculty). In fact, Śaṅkara quotes B.A.U. 3.9.4 in support : 'Ten are these prāṇas in man, and Ātman is the eleventh.' He points out, however, and Rāmānuja again concurs, that

> 'By the word Ātman we have to understand the internal organ, on account of its ruling over the organs.'[73]

These organs, as the passage quoted above (under note 71) reveals, are the buddhīndriyas and karmendriyas of the Sāṃkhya system, much of which was incorporated into the cosmology of the later Vedānta. We may note, however, that not one scriptural reference demonstrating that the karmendriyas are called 'prāṇas' is forthcoming.

As was shown in the two preceding chapters of this study, the plural 'prāṇās' is primarily employed in śruti to mean either the five prāṇas : prāṇa, apāna, vyāna, udāna and samāna, or the faculties of breath, speech, mind, sight and hearing, or to refer to both together, which is probably the case in this B.A.U. quotation. Such an interpretation of the passage is not acceptable to Śaṅkara and Rāmānuja since that would require mind (manas) to be included among the ten prāṇas and it could not, therefore, be taken as the referent of 'ātman'. This would then have to be taken to mean 'body', as was argued in chapter two, or 'self', which would be problematic, for neither commentator wants ātman to be classed as one of the prāṇas since these are deemed to be non-intelligent upādhis. Analysis of the contents of these sūtras and commentaries thus reveals, once again, that the earlier conceptions of prāṇa and prāṇas constituted problems for the teachers of the later Vedānta tradition and that they dealt with it by misrepresenting the older teaching.

Sūtra seven (six in Rāmānuja) states that the prāṇas are minute (aṇu). Exactly why the sūtrakāra chose this term to describe the prāṇas is not clear from either of the commentaries. If taken literally it leads the sūtrakāra into obvious conflict with such śruti texts as Kauṣ.U. 4.20 where prāṇa (in which all speech and names, eye and forms, ear and sounds, mind and thoughts merge) enters the bodily self (śarīrātman) up to the hairs and nails. Hence Śaṅkara explains that by 'aṇu',

> '... we have to understand subtility and limited size; but not atomic size ...'[74]

They must be subtle, for otherwise they would be seen departing at death, and they must be limited for,

> '... if they were all-pervading the scriptural statements as to their passing out of the body, going and coming, would be contradicted thereby.'[75]

For some unstated reason Rāmānuja keeps to the literal statement of the sūtra, that the prāṇas are atomic in size, and neither mentions the view of Śaṅkara nor provides any argument which might indicate that he was aware of the clash between the sūtra and śruti passages. In terms of exegetical accuracy, of course, only Śaṅkara's view can be substantiated by reference to Upaniṣadic texts.

The next six sūtras, 8-13 (7-12 in Rāmānuja), deal with the mukhya prāṇa and its nature. They read,

> 'And the best (8) [is] neither air nor function, on account of its being stated separately. (9) But [it is] like the eye and the rest, on account of being taught with them, and for other reasons. (10) And there is no objection on account of its not having an activity (karaṇa); for (Scripture) thus declares. (11) It is designated as having five functions like mind (12) and (it is) minute. (13)'[76]

Śaṅkara and Rāmānuja interpret some of these sūtras in more or less the same way but differ considerably about the import of others. I will thus present the views of each in turn before commenting on the nature of their arguments.

Both writers take the first sūtra to mean something like, 'just as the prāṇas have been created so too has the mukhya prāṇa been created.' The next sūtra, according to Śaṅkara, represents two pūrvapakṣa positions which need to be refuted. The first is that prāṇa is air (vāyu); the second, that it is the function of an organ. The first alternative is based on a number of equations between prāṇa and vāyu found in śruti, e.g. A.V. 11.4.15; Ś.B. 11.1.2.3.; the second on a Sāṃkhyan interpretation of prāṇa.[77] His response to the first alternative is that since some śruti passages distinguish prāṇa from vāyu they cannot be the same. His response to the Sāṃkhya view is three-fold: (a) if prāṇa were merely the function of an organ or organs it would not be mentioned separately from the organs in śruti texts; (b) all the organs together cannot produce prāṇa because each has its own specific function; (c) furthermore,

> '... we have no right to assume that the different prāṇas with their subordinate functions such as hearing etc. can, by combination, produce the function of vital breath; for there is no means to prove this, and the vital breath is in kind absolutely different from hearing and so on.'[78]

Despite having an existence separate from either vāyu or the other organs the mukhya prāṇa is, as the next sūtra (10) points out, subordinate to the ātman. Its relation to the ātman, says Śaṅkara, is like that of a minister in relation to a king, i.e. superior to ordinary subjects but subordinate to the monarch. However, even though prāṇa is often linked with the other prāṇas such as the eye/sight because like them it has a specific effect (that of supporting the body and the senses), unlike them it has no sense object to which it relates. Its functions, like those of mind, are fivefold. For Śaṅkara the functions of mind are : sight, hearing, smelling, tasting and touching; those of prāṇa are : prāṇa (which controls aspiration), apāna (which controls inspiration), vyāna (which controls life in the interval between prāṇa and apāna), udāna (which leads the soul from the body at death) and samāna (which controls the nourishment of the body).[79]

Like the other prāṇas, the mukhya prāṇa is minute (aṇu) and, again, this is to be understood as being subtle and limited. The pūrvapakṣin objects to this suggestion, however, for in texts such as B.A.U. 1.3.22 it is said that prāṇa is 'equal to a grub, equal to a gnat, equal to an elephant, equal to these three worlds, equal to this universe' and this must mean that it is all-pervading. 'Not so,' says Śaṅkara,

> '... the all-pervadingness to which this text speaks belongs to the Self of the prāṇa in its adhidaivata relation, according to which it appears as Hiraṇyagarbha in his double-universal and individual-form, not in its adhyātma relation.'[80]

Unlike Śaṅkara, Rāmānuja does not take the words 'neither air nor function' as relating to two quite different pūrvapakṣa positions. Instead, he reads it to mean 'neither air nor a function or air.' It is not air because śruti texts list it separately; it is not a function of air since śruti does not mention the function of other elements such as fire, water etc. As far as the pūrvapakṣin's text 'prāṇa is air' is concerned, this simply intimates,

> '... that breath is air having assumed a special form, not a thing altogether different from it, like fire. In ordinary language, moreover, the word 'breath' does not mean a mere motion but a substance to which motion belongs; we say "the breath moves to and fro in inhalation and exhalation".'[81]

Thus, for Rāmānuja, the next sūtra, sūtra 10 (9 in Rāmānuja), makes it clear that prāṇa is an instrument of the soul, like eye or ear, and not an element, like air or fire. That prāṇa is an instrument of the soul is a conclusion shared by Śaṅkara. Where he differs is on the reason for the sūtrakāra making the statement. Nevertheless the treatment of sūtras 10 and 11 (9 and 10 in Rāmānuja) is essentially the same in both commentaries.

When it comes to the functions and size of the mukhya prāṇa Rāmānuja again makes a considerable departure from Śaṅkara. Whilst he agrees that the five functions of prāṇa are : prāṇa, apāna, vyāna, udāna and samāna (none of which is described) he regards the functions of mind as being desire, purpose, doubt, faith, want of faith, firmness, absence of firmness, shame, reflection and fear (taken from B.A.U. 1.5.3). Similarly, as in the case of the prāṇas, he rejects Śaṅkara's view that 'aṅu' means 'subtle' and 'limited'. For him, the fact that it is not seen when leaving the body means it is atomic in size. As far as the texts describing prāṇa as all-pervading are concerned, they are contradicted by other texts and, moreover,

> '... the all embracingness ascribed to prāṇa in those other texts must be interpreted to mean only that the life of all living and breathing creatures depends on breath.'[82]

As far as the three areas of disagreement between the two commentators are concerned : (1) that function relates to 'organs' (Śaṅkara) or 'air' (Rāmānuja); (2) that 'aṇu' means 'subtle' (Śaṅkara) or 'atomic' (Rāmānuja) and (3) the functions of manas, Śaṅkara presents the more convincing interpretation of (2) and (3). The interpretation of (1) however, is a complex matter and it is not clear which exegesis is closest to the intent of the sūtrakāra.

With regard to the first area of disagreement, in Śaṅkara's favour is the fact that we know the sūtrakāra to be concerned with the refutation of Sāṃkhyan interpretations of śruti. It is unlikely, therefore, that he would pass by an opportunity to demonstrate that the Sāṃkhyan view of prāṇa had no foundation in scripture and, as was mentioned above, Śaṅkara often seems to be more alert to the concerns of the sūtrakāra than does Rāmānuja. On the other hand, Rāmānuja's interpretation provides a smoother continuity between sūtras 9 and 10 (8 and 9 in Rāmānuja) than does Śaṅkara's. From Rāmānuja's perspective the gist of these sūtras would be: 'prāṇa is neither air nor a function of air, on account of its being mentioned separately from air in scriptural texts. Rather it should be understood as being like the eye and other faculties because it is usually mentioned with them in śruti accounts as well as for other reasons.' Śaṅkara's interpretation produces immediate problems if rephrased in this way. There is no problem with 'prāṇa is not air because it is mentioned separately from air in scriptural texts' but 'prāṇa is not a function of the organs because it is mentioned separately from them in scriptural texts' does not fit with the next sūtra, which states exactly the opposite.

Against this 'continuity' argument is the fact that Rāmānuja's argumentation in support of his views is rather muddled. As was noted above, in his commentary on 2.4.9 (2.4.8 in Rāmānuja), Rāmānuja states that 'breath is air having assumed a special form' but immediately goes on, in his comments on the next sūtra, to claim that 'breath is not an element.' It is unlikely that the sūtrakāra would want to maintain that prāṇa is both a modification of air (vāyu) which would give it the nature of an element, and yet maintain that it is not an element (bhūta) but an organ of the self. In fact, the pūrvapakṣa view that 'prāṇa is vāyu' would seem to be the position most well grounded in śruti for, on the one hand, he can maintain, just as strongly as Śaṅkara can maintain his view, that since some śruti texts equate prāṇa and vāyu they must be the same; where the two are distinguished the difference is not absolute but simply one of manifestation. Such an argument fits well with the conclusion of the first two chapters of this study but, since my own conclusions entail that prāṇa is the source of the faculties and not just one of them neither the sūstrakāra nor Śaṅkara nor Rāmānuja can accept this.

With regard to the size of the mukhya prāṇa, Rāmānuja's view that references to the all-pervadingness of prāṇa simply mean that all creatures depend on breath is a complete mis-representation of the Upaniṣadic statements. Śaṅkara's view is more consistent with the texts but, again, is probably less well-grounded than the pūrvapakṣa position he is trying to refute. As far as the functions of manas are concerned, it is interesting to note that Śaṅkara provides no scriptural statements in support of his view, because there are none, whilst Rāmānuja's reference gives manas more than five functions mentioned in the sūtra. What seems to be happening here is that the sūtrakāra is trying to (1) incorporate a Sāṃkhya-derived categorization into the Vedānta cosmology and (2) restrict the function of prāṇa to the five prāṇas and make mind rather than prāṇa the source of eye, ear, etc. There is some foundation in the Upaniṣads for the first move since texts like the Kaṭha, Śvetāśvatara and Maitrī Upaniṣads employ terminology found in the later Sāṃkhya tradition. The second move, however, is totally unwarranted and goes directly against numerous scriptural statements about prāṇa dividing itself into the faculties of speech, breath, mind, eye and ear. Once again we have here a demonstration of the extent ot which the Vedānta teachers were prepared to misrepresent the texts of the Upaniṣads in order to develop a doctrine of their own which possessed a high degree of internal consistency.

The next issue dealt with in these sutras is the autonomy of the prāṇas. The question for Śaṅkara is, if the prāṇas have effects, are these brought about by their own power or by the power of superintending divinities? For Rāmānuja it is whether the prāṇas are controlled by the deities and the individual soul or by the highest self. In Śaṅkara's text the pūrvapakṣin maintains that the effects of the prāṇas are produced by their own power. Śaṅkara, on the other hand, holds the effects to be produced by the power of superintending divinities. But, although these divinities motivate the prāṇas they are not the enjoyers of their effects. As his commentary on 2.14.16 explains, the gods, which 'exist in the state of highest power and glory' cannot enter the body as enjoyers for 'there is in this body only one embodied enjoyer' : the ātman.[83]

Not only is this whole discussion rather tortuous and peculiar, it is not very well grounded in scripture. For some reason, which Śaṅkara does not make clear, the sūtrakāra or Śaṅkara himself wants to maintain that the ātman experiences the effects of the prāṇas' activities but does not motivate them. This is done by divinities which are external to the body. It could be that in these comments Śaṅkara is laying some foundations for his treatment of the problem of evil. From the point of view of scriptual exegesis, however, it leaves much to be desired. In B.A.U. 1.3. and C.U. 1.2 the faculties of breath, speech, mind, sight and hearing are called gods (deva) but there is no intimation that external divinities control either those faculties or the five prāṇas. Other texts, e.g. Kauṣ.U. 4.20, present the gods (probably meaning senses) as being derived from the prāṇas. Consequently, as exegesis the solutions of both the sūtrakāra and Śaṅkara are manifestly inadequate. In fact, from an exegetical point of view the whole issue is really a non-issue.

Rāmānuja's comments are less convoluted because he is not concerned with separating the motivation of the prāṇas from the enjoyment of their effects. For him it is simply a matter of demonstrating that everything is under the control of the highest self. Once again, however, it hardly constitutes an exegesis of passages relevant to the question of the prāṇas' autonomy.

A related question is introduced in 2.4.18 (2.4.15 in Rāmānuja). It is whether the prāṇas are to be put into the same category as the mukhya prāṇa or not. The pūrvapakṣin's view is that they *are* to be placed in the same category but the sūtrakāra's is that they are not. From the point of view of the present investigation, the pūrvapakṣa view is the most faithful to scripture since the Upaniṣads frequently present prāṇa as dividing into vāc, prāṇa, manas, cakṣus and śrotra, or into prāṇa, apāṇa, vyāna, udāna and samāna, or both. Śaṅkara, however, argues that the eleven prāṇas (= manas, buddhīndriyas and karmendriyas) are organs (indriya) whereas the mukhya prāṇa is not, and a number of scriptural passages are quoted to demonstrate that prāṇa has qualities not shared by the indriyas, e.g. whilst the indriyas sleep the prāṇa remains awake. As was pointed out above, however, there is no scriptural justification for categorizing the karmendriyas as prāṇas. Moreover, Śaṅkara's solution either requires that prāṇa, apāna, vyāna, udāna and samāna are referred to by a name other than 'prāṇas' or means that there are either twelve, sixteen or seventeen prāṇas (11 plus mukhya prāṇa *or* 11 plus the five forms of mukhya prāṇa: prāṇa, apāna, vyāna, udāna and samāna *or* 11 plus mukhya prāṇa plus the five forms of mukhya prāṇa). In fact, the dictates of consistency required that the first alternative had to be accepted, though no collective term to refer to these five is ever suggested.

The upshot of this treatment of prāṇa is that it loses all involvement with the faculties or sentience in general, its activities are restricted to those of prāṇa, apāna, vyāna, udāna and samāna and since all passages attributing the characteristics of the ultimate principle to it are deemed to be actually referring to brahman it becomes a concept which is completely peripheral to the Vedānta system. A more crushing defeat for the teachers of the 'older school' can hardly be imagined.

What this examination of Brahma Sūtra passages dealing with the relationship between prāṇa and the prāṇas has revealed, amongst other things, is a number of exegetical procedures which contributed significantly to the character of the later Vedānta tradition. One is that, despite the fact that the sūtrakāra regarded the Sāṃkhya tradition as essentially heretical he was prepared to incorporate some of its categorizations into the Vedānta system. The organs of knowledge (buddhīndriyas) and the organs of action (karmendriyas) are good examples. These are clearly Sāṃkhya concepts and are not prominent in the teachings of the Upaniṣads. The concept of the prāṇas, embracing the five vital energies, the five senses plus mind and speech, is, by contrast, well attested in the Upaniṣads. To take the term 'prāṇas' to refer to the buddhīndriyas plus the karmendriyas, as Śaṅkara does, is to misrepresent the tradition and to give the Vedānta characteristics of a system of thought which (as will be argued in the next chapter) in all likelihood had its origins outside of Vedic circles.

Another factor that features prominently in these passages is the tendency of the pūrvapakṣa view to be more in accord with the actual contents of the Vedic literature than are the views of the sūtrakāra, Śaṅkara or Rāmānuja, at least in cases where the pūrvapakṣa argument does not play an obvious part in the presentation of the commentator's interpretation. On the issue of the relationship between prāṇa and the prāṇas the pūrvapakṣin maintains a position which is generally in accord with that presented in the first two chapters of this study, namely that the term 'prāṇas' covers both vital energies and perceptual faculties and that they are derived from the adhyātma manifestation of the unitary prāṇa which, at the adhidaivata level is frequently referred to as vāyu and from which the other divinities (the cosmic correlates of the prāṇas) arise.

Here, perhaps more clearly than anywhere else, we witness the tendency on the part of influential Vedāntins to engage in what I have described as the subordination and marginalization of the prāṇa concept. The reasoning behind such a consistent and sustained campaign of this nature, which required such violent misrepresentation of Upaniṣadic texts, can only be that vitalistic thinking of the kind set out in chapters one and two of this study was anathema to the inheritors of the 'younger school' orientation within the Vedānta. The thoroughness of the attack presumably stems from the fact that the vitalists of the 'older school' were actually in a stronger position than other challengers, such as the Sāṃkhyans, to contest the younger school's claim to be the authoritative interpreter of the Upaniṣads.

Prāṇa and the process of dying

The first seven sūtras of adhyāya three deal with the issue of whether the soul takes subtle forms of the elements with it when transmigrating from one body to another. The pūrvapakṣin says 'No!' the sūtrakāra, Śaṅkara and Rāmānuja says 'Yes !' Their view is supported by a rather tenuous interpretation of C.U. 5.3-10. They argue that water transmigrates with the soul and that this water must necessarily contain the essences of the other elements. In addition, Śaṅkara points out that when passages such as B.A.U. 4.4.2 state that on the departure of the self prāṇa and then the prāṇas depart after it,

> '... this going of the prāṇas is not possible without a base ... the prāṇas cannot, without such a base, either move or abide anywhere; as we observe in living beings.'[84]

Both of these arguments are unconvincing. In the first place, the absence of a clear scriptural statement to the effect that the soul takes these 'fine parts of the elements which form the seed of the body' (deha-vījāni bhūta-sūkṣmāni)[85] with it at death suggests that such was not the view of the Upaniṣadic teachers. In the absence of any corroborating statements the convoluted exegesis of C.U. 5.3-10 can hardly be regarded as authoritative. The argument that nothing can exist without a material base is likewise difficult to reconcile with scripture. In fact, this whole theory is probably derived from Sāṃkhya (see S.K. 40-43). The prominent cosmology of the Upaniṣads has the material world evolving out of the ātman, whether this be regarded as being essentially vitality or consciousness. In other words, the creative source and the principles which emerge from it prior to the manifestation of the material world contain within themselves the potential to manifest material elements. There is thus no need for the self and the prāṇas to carry any seeds of materiality with them as these are intrinsic to their nature.

The topic of transmigration is taken up again at B.S. 4.2.1-11. These sūtras are dominated by the account in C.U. 6, which, as was argued in chapter two, is unique in the Upaniṣads. Consequently, these sūtras give rise to some convoluted interpretations. Ṣaṅkara and Rāmānuja do not differ markedly on this issue, though where Śaṅkara maintains that it is the functions of the various faculties which are merged or joined (sampadyate) with mind, then with prāṇa, then with heat (tejas) at death Rāmānuja argues that it is the actual faculties which join with mind etc.. He writes,

> 'The text says distinctly that speech itself, not merely the function of speech, becomes one with the mind. And when the function of speech comes to an end, there is no other means of knowledge to assure us that the organ itself continues to have an independent existence. The objection that speech cannot become one with mind because the latter is not the causal substance of speech, we meet by pointing out that the purport of the text is not that speech is merged in mind, but only that it is conjoined with it.'[86]

Such a view appears reasonable so long as the discussion is restricted to the C.U. 6 account. However, things become problematic if it is extended to include other versions of the death process. Both Śaṅkara and Rāmānuja are committed to such extension, as their commentaries on B.S. 4.2.2 '("And for the same reason all (sense organs) (follow) after (mind)")'[87] make clear. Since eyes, ears, etc. obviously remain with the body at death Rāmānuja's argument seems unbelievably clumsy. It is also at variance with the text of the C.U. for whereas he maintains that 'breath is a modification of ether and other elements' C.U. 6.5.2 clearly states that it is composed (maya) of the subtle part of water. Once again, Śaṅkara's interpretation of this material is the more plausible of the two.

One of the problems with the C.U. account is that it is far from easy to interpret. We are told that in the beginning the one being divided itself into three forms each emerging from the preceding one in the following order: heat (tejas), water (ap) and earth or food (anna). Each of these then divided itself threefold, the subtle parts becoming speech (vāc), breath (prāṇa) and mind (manas) respectively. The medium and coarse parts of heat are marrow and bone; those of water are blood and urine whilst those of earth are flesh and faeces. The complete picture can be represented by the following table :

TABLE 5

	TEJAS	*AP*	*ANNA*
subtle	vāc	prāṇa	manas
medium	marrow	blood	flesh
coarse	bone	urine	faeces

At death the medium and coarse forms of the three elements, which together constitute the body, are left behind. One would then expect each of the faculties (vāc, prāṇa and manas) to merge with the element from which it evolved and then each element to be absorbed by the one which preceded it. The order of reabsorbtion presented in C.U. 6.8.6, however, bears little resemblance to this pattern. There, vāc is said to merge into manas, manas into prāṇa, prāṇa into tejas and tejas into the highest divinity (parasyām devatāyām). Although the purvapakṣin, Śaṅkara and Rāmānuja all try to make the creation and reabsorbtion accounts square with each other none succeeds in any convincing manner, not surprisingly since the text is actually incompatible with itself.

In an attempt to harmonise this C.U. 6 account with other Upaniṣadic versions of the death process the sūtrakāra introduces 'the ruler', i.e. the individual soul, between prāṇa and tejas in the reabsorbtion process. This is because other texts, e.g. B.A.U. 4.3.38, state that the prāṇas go to the self at the time of death or, as in B.A.U. 4.4.2, that after the self quits the body at death prāṇa, followed by the other prāṇas, departs also. Both Śaṅkara and Rāmānuja subscribe to this move and thus insert 'ātman' into an Upaniṣadic passage where it clearly has no place. They are thus in breach of their own principle that separate vidyās (items or accounts of doctrine) have to be acknowledged where the texts show a difference of subject matter. Of course both commentators would argue that this C.U. passage and the B.A.U. passages do not exhibit a difference of subject matter but 'are the same in all essential points.'

This interpretative device concerning separate vidyās is established in the treatment (B.S. 3.3.6-10) of passages discussed at some length in chapter two of the present study : B.A.U. 1.3 and C.U. 1.2, which are similar versions of the contest of the faculties. It was noted in chapter two that the C.U. version, as Deussen points out, '... deals not with the singing of the Udgītha by Prāṇa, but with the glorification of Prāṇa as one of the symbols of the Udgītha; on account of this, the original point of the narration [:the presentation of prāṇa as the ultimate principle] gets lost.'[88] There is, thus, an obvious problem in reconciling the two passages. Since the sūtrakāra, Śaṅkara and Rāmānuja are all committed to producing a consistent overall account of Upaniṣadic teaching they maintain, despite the close similarity of the texts, that these passages are to be regarded as not one but two vidyās.

The pūrvapakṣin, on the other hand, argues that since both texts deal with the udgītha, both are called 'udgītha vidyā' and they are fundamentally the same in structure, they should be regarded as one vidyā, a claim which would probably have been true for the original account before it was reworked by the redactors of the C.U. The actual situation, as Śaṅkara and Rāmānuja point out, is, however, that

> '... the object of meditation for the Chāndogyas is the praṇava viewed under the form of prāṇa; while for the Vājasaneyins it is the Udgatṛ (who sings the Udgīstha), imaginatively identified with prāṇa'[89]

Hence for exegetes of the Vedānta the way to deal with incongruences between different redactions of the same material which present problems for one's own position is to treat each as a separate vidyā. However, where one wishes to supplement one account with another, as the sūtrakāra does in B.S. 4.2.4, one recognizes that the vidyās are 'the same in all essential points' and therefore 'the qualities mentioned in one text are to be inserted in the other corresponding texts also.'[90]

The fact that the principal commentaries on the B.S. devote considerable space to an unsatisfactory treatment of a passage, where, as was argued in chapter two, interpolations have been made for the purpose of lowering the status of prāṇa, can only be taken as support for that contention. It also demonstrates that such reworkings continued to be a problem for Vedāntins of the 'younger school' at least until the time of Śaṅkara. The fact that these commentators are meticulous in establishing the 'younger school's' interpretation of this passage also supports the contention that the concept of prāṇa was essentially problematic for the teachers of the later Vedānta. Interestingly, the other case of interpolation identified in chapter two of this study : C.U. 7, is also the subject of considerable discussion in the commentaries of both Śaṅkara and Rāmānuja.

Prāṇa in C.U. 7

One topic division in B.S. 1.3, sūtras 8-9 (9-10 in Rāmānuja), is devoted to a consideration of the place of prāṇa in the teaching of C.U. 7. It was noted in chapter two that the extraction of a coherent account from C.U. 7 presented considerable difficulties and it was suggested that this was because one or more additions had been made to the root text : C.U. 7.1-15. The early Vedāntins were obviously alert to the problematic nature of this material and hence the sūtrakāra offers his own view about how the issues are to be resolved. He writes,

> 'The bhūman (is the highest Self), as the instruction about it is additional to that about serenity (8). And on account of the suitability of the attributes (9).'[91]

Exactly why the problems of the integrity of C.U. 7 should be put in this form is not readily apparent, though a sceptical mind might surmise along the following lines : it is clear that the verses referring to the bhūman ('the infinite' or 'that which is much'– Pāṇini 6.4.158), fall in the supplementary part of the chapter and therefore relate to the principle which is put at the apex of that supplement namely 'ātman'. So the 'issue' of whether bhūman is to be understood as referring to prāṇa or ātman is really a 'non-issue'. However, resolving it in terms of a conclusion which is obviously legitimate has the effect of inculcating a confidence in the sūtrakāra's exegetical ability and of taking attention away from the real issue, which is why a text presenting prāṇa as the supreme principle and one who knows this as an ativādin (one who makes the highest statement) immediately proceeds to negate its own teaching.

Both Śaṅkara and Rāmānuja devote a considerable amount of space to the elucidation of these sūtras. Once again, their interpretations are very similar, though Rāmānuja does tend to read more of his own system into the sūtras than does Śaṅkara. Like all Vedāntins, the pūrvapakṣin has to accept the overall coherence of the text, and since the teaching of C.U. 7 has already been reworked to produce a doctrine acceptable to the 'younger school', his arguments are neither radical nor convincing. But this does not eliminate the obvious problems of coherence that the text itself presents, and the fact that both Śaṅkara and Rāmānuja devote so much space to these sūtras is indicative of the very real problems of exegesis that they faced. This, in turn, I would suggest, strengthens the case for C.U. 7.16-26 being regarded as an interpolation.

The pūrvapakṣa view, according to Śaṅkara, is that the bhūman mentioned in C.U. 7.23-24 is prāṇa, which for Śaṅkara is an 'unreal product' and for Rāmānuja, means 'the individual soul which is associated with breath, not a mere modification of air'.[92] The pūrvapakṣin's reason for holding this view is that in C.U. 7.15 prāṇa is said to be greater than all the previously mentioned principles and no principle is said to be greater than it. Prāṇa is said to be everything, and one who knows this becomes an ativādin (one who makes a supreme or definitive statement). This view is easy to refute because of the structure of the text and Śaṅkara and Rāmānuja accomplish the refutation by almost identical moves. That 'bhūman' refers to the highest self is clear, says Rāmānuja, because,

> 'The text, after having declared that he who knows the prāṇa is an ativādin, goes on, "But really that one is an ativādin who makes a supreme declaration by means of the True." The "but" here clearly separates him who is an ativādin by means of the True from the previous ativādin, and the clause thus does not cause us to recognise him who is ativādin by means of Prāṇa; hence "the True" which is the cause of the latter ativādin being what he is must be something different from the Prāṇa which is the cause of the former ativādin's quality ... The conjunction "but" shows that the section gives instruction about a new ativādin and does not merely declare that the ativādin previously mentioned has to speak the truth.'[93]

And just in case this argument fails to convince the pūrvapakṣin Śaṅkara and Rāmānuja offer a detailed explanation for the disjointed effect created by the transition from 7.15 to 7.16. In the words of Rāmānuja,

> '... the reason why the pupil does not ask the question whether there is anything greater than Prāṇa [is that] with regard to the non-sentient objects extending from name to hope–each of which surpasses the preceding one in so far as it is more beneficial to man–the teacher does not declare that he who knows them is an ativādin; when, however, he comes to the individual soul, there called Prāṇa, the knowledge of whose true nature he considers highly beneficial, he expressly says that "he who sees this, notes this, understands this is an

> ativādin" (7.15.4). The pupil therefore imagines that the instruction about the self is therefore completed, and hence asks no further question. The teacher, on the other hand, holding that even that knowledge is not the highest, *spontaneously* continues his teaching, and tells the pupil that truely he only is an ativādin who proclaims the supremely and absolutely beneficial being which is called 'the True', i.e. the highest Brahman.'[94]

In addition to these arguments both Śaṅkara and Rāmānuja point out that since 7.26.1 states that prāṇa springs from the self (ātman) it is clear that there is a subject other than the individual self [= prāṇa] to know. This other subject is what 7.16.1 refers to as 'the True' and what 7.23-25 refer to as the bhūman; it is, in fact, brahman. Ṣaṅkara also offers a version of the 'characteristics' argument in support of this conclusion. In C.U. 7.3 Nārada requests Sanatkamāra to help him to cross over to the other side of sorrow through knowledge of the self (ātman) and the fact that Sanatkumāra seems to terminate his instruction in 7.15 makes it appear as though prāṇa is the ātman to be known in order to cross over sorrow. Śaṅkara, however, points out that the cessation of sorrow can only take place through knowledge of the highest self, a claim which carries the implicit statement 'we know from elsewhere that prāṇa is not the highest self and hence prāṇa cannot be that self by which one crosses over sorrow.'

The shortcomings of these exegeses are readily apparent to even a casual reader of the text. In the first place, the text of C.U. 7 provides no support for taking 'prāṇa' to mean either an 'unreal product' (Śaṅkara) or 'the individual self' (Rāmānuja). We may note that Rāmānuja is rather crafty here, for the view that prāṇa means individual self is put into the mouth of the pūrvapakṣin. This, of course, is a view congenial to Rāmānuja, who accepts it and thereby seems to make a conciliatory gesture to the pūrvapakṣin. We thus have here a clear example of how the pūrvapakṣa view is employed to facilitate the argument of the sūtrakāra and the commentators as often as it is included to present a genuinely alternative interpretation.

In the second place, the claim made by both commentators, that Nārada became silent after Sanatkumāra's statement that the knower of prāṇa was an ativādin because he was unaware of the fact that such a view was only a provisional step to knowledge of the highest self and hence Sanatkumāra had to 'spontaneously' recommence the teaching, is highly suspect. If Sanatkumāra had intended to say that only the knower of ātman/brahman is an ativādin, as Śaṅkara maintains, why did he 'spontaneously' tell Nārada that the knower of prāṇa is an ativādin? Śaṅkara's exegesis can only be convincing to those who are committed to the unity of the C.U. 7 text and the coherence of the doctrine presented therein. Rāmānuja's solution, that there are two ativādins, one lower than the other, is only slightly better, for if an ativādin is really 'one who makes a final supreme declaration'[95] then people who make different declarations about what is the greatest cannot both be ativādins.

The third dubious aspect of this exegesis concerns Rāmānuja's commentary only. In order to establish that in the context of this C.U. chapter the term prāṇa refers to the individual self he states that all the principles listed in descending order of greatness before prāṇa are non-intelligent and hence the reason why Sanatkumāra calls the knower of prāṇa an ativādin is because this being, (according to Rāmānuja, a synonym for the individual soul) is the first intelligent principle on the list. Such an argument is completely without foundation in the text. The principles preceding 'prāṇa' in the C.U. 7 list are, in descending order, hope (āśā), memory (smara), space (ākāśa), heat (tejas), water (apas), food (anna), strength (bala), consciousness (vijñāna), meditation (dhyāna), thought (citta), conception (saṃkalpa), mind (manas), speech (vāc) and name (nāma). At least some of these, e.g. manas, citta, vijñāna, could legitimately be argued to be intelligent or sentient or indicative of the same.

Thus, both commentators take considerable liberties with the text under discussion in order to develop their own view. Rāmānuja is more guilty of this than Śaṅkara. Where they do try to resolve genuine difficulties in the text, i.e. on the disjunction between 7.15 and 7.16 their arguments are unconvincing and merely serve to draw attention to the possibility of interpolation at this point.

A final example of such liberties being taken with Upaniṣadic texts in order to maintain the commentators' own views, here that, once again, prāṇa really means brahman and that only brahman is the abode of a person in deep sleep, can be found in the commentaries on B.S. 3.2.7. It reads,

> 'The absence of that (i.e. of dreams, i.e. dreamless sleep) takes place in the nāḍīs and in the self; according to scriptural statement.'[96]

Śaṅkara provides a number references which indicate that a person abides in the nāḍī/hitā during sleep, e.g. C.U. 8.6.3; B.A.U. 21.19. He also quotes Kauṣ.U. 4.19 and 20, where it states that when a person has entered the hitā during sleep he sees no dream. 'Then he becomes one with prāṇa alone'.

Here Śaṅkara again takes prāṇa to mean 'brahman' for it is presented as the supreme principle. However, he suggests that a person enters the prāṇa/brahman *by means* of the nāḍīs not *in* the nāḍīs. He writes,

> '... scripture mentions only three places of deep sleep, viz. the nāḍīs, the pericardium [puritat], and Brahman. Among these three again Brahman alone is the lasting place of deep sleep; the nāḍīs and the pericardium are mere roads leading to it.'[97]

Such a view goes directly against the evident meaning of the text which explicitly states

> 'In these (tasu - locative plural) (hitā), one remains, while asleep he sees no dream whatsoever.'[98]

More cautiously, Rāmānuja suggests that

> 'When different alternatives may be combined, on the ground of there being different effects in each case, it is improper to assume an option which implies sublation of some of the alternatives.'[99]

Nevertheless, despite this concession to what is unambiguous in the text, Rāmānuja, like Śaṅkara, has to take 'prāṇa' in this context to mean 'brahman'. Furthermore, his concession actually conflicts with his claim, when commenting on B.S. 1.4.17, that the veins (hitā/nāḍī) are *not* the abode of a person in deep sleep, only brahman constitutes such an abode.

Conclusion

When assessing the development of the prāṇa concept in the epic and post-epic periods of Vedānta development it is clear that the trends of doctrinal elaboration and systematization taking place at that time had their roots in much earlier processes of Upaniṣadic redaction which had, as one of their goals, the lowering of the status of prāṇa. The two passages where clear interpolations to this end have been identified are both from the Chāndogya Upaniṣad. Furthermore, Uddālaka's teachings in C.U. 6 not only offer a cosmology unique in the Upaniṣads they also present a cosmology which unambiguously makes prāṇa a purely derivative principle. It seems highly likely, therefore, that the Vedāntins of the Sāmaveda, identified by Nakamura as instigating the production of what is now known as the Brahmasūtra, were heirs to, or even the same as, those early upaniṣadic redactors. As far as the concept of prāṇa was concerned, the fact that this school or schools dominated the evolution of the Vedānta tradition meant that its future became one of virtual extinction. However, the concept of prāṇa did manage to find a place in other systems of religious thought and practice though these were often regarded with some suspicion by the so-called more orthodox Vedāntins. It is to a consideration of two such systems that this study now turns.

REFERENCES

1. Each of the four Vedas was preserved by a number of schools which composed or compiled supplementary texts for their own guidance. The Brāhmaṇas are the works deemed to offer, in the main, guidance or ritual matters whilst the Āraṇyakas supply guidance on doctrinal and philosophical issues. Not all śākhās have survived or left their supplementary texts for posterity. Those which have bequeathed Upaniṣads to us are the Aitareyins and the Kauṣītakins of the Ṛgveda, the Tāṇḍins and Jaiminiyas (or Talavakāras) of the Sāmaveda, the Taittirīyakas, Kaṭhas and Maitrāyaṇīyas of the Kṛṣṇa Yajurveda and the Vājasaneyins of the Śukla Yajurveda. For further details see Deussen (1906) p.p. 1-15 and (1912) p.p. 1-19. The exception to this is the Atharvaveda, whose Upaniṣads do not, on the whole (the Māṇḍūkya and Jabala constituting what Deussen, (1980) (2) p. 555, calls 'suspect exceptions'), have any clear connections with the śākhās of that Veda.

2. Nakamura (1983) dates the Maitrī around 200 B.C.E. and the Māṇḍūkya somewhere between 1 and 200 C.E. He also points out that when the writings of interpreters of the Upaniṣads are examined, the later the interpreter the more the number of Upaniṣads which are accepted as canonical. This tendency to indicate or circumscribe what it to be regarded as canonical began, he suggests, with the compliers of the middle period Upaniṣads : Kaṭhaka, Muṇḍaka, Praśna and Śvetāśvatara. He writes ;... the Upaniṣads of the middle period clearly state that they find a special significance in the "vedānta:, and that they themselves are based upon it. Because the poets who composed the Old Upaniṣads of the middle period had no longer any concern with rituals, and must have differed also in their social lives from the authors of the early period Old Upaniṣads, I think that we can recognize that these were new Vedāntins devoted to the Sacred Upaniṣads ... not only did the Vedānta students follow the early period Upaniṣads as sacred canon, they were also continually producing Upaniṣads and they ascribed canonical authority to these as well. The history of the composition of the Upaniṣads is exactly the same as the history of the Vedānta school.' (p.p. 46-47). Whilst there is obviously much truth in this claim it is probably more accurate with regard to the earlier period than the later in so far as in the post-Bādarāyaṇa period the composers of the Upaniṣads appear to be different from the principal interpreters of the Vedānta tradition. In other words, there is no evidence I am aware of that Śaṅkara, Bhāskara, Rāmānuja or any of the other prominent Vedānta teachers of the middle ages composed Upaniṣads.

3. Thibaut (1890) p. xviii.
4. op. cit. p. xi.
5. Also called the Vedāntasūtra(s), the Śarīraksūtra(s), Caturlakṣanī, Śarīraka-śāstra, Śarīraka and Vedānta-mīmāṃsā-śāstra. For details see Nakamura (1983) pp.425-428.
6. Dasgupta (1922) pp. 24-25.
7. Pandey (1983) pp. 114-177.
8. Radhakrishnan (1931) (2) pp. 432-433.
9. Deussen (1912) pp. 24-25.
10. Winternitz, quoted in Nakamura (1983) p. 408.
11. Dasgupta (1922) pp. 418-422 and 429; Pandey (1983) p.p. 114-177.
12. Nakamura (1983) p. 429 f.f.
13. Mayeda (1979) p. 12.
14. Nakamura (1983) pp. 425-437.
15. Thibaut (1890) pp. xiii-xiv.
16. op. cit. p. xiv.
17. Śaṅkara's dates are a matter of some controversy but the consensus of scholarly opinion at the present time seems to favour 700-750 C.E. For details see Mayeda (1979) p. 3f.
18. Rāmānuja's dates are traditionally 1017 to 1137 C.E. John Carmen (1974) p. 27 suggests 1077 to 1157 but goes on to qualify this by saying that 'the most probable dates of the important events in Rāmānuja's life indicate that he lived to be at least 80, and he may well have lived to be much older than that' (op. cit. p. 280).
19. For details see Dasgupta (1975) (3) pp.1-11, Radhakrishnan (1960) p.p. 39-45 and Srinivasachari (1934). Both Dasgupta (p.3.n.) and Radhakrishnan (p.39.n.) find Bhāskara in general agreement with the Pañcarātrins, from which Rāmānuja's Śrī Vaiṣṇava movement developed.
20. Srinivasachari (1934) pp.287-292.
21. Thibaut (1890) p.lxxxvi.
22. Srinivasachari (1934) pp. 287-292.
23. Mayeda (1979) pp. 6.
24. loc. cit.
25. 17.27, in Mayeda's translation, reads as follows:

    'Just as one and the same seed becomes different in accordance with [differences of] vital air [prāṇa], dreaming state etc., so Ātman like the moon on the water becomes different in bodies in the dreaming and waking states' (p. 162). Mayeda suggests that in this context 'prāṇa' probably means the state of deep sleep for, in

17.57, the last reference to prāṇa in the Upadeśasāhasrī, it seems to mean, according to Rāmatīrtha, the three states of waking, dreaming and deep sleep. 17.57 reads as follows: 'He who has thus given up the triad, viz. the vital air (= the state of deep sleep) goes across the goat ocean of ignorance for he is by nature abiding in his own Ātman, attributeless, pure, awakened and released' (p. 165). However, his insertion of '(= the state of deep sleep)' here is surely wrong for in the note to this verse he quotes Rāmatīrtha, who interprets 'prāṇady ... trikaṃ' as all three states. This insertion would be more accurately placed after 'vital air' in 17.27 since there it *does* appear to mean 'deep sleep'.

26. 13.2 reads as follows : 'As I am devoid of the life principle [prāṇa], I do not act. Being without intellect [buddhi] I am not a knower. Therefore I have neither knowledge nor nescience, having the light of Pure Consciousness only' (p. 132). When commenting on this verse Mayeda suggests that here 'prāṇa is probably employed to mean the buddhīndriyas, the karmendriyas, the antaḥkaraṇa and the mukhya prāṇa. This seems unlikely to me as 'I' is said to be devoid of both prāṇa and buddhi. For Śaṅkara, buddhi is the same as antaḥkaraṇa and thus antaḥkaraṇa cannot be a constituent of prāṇa if this term does not include buddhi within it. Furthermore, since the buddhīndriyas and karmendriyas in Śaṅkara's system are closely connected with buddhi the reference is most likely to the mukhya prāṇa alone. 14.15. reads as follows: 'As the vital air [prāṇa] is the universe including the sun, there is neither day nor night for a knower of the vital air. How can there be [day or night] for a knower of Brahman, since He is non-dual?' (p.137). In his note on this verse Mayeda indicates that the references are to B.A.U. 1.5.4; C.U.5.1.5 (= 7.15.4 [?]); 3.16.5 and 6; P.U.1.5; 3.8. Certainly C.U. 7.15.4 presents prāṇa as 'all this' and P.U. 3.8 informs us that the sun is the external form of prāṇa (ādityo ha vai bāhyaḥ prāṇa), but the others either make no clear statement on the issue (e.g. C.U.5.1.5; 3.16.5 and 6) or actually present a view which is in conflict with the claim that prāṇa is 'the universe including the sun.' B.A.U. 1.5.4, for example, presents prāṇa as only one of three parts of the ātman (the other two being manas and vāc). It is identified with heaven whilst manas is identified with the atmosphere and vāc with the earth. In the same vein P.U. 1.5 informs us that whilst the sun is prāṇa, matter (rayi) is both the moon and 'all this, whetever is formed and formless.'

27. Deussen (1912) p.37.

28. But see the discussion in Carmen (1974) pp. 49-64.

29. Raghavachar (1978) p. 38.

30. op. cit. pp. 78 and 182.

31. op. cit. p. 111.

32. op. cit. p. 44. The text runs as follows:

pūḥ prāṇinassarva-guhāśayasya iti/sarve prāṇinaḥ guhāsayasya paramātmanah pūḥ puraṃ śarīram ityartha/prāṇina iti/ jīvātmakabhūtasaṅghātāḥ/ 'Pūḥ (city or body) is all the prāṇins (living ones) of the secret place (of the heart); the highest self is in all prāṇins of the secret place. Now pūḥ is city [which means] body. A prāṇin is a living self (jīvātman) combined with the elements (bḥūta-saṅghātāḥ).'

33. These are 1.33; 4.29-30;8.10 and 12; 18.33.

34. Hume (1931) pp. 463-437.

35. Zaehner (1969) pp. 263-264.

36. Sastry (1981) pp. 227 and 229.

37. Van Buitenen (1968) p. 229.

38. Radhakrishnan (1960) p. 243.

39. loc. cit.

40. Thibaut (1890) p. 85.

41. Thibaut (1904) p. 246.

42. loc. cit.

43. op. cit. pp. 250-253. The sanskṛt is: prāṇas tathānugamāt/na vakyur ātmopadeśād iticed adhyātma-sambandhabhūmā hy asmin/śāstra-dṛṣṭyā tūpadeśo vāmadeva-vat/jīva-mukhya-prāṇa liṅgān neti nopāsat traividyād aśritatvād iha tad-yogāt// (Taken, as are all sanskṛt quotations from the Brahmasūtra, from Radhakrishnan (1960).

44. Thibaut (1890) p. 97.

45. Here we see in the clearest of terms the attempt on the part of the later Vedānta spokesmen to separate prāṇa from any kind of mental or conscious activity. Rāmānuja makes the same kind of statement about prāṇa in his comments on 1.1.13, '... the text does not ascribe agency to the other Selfs (the prāṇamaya and so on) which are mentioned [in T.U.2] before the vijñānmaya; for they are non-intelligent instruments of intelligence ...' (Thibaut (1904) p. 213).

46. See B.A.U.1.4.10.

47. Thibaut (1890) pp. 103-106.

48. Thibaut (1904) p. 254.

49. Here Śaṅkara and Rāmānuja disagree about the topic division. Śaṅkara takes 1.3.39 as constituting a complete topic division and 1.3.40 as constituting another. Rāmānuja, on the other hand, puts the two together. Consequently they disagree about the Upaniṣadic passages referred to by B.S. 1.3.40 (41 in Rāmānuja). For Śaṅkara the reference is to C.U.8.12.3, for Rāmāṇuja it is to Kaṭh.U. 2.5.15.

50. Thibaut (1890) p. 229.

51. loc. cit. In his note on this passage Thibaut writes, 'As the words stand in the original they might be translated as follows (and are so translated by the purvapakṣin), 'Whatever there is, the whole world trembles in the prāṇa, there goes forth (from it) a great terror, viz. the raised thunderbolt.'

52. op. cit. p. 230.

53. op. cit. p. 230.

54. loc. cit.

55. Thibaut (1904) p. 348.

56. Thibaut (1890) pp. 268-269.

57. op. cit. p. 279.

58. Thibaut (1904) p. 382.

59. Thibaut (1890) p. 273.

60. Thibaut (1904) pp. 383-384.

61. op. cit. p. 384.

62. My translation.

63. Carmen (1974) p. 57.

64. Thibaut (1869) p. 76.

65. Sato bandham-asati nir-avindan-hṛdi pratiṣya kavayo manīṣā. Miller (1974) pp. 218-219.

66. Thibaut (1896) p.77.

67. Thibaut (1904) p. 569.

68. op. cit. p. 570.

69. Thibaut (1896) pp. 79-80. The sanskṛt is: saptagater viśeṣitatvāc ca/ hastādayas tu sthite' to naivam.

70. op. cit. p. 80.

71. loc. cit.

72. op. cit. p. 81.

73. loc. cit.

74. op. cit. p. 84.

75. loc. cit.

76. Thibaut (1904) pp. 572-575. The sanskṛt is: śreṣṭhaś ca/na vāyukriye pṛthag upadeśāt/cakṣurādivat tu tat-saha-śiṣṭyādibhyaḥ/ akaraṇatvāc ca na doṣas tathā hi darśayati/pañcavṛttir manovad vyapadiśyate/aṇuś ca.

77. Both Thibaut and Radhakrishnan state that this refers to Sāṃkhya Sūtra 2.31, but, as Deussen points out, this verse is itself based on

Sāṃkhya Kārikā 29: 'With respect to the specific characteristics of the three (i.e. of the buddhi, ahaṃkāra and senses) each functions differently; the five vital breaths (or winds) (make up) their common function'. Larson (1979) p. 265.

78. Thibaut (1896) p. 87.
79. This list of functions is composite, derived from Kaṭh.U. 5.3 and 5 (prāṇa and apāna) and P.U. 3.5-7 (vyāna udāna and samāna).
80. Thibaut (1896) p. 91.
81. Thibaut (1904) p. 573.
82. op. cit. p. 575.
83. Thibaut (1896) p. 93.
84. op. cit. p. 105.
85. Deussen (1912) p. 370.
86. Thibaut (1904) p. 728.
87. Thibuat (1896) p. 365.
88. Deussen (1980) p. 404.
89. Thibaut (1904) p. 634.
90. Thibaut (1896) p. 200.
91. Thibaut (1904) pp. 299 and 307.
92. op. cit. p.300.
93. op. cit. p. 303.
94. op. cit. p. 304-305.
95. op. cit. p. 301.
96. Thibaut (1896) p. 141.
97. op. cit. pp. 144-145.
98. Radhakrishnan (1953) p. 790.
99. Thibaut (1904) pp. 604-605.

PART TWO :
The Concept of Prāṇa in the Sāṃkhya tradition

Systems of thought and practice called 'Sāṃkhya' display considerable antiquity in the religious literature of India. The teaching to which this term refers is, however, not always clearly delineated. In fact, the earliest references to the system indicate that it existed in a number of forms. There is thus considerable controversy in scholarly circles about the early history of Sāṃkhya. Unlike the Vedānta, it does not trace its origin back to the Veda but to the sage Kapila.[1] Likewise, some of its key terms have no Vedic background.[2]

The Sāṃkhya Kārikā (S.K.) of Īśvarakṛṣṇa has been the normative statement of the school since the time of its composition (fifth century C.E.), though it is possible that earlier systematic formulations of Sāṃkhya did exist but are now lost. One reason for thinking along these lines is that whilst the other five orthodox (astika) darśanas have sūtra collections as their root texts the Sāṃkhya possesses kārikās or aphoristic verses, which are less concise than sūtras. This text has attracted many commentaries and elaborations and is the work most frequently quoted by Mādhava in his treatment of Sāṃkhya in the Sarva-Darśana-Saṃgraha (14th century C.E.).

The principal features of the system represented by Īśvarakṛṣṇa are that the universe exists because of the conjunction (saṃyoga) of two self-existent realities : puruṣa (spirit/awareness) and prakṛti (matter/energy). There are many puruṣas, all identical. In kārikā

19 we are informed that puruṣa is a witness (sākṣitvam), is isolated or alone (kaivalyam), is indifferent (mādhyasthyam), is a spectator (draṣṭṛtvam) and is not an agent or doer (akartṛbhāvam).

Prakṛti, on the other hand, is unitary. It exists in two modes, an unmanifest (avyakta) and a manifest (vyakta). The manifest is not a coming into being of new existence, however, but merely an actualizing at the manifest level that which already existed at the unmanifest one. This is the teaching of satkāryavāda, that the effect or manifestation (vyakta) already exists in the cause (avyakta).

Prakṛti's unfolding is accomplished initially through the manifestation of psychological faculties: intellect (buddhi) and egoity or self-formulation (ahaṃkāra).[3] The latter, in its different modes as conditioned by the qualities (guṇa) of sattva, rajas and tamas, then proceeds to evolve the remaining principles (tattvas) which make up the world of our experience. The order of evolution can be seen from the following table :

TABLE 6

- puruṣa
- prakṛti (2 modes)
  - avyakta (the state of the guṇas in equipoise).
  - vyakta
    - intellect (buddhi or mahat)
      - ahaṃkāra
        - sāttvic
          - buddhīndriyas: eye, ear, nose, tongue, skin
          - mind (manas)
          - karmendriyas: hands, feet, speech, anus, genitals
        - tāmasic
          - tanmātras → mahābhūtas:
            - sound → ether
            - touch → air
            - form → fire
            - flavour → water
            - smell → earth

The relationship between the guṇas and tattvas is not very clear in the S.K. and Van Buitenen has suggested that they were originally distinct but combined in the classical Sāṃkhya of the Kārikā.[4]

When prakṛti is manifest, the experience of the individualised psychic organs as illumined by puruṣa, who has no ontological involvement with the prakṛti is permeated by suffering, primarily because the vyakta universe is in a constant state of flux. This suffering leads, on the one hand, to a search for pleasure, which does nothing to bring about any kind of ultimate change in the way things are, or for release, which is brought about by discrimination (viveka). When the tattvas are known for what they are, namely aspects of prakṛti, the knower (puruṣa) becomes aware of his own identity as something different from prakṛti. This realisation obviates the need for further prakṛtic activity with regard to the particular puruṣa in question. Thus suffering is overcome and the aims of the Sāṃkhya system are realised. However, for those puruṣas not obtaining liberation a periodic rest is provided by prakṛti who, at the end of each aeon, reverses the creative process and returns to the unmanifest state, known in this context as pralaya. After a period (time does not exist in pralaya) the karma of the puruṣas, which was responsible for bringing about the pralaya, becomes expended and a re-manifestation of prakṛti begins.

In essence then, the Sāṃkhya system describes the nature of existence by postulating that many identical puruṣas, whose only defining characteristic appears to be that they are conscious, become involved in some way with prakṛti, who is not conscious but subject to modification under stimulus and who responds to the presence of puruṣa by generating the universe in order that puruṣa may realise that the nature of his involvement with prakṛti has no effect upon him whatsoever. In Sāṃkhya then, there is no need for the postulation of any kind of creator or superintending divinity. It is therefore classed as an atheistic (anaiśvarya) system.

Proto-and Epic Sāṃkhya

When authors write about the existence of proto-Sāṃkhya traditions they are referring to pre-Kārikā accounts of existence which, in structure or terminology, overlap in some way with that found in the Sāṃkhya Kārikā. The most recent thorough survey of such speculations is that of Larson (1979), whose approach makes it clear that he would like to locate the origins of the Sāṃkhya system in the pre-Upaniṣadic Vedic tradition. However, after surveying the evidence the most he can say is, '... the Sāṃkhya in any of its forms is not present in those early speculations. Yet it is *possible* to point to certain trends of thought which *might* have later *been assimilated* into Sāṃkhya. To point to such trends is not to make the claim that these trends can be precisely traced into later Sāṃkhya. The claim is only that certain trends *provide a context* from which later Sāṃkhya *may* have arisen.'[5]

Not until we reach the Kaṭha and, later, the Maitrī and Śvetāśvatara Upaniṣads does the existence of embryonic Sāṃkhya or of Sāṃkhyan influence become self-evident. There are clear parallels between the Kārikās and the earliest of these Upaniṣads, the Kaṭha, in terms of the description of the self (ātman) (Kaṭh.U. 2.18-25) and in terms of the relation between self and body and the constituents of the person (Kaṭh.U. 3.3-12 and 6.6-9) and I would suggest that here we have the earliest clear indication of the existence of Sāṃkhya-like analyses in Indian literature.

Some writers, however, identify such analyses in earlier Upaniṣads, most notably the Chāndogya. C.U. 6 (discussed in some detail in chapter two and chapter three part one of this study) contains an account of how the one being (sat) evolved from itself in the beginning, three forms (rūpa): fire or light (tejas), water (apa) and earth (anna). From these everything else was produced. Larson thinks it 'quite likely' that the Sāṃkhya of the Kārikās could have developed out of such speculations[6] and Beidler[7] thinks it clearly lays the foundation for the development of the Sāṃkhyan guṇa theory. When the text of C.U. 6 is examined, however, the similarities between it and the Kārikā account of evolution are few and far between. The last evolutes in the Kārikā scheme are the mahābhūtas: ether (ākāśa), air (vāyu), fire or light (tejas), water (apa) and earth (pṛthivī). In the C.U. account the first evolutes of the one being are the three 'forms' (rūpa) of tejas, apa and anna (=pṛthivī). Whatever exists, according to Uddālaka, is merely a modification of one of the forms, 'the reality is just "the three forms"'.[8]

From these three forms emerge the subtle faculties of speech (vāc), breath (prāṇa) and mind (manas), which evolves from earth. Thus, in this C.U. account the mental evolves from the physical. In the Kārikā the reverse is the case. Mind (manas) evolves from ahaṃkāra, which in its tāmasic manifestation, produces the tanmātras (sense faculties) from which, in turn, emerge the mahābhūtas, the last three of which are the same as the three 'forms' of C.U. 6. That the former should be a prototype of the latter is hardly credible. In fact, the only thing in common between the C.U. and Kārikā accounts would seem to be that the 'forms' of the one being are three in number as are the qualities (guṇa) of prakṛti.

But even if it is accepted that the Kaṭh. U. passages constitute the earliest references to Sāṃkhya thought in Indian literature there still remains the vexed question of whether the compilers of the Kaṭha Upaniṣad were developing or just borrowing these Sāṃkhya concepts. Not until the period of the later prose Upaniṣads and the great epic, the Mahābhārata, do we find specific references to the existence of a school designated as Sāṃkhya.

Larson suggests that the first recorded mention of 'Sāṃkhya' in the literature of India is to be found in the Śvetāśvatara Upaniṣad 6.13.[9] In fact, the reference is to Sāṃkhya-Yoga, the common term employed in the Mahābhārata to denote the system of Kapila.[10] Moreover, the claim itself is controversial since the date of the Ś.U. is actually a matter of some dispute. Hume's chronology of the Upaniṣads follows Deussen's with regard to all the principal Upaniṣads except the Śvetāśvatara, which he places in Deussen's third group along with the Praśna, the Maitrī and the Māṇḍūkya.[11] K.B.R. Rao goes even further. He argues that the Ś.U. succeeds rather than precedes the various formulations of Sāṃkhya in the Mahābhārata.[12]

Rao's view receives some indirect support from the observations of two other scholars : E.W. Hopkins and J.A.B. Van Buitenen. The former argues that both the Kaṭha and Maitrī Upaniṣads (which contain undisputed 'Sāṃkhya' material) 'were certainly copied by the epic poets.'[13] With regard to the Ś.U. however, all he can say is, 'This may be loosely copied, but, except for one parallel, the mutual passages are common to this and other sources.'[14] There is thus little evidence from the Mahābhārata to support the claim that the compilation of the Ś.U. was carried out in a period anterior to that of the epic.

When commenting on the relationship between Vedic and epic material in general, Van Buitenen points out that the notions of a 'vedic age' and an 'epic age', with their suggestions of chronological continuity are perhaps misleading. He suggests that the substitution of the terms 'milieu' for 'age' may be a closer approximation to the true state of affairs since 'chronological priority of Vedic to post-Vedic notions is not necessarily a fact.'[15] This in turn goes some way towards supporting Grierson's claim that the developments of the Vedic tradition took place primarily in the 'midland' (madhyadeśa), the area around and to the north of Delhi, whilst less brahmanically influenced systems such as Sāṃkhya and Pañcarātra developed in the 'outland', mainly to the east of Delhi.[16]

Grierson's answer to the question posed earlier about whether 'Sāṃkhya' was developed by Upaniṣadic teachers or borrowed by them would thus be strongly in favour of the latter alternative, an option also favoured by a number of more recent scholars.[17] The evidence of the Mahābhārata can also be seen to support such a view since most of the references to Sāṃkhya suggests that it was a well established system, though perhaps not always uniform in its manifestations. In fact, as Hopkins points out, the system of Kapila 'is *repeatedly* declared to be the oldest.'[18]

In the mokṣadharma section of Mahābhārata 12 a number of teachers are quoted as offering instruction about some form of Sāṃkhya. They are Pañcaśikha, Bhīṣma, Vyāsa, Yajñavalkya, Vaśiṣṭha, Asita Devala, Sulabhā and Vaiśampāyana. None of these teachers offers exactly the same version of Sāṃkhya teaching as the others and all differ in one way or another from that presented in the Sāṃkhya Kārikā. Nevertheless, features which differentiate the classical Sāṃkhya of the Kārikās from the teaching of the Upaniṣads : the plurality and separateness of the puruṣas and the lack of a god figure, are in evidence in some epic versions of Sāṃkhya, a fact which indicates that the system of Īśvarakṛṣṇa is not some deviation from a genuine theistic and possibly monistic Sāṃkhya which developed out of the teaching of the Upaniṣads but one which stands in an ancient and well-established tradition of thought. Most epic descriptions of Sāṃkhya are not provided by actual Sāṃkhya teachers but are reports of what Sāṃkhyans believe. In fact, Yajñavalkya distinguishes between those Sāṃkhyans, whom he calls 'yatis', who regard puruṣa 'as existing by himself without a second, immutable, unmanifest (in the form of cause), unstable, and manifest (in the form of effects)' and those who 'depend on knowledge only (for their emancipation) and the practice of compassion for all creatures [and who] say that it is prakriti which is one but Purushas are many.'[19] King Janaka, disciple of Pañcaśikha, makes a similar distinction between those who claim that knowledge is the only means of emancipation and those, called Yatis, who argue that actions are the means.[20] In

12.308, Vaśiṣṭha too, uses the term 'Yati' to denote those Sāṃkhyans who believe in the singularity of puruṣa. In 12.351 Vaiśampāyana goes further, stating boldly that the followers of Sāṃkhya and Yoga do not accept that there is just one puruṣa in the universe.[21] Implicit in such a claim is the argument that those who do accept the singularity of puruṣa are not followers of Sāṃkhya or Yoga. We may also note that it is the Sāṃkhyans who maintain the plurality of puruṣa who practise compassion for all creatures. This clearly links them with Kapila who, in 12.269.9 criticises the Vedic tradition's adherence to animal sacrifice.[22]

Some schools of Sāṃkhya during the epic period appear to have been atheistic. Chakravarti perhaps goes too far when he claims that the Mahābhārata 'is always found to represent the atheistic school of Sāṃkhya,'[23] but that the epic knows an atheistic form of Sāṃkhya is clear from 12.301, where Bhīṣma contrasts the followers of Sāṃkhya with those of Yoga. The latter hold that unless a person accepts a lord (īśvara) they cannot attain liberation; the former, however, are said to hold that a person 'by acquiring true knowledge of all ends, becomes disassociated from all worldly objects, and, after departing from this body, it is plain, becomes emancipated ...'[24] In other words, god (īśvara) is not necessary for emancipation.

Unfortunately, the epic nowhere provides anything like a detailed account of the Sāṃkhyans who practise compassion towards all creatures, who teach that puruṣas are many and that a person does not need god to attain liberation. Only versions of the other kind of Sāṃkhya are presented at any length. One noticeable detail about these 'one-puruṣa' schools is that they generally subscribe in some way or other to Vedic values, world-view and terminology. For example, Vaśiṣṭha, one who knows both Sāṃkhya and Veda, incorporates Hiraṇyagarbha, Virāj and Viṣṇu into his exposition of Sāṃkhya. He also describes the ones who experience 'the supreme soul' as 'high-souled Brahmanas endued with intelligence and wisdom and conversant with the Vedas ...'[25] The Vedas, for their part, are authoritative and eternal.[26] Likewise, Asita Devala is called a brāhmaṇa and maintains that his teachings are compatible with both śruti and reason. For him, emancipation is the attainment of brahma. Bhīṣma too, although attempting to be a neutral expositor, presents a rather Vedic view of Sāṃkhya. Yama and Prajāpati find a place in his version and liberation is the merging of the jīva-soul with the supreme soul through the help of Nārāyaṇa.

Pañcaśikha is even more noteworthy in this respect for, since he is described as 'the son of Kapila', one would expect him to offer a version of pluralistic, non-violent (and atheistic?) Sāṃkhya. However, like the teachers just mentioned, he incorporates Vedic terminology into his teaching, regards the Vedas as sources of right knowledge which guide people along the true path, is conversant with Upaniṣadic teachings such as the five sheaths of the Taittirīya Upaniṣad and holds that emancipation is the attainment of brahma.[27] He is also described as 'the foremost of all persons conversant with the Vedas'[28] and he teaches his disciple, King Janaka, that one does not have to renounce kingdom or householder life in order to win emancipation for, 'If men leading the domestic mode of life be endued with Yama and Niyama, they become the equal of Sannyasins.'[29]

Can this be the son of the Kapila who criticised the brahmins for conducting animal sacrifices ? If so, the view that Sāṃkhya evolved out of the Vedic milieu would seem to be quite well founded. The answer of the Mahābhārata, however, is negative for we read in 12.218-219 that Pañcaśikha was 'foremost of all the disciples of Asusri' and that 'There was a certain Brahmani of the name of Kapila. She was the wife of Asuri. Pañcaśikha was accepted as her son and he used to suck her breasts. In consequence of this, he came to be known as the son of Kapila and his understanding became fixed on Brahma.'[30] Pañcaśikha, son of Kapila, has thus no evident connection with the reputed founder of the Sāṃkhya system. That others doubted the authenticity of Pañcaśikha's Sāṃkhya is clear from the Janaka-Sulabhā dialogue in 12.321. The latter instructs the former, in what Roy regards as the doctrines of the atheistic Sāṃkhya.[31] She informs him that whilst he might have moved a little beyond conventional domestic life he has not attained emancipation but is stuck between the two, pretending to have reached the goal.[32]

In some respects the 'one puruṣa' schools of Sāṃkhya appear to be in a similar situation. Their basic structure is determined by their versions of the guṇa and tattva categories found in the S.K. though the details of each set of categories varies from teacher to teacher. They are also claimed to be in accord with the Veda, even though none of their basic concepts can be clearly derived from pre-Kaṭha Upaniṣad Vedic literature. Also noticeable in these 'one puruśa' versions of Sāṃkhya, despite their conformity to the Veda, is the minimal or non-existent role they give to prāṇa.

Prāṇa, as is clear from the Kārikās, figures little in Sāṃkhya thinking; Sulabhā does not mention it at all in her exposition. In the Veda, however, the opposite is the case. Prāṇa is one of the most prominent cosmological principles. The minimal presence of the prāṇa concept, along with the inclusion, here and there, of other notions and deities suggests, when added to the fact that there appears to be Vedic and non-Vedic forms of Sāṃkhya in the epic, that these 'one puruṣa' schools are attempting some kind of synthesis between Vedic and Sāṃkhya thought albeit one which is structurally dominated by the Sāṃkhya side of the combination.

None of the 'one puruṣa' Sāṃkhyans present prāṇa in anything like the way it is found in the Upaniṣads. In fact, their treatment is much closer to that found in the writings of Śaṅkara. Hence, for Pañcaśikha the prāṇas are modifications of vāyu, classed by him as one of the three organs of action.[33] In Vyāsa's teaching vāyu (including the prāṇas) is classed as a mahābhūta. Yajñavalkya's view is different again, though perhaps more akin to Pañcaśikha's than Vyāsa's. After explaining how mahat/buddhi proceeds from the avyakta, ahaṃkāra from mahat, manas from ahaṃkāra, the mahābhūtas from manas, the sense of faculties from the mahābhūtas and the sense organs from the sense faculties, he states,

> 'Then, O Monarch, come the breath that rises upward (viz. Prana) and these that have a transverse motion (viz. Saman [a], Udana, and Vyana). This is the eighth creation and is called Arjjava. Then come those breaths that course tranversly in the lower part of the body (viz. Samana, Udana and Vyana) and also that called Apana coursing downwards. This ninth creation, is also called Arjjava, O King.'[34]

In a note on this passage the translator states that '"Arjjava" mean[s] "relating to straight paths or courses", so called from the straight courses of these winds or breaths.'[35] Here then, is another tantalizing and ambiguious suggestion that the prāṇas might traverse the body in channels. However, the straight coursing could well refer to the movement in the limbs and the text provides no further details on this material.

Only Asita Devala places prāṇa in any position of prominence. For him,

> 'There is a being called Mahat, which with the aid of the wind (called Prana), upholds this combination containing the

twenty things that have been named [: five buddindriyas, five karmendriyas, muscular power, mind, understanding, citta, sattva, rajas, tamas, the owner of the body, avidya and stomachic heat], and in the destruction of that body the wind (which is generally spoken of as the cause) is only the instrument of the hands of that same Mahat.'[36]

In these four short passages we have four different accounts of Sāṃkhya cosmology and four different descriptions of prāṇa/prāṇas, all of which give them a very minor role. What is more, these accounts which include the prāṇas in their expositions of Sāṃkhya are ones which are particularly Vedic in their orientation. It is thus possible and I would regard it as likely, that the prāṇas only feature in epic versions of Sāṃkhya which are synthetic, i.e. Veda plus Sāṃkhya. I would also suggest that the concept of the prāṇas was brought into these synthetic accounts from the Vedic side as they fit very poorly into the guṇa-tattva enumerations of the principles of existence. If this is so it would seem likely that the Sāṃkhya of Kapila, like Jainism and early Buddhism, had no place for an ultimate or cosmic principle like prāṇa and could only with difficulty accommodate the doctrine of prāṇas. In this, as is clear from the material in chapters one and two of this study, it represents a considerable divergence from the Vedic world-picture. Such a view of Sāṃkhya finds considerable support in the Sāṃkhya Kārikā and subsequent Sāṃkhya texts.

Prāṇa in the Sāṃkhya Kārikā, Tattva Samāsa, Yukti Dīpikā and Sāṃkhya Sūtra

The Sāṃkhya Kārikā and Sāṃkhya Sūtra have little to say on the topic of prāṇa. This, as I intimated above, is because it is a concept essentially alien to Sāṃkhya thinking and, in all likelihood, was only introduced into the system as one way of reconciling the teaching of Sāṃkhya with that of the Upaniṣads. What was incorporated into Sāṃkhya initially, however, was simply the Vedic notion of the five prāṇas. As later commentators sought to justify this inclusion they expanded the concept of prāṇas (plural) to include prāṇa (singular). Whilst this might have gone some way towards reconciling Sāṃkhya with the Veda it had the effect of demonstrating that the whole notion of prāṇa and prāṇas had no authentic place in the cosmology of Sāṃkhya. The substantiation for these suggestions is set out below.

There is just one reference to prāṇa in the Sāṃkhya Kārikā and only two in the much longer Sāṃkhya Sūtra. All have more or less the same purport. The first reference, S.K. 29, reads as follows :

> 'With respect to the specific characteristics of the three ... each functions differently; the five vital breaths (or winds) (make up) their common function.'[37]

Sāṃkhya Sūtra (S.S.) 2.31 makes an almost identical statement:

> 'The five airs (vāyu) beginning with Prāṇa [result from] the joint functioning of the instrument(s) (karaṇa) [=antaḥkaraṇa]'[38]

Finally, S.S. 5.113 makes the same kind of claim but adds a further item :

> 'Prāṇa is not a characteristic of the source of the body because that is accomplished (tat siddheḥ) through the power of the indriyas.'[39]

In commenting on this verse, Vijñānabhikṣu writes,

> 'The import is this: Prāṇa which is the form of a modification of the instruments (i.e. Indriyas), does not subsist in the absence of the Instruments. Therefore, since in a dead body, by reason of the absence of the Instruments, there is the absence of Prāṇa, (it follows that) Prāṇa is not the originant of the body.'[40]

Aniruddha's vṛtti makes it clear that 'tat siddheḥ', 'the accomplishment of that' refers to the accomplishment of prāṇa's existence rather than the body's existence. 'Prāṇa', he states, 'is supported or upheld *by the power of all the Indriyas...* [It is] a *modification of all the Indriyas.*'[41]

This sūtra, and especially Aniruddha's comments, supports Larson's understanding of 'the three' in S.K. 29 as buddhi, ahaṃkāra and the senses and conflicts with Sinha's view, presumably based on S.S. 2.31, that 'the three' are the three components of the antaḥkaraṇa: buddhi, ahaṃkāra and manas (see note 37). This is not just a recent scholarly controversy, however, for, as Larson points out,[42] Gauḍapāda's bhāṣya on the S.K. and the Jayamaṇgalā both suggest that the prāṇas circulate throughout the thirteenfold instrument (buddhi, ahaṃkāra, manas, five buddhīndriyas and five karmendriyas) whilst Vācaspatimiśra's Sāṃkhyatattvakaumudī and Vijñānabhikṣu restrict their activities to the antaḥkaraṇa. In itself, this disagreement between texts, and even different passages from the same text, is indicative of the rather tenuous connection that the prāṇa concept has with the Sāṃkhya scheme. This lack of fit was obviously noted by contemporary critics too, for in his comments on S.S. 2.31, Vijñānabhikṣu attempts to meet an objection to that effect.

The question posed by the objector is that if prāṇa, apāna etc. are modifications of 'the Internal Instrument'[43] why are they not listed along with the other components of the liṅga śarīra (S.K. 39-41; S.S. 3.7-16) and why is prāṇa often identified with air (vāyu)? Vijñānabhikṣu's response represents a neat way of dealing with the problem which simultaneously makes Sāṃkhya doctrine more compatible with the Upaniṣads. Nevertheless, it underlines quite clearly that the concept of prāṇa/prāṇas has no real home in the Sāṃkhya system. He states,

> '... Buddhi itself, by reason of its power of action, takes the names of Sūtra-ātma, Prāṇa etc. ... Although it is a modification of the Internal Instrument, still the use of the term, air, is accounted for by the fact of its having peculiar movements like those of air, and also of its being presided over by the Deva, Vāyu.'[44]

This helps him to deal with statements in śruti such as P.U. 6.4. and Muṇḍ.U. 2.1.3, where prāṇa is presented as the first of the created principles but puts him in conflict with other Sāṃkhyan statements to the effect that the prāṇas are the result of the joint function of either the components of the antaḥkaraṇa or of all the indriyas together. Moreover, there is no support whatsoever in either the Sāṃkhya Kārikā or the Sāṃkhya Sūtra for such a claim. S.K. 23 and S.S. 2.13-15 are definitions of buddhi. Both state that it is 'ascertainment' (adhyavasāyaḥ) and that its sāttvic manifestations are virtue (dharma), knowledge (jñāna), dispassion (vairāgya) and power (aiśvarya) whilst its tāmasic ones are the opposites of these. Vijñānabhikṣu, in his comments on S.S. 2.15 explains how adharma, ajñāna avairāgya and anaiśvarya can be modifications of mahat. He writes,

> '... the principle of Mahat, through the tincture received from the adjacent Rajas and Tamas, becomes also "the reverse" i.e. small (the opposite of great), i.e. endowed with the properties of Demerit, Ignorance, Passion and Impotence. Such is the meaning.'[45]

He thereby closes off the possibility of taking the rājasic modifications of buddhi to be the five prāṇas.

It would appear that when the authors of the Kārikā and the Sūtra wanted to explain the nature of buddhi/mahat they either forgot to mention its synonymity with prāṇa and that one of its manifestations was the five prāṇas *or* they did not think of it as possessing these characteristics. The latter alternative seems by far the most likely. But if this is the case and buddhi is not a synonym for prāṇa the objector's question still stands: 'Why are praṇa and the rest not included in the components of the liṅga śarīra?.' The real answer is probably that they have no place there. The Sāṃkhya system gains no explanatory benefits from the inclusion of prāṇa/prāṇas into its cosmological scheme. Their inclusion as a function of the antaḥkaraṇa or the indriyas is, as Śaṅkara pointed out in his commentary on B.S. 2.49, absurd since life/breath is is clearly independent of sensory and intellectual activity. This is demonstrated by the fact that the activities of prāṇa continue during sleep whilst those of the intellect and senses remain inoperative.

When the more detailed descriptions of the prāṇa are set out in Sāṃkhya texts such as Narendra's commentary on the Tattvasamāsa and the Yuktidīpikā it is immediately apparent that they are derived from similar accounts in the Upaniṣads. Verse ten of the Tattva Samāsa states that the airs (vāyava) are five in number and Narendra names them as prāṇa apāna, vyāna, udāna and samāna. Then he locates them in the various parts of the body, thereby falling in with Gauḍapāda and the author of the Jayamaṅgalā on the issue of the extent of prāṇa activity. He writes,

> 'The function operating in the mouth, nose, etc., belongs to Prāṇa, the function operating in the back, anus, the organ of generation, etc. belongs to Apāna; the function operating in the heart, navel and all the joints belongs to Udāna; the function operating in the skin, etc. belongs to Vyānā'.[46]

The locations of prāṇa and apāna in this account are the same as are found in P.U. 3 and Mait.U. 2.6. In Narendra's list, udāna seems to be taking the place of samāna in the P.U. and Mait.U. accounts. The former locates it in the middle of the body, whilst the latter has it distributing the essential ingrediients (dhātu) of food to the limbs. Narendra's link between vyāna and the skin, however, has no Upaniṣadic precedent but, as was noted in chapter two, none of the

Upaniṣadic accounts are exactly in agreement either. Here though, it is possible that Narendra has been influenced by Vyāsa's commentary of Yoga Sūtra 3.39, where he states that vyāna is all-pervading.

In its treatment of these prāṇas, the Yukti Dīpikā, whilst obviously influenced by the Upaniṣadic material, introduces a novel distinction: that between internal and external functions. The internal functions are much the same as those listed in the Praśna and Maitrī Upaniṣads: prāṇa functions as breath through the mouth and nostrils; apāna carries urine etc. downwards; samāna is located between prāṇa and apāna though it does not seem to distribute the dhātu to the limbs; vyāna is diffused throughout the system, 'through its instrumentality blood and other such fluids are circulated even upto the extremity of nails and pores';[47] Finally, udāna pushes fluids and semen up to the brain, or, if obstructed, is the cause of the production of letters, words, sentences etc. This probably means it either facilitates spiritual awareness or conceptualization and language use.

The external functions have no antecedents that I am aware of. Prāṇa produce feelings of obedience or suceptibility to something; apāna initiates changes in an individual's orientation, e.g. from vice to virtue; samāna manifests as feelings of pleasure in sharing with others; vyāna manifests as feelings of connection with other individuals and udāna generates feelings of superiority over other people.[48] Whilst these external or perhaps 'feeling' functions of the prāṇas are rather novel their derivation from Upaniṣadic accounts of their activities is unmistakable.

Conclusion

The evidence presented above makes it clear that there is no genuine place for prāṇa/prāṇas in the Sāṃkhya scheme. The reason for their inclusion, I would suggest, was partly historical and partly tactical. On the historical side, the evidence of the epic suggests that most of the 'one puruṣa' schools of Sāṃkhya were, at that time, seeking to demonstrate agreement between Vedic and Sāṃkhyan teachings. Whilst such accommodation is hardly in evidence in the Sāṃkhya Kārikā, even though Īśvarakṛṣṇa states that he received his teachings through the tradition of Asuri and Pañcaśikha (S.K. 70-71), I would suggest that the reference to prāṇa in kārikā 29 represents one step in this direction. That Sāṃkhyans consistently sought to claim orthodoxy for their views is attested by the facts that the Brahmasūtra seeks to refute their interpretations of śruti and that the later Sāṃkhya Sūtra along with Vijñānabhikṣu, seeks to demonstrate their validity.

However, the traffic was not all one-way. As was noted in part one of this chapter, the Vedāntin idea of subtle forms of the elements accompanying the subtle body during transmigration has no antecedents in the Upaniṣads but is an integral part of Sāṃkhya teaching. Likewise, the inclusion of the karmendriyas as faculties of the ātman is not Upaniṣadic but probably borrowed from Sāṃkhya. In fact, what appears to have happened in the post-Upaniṣadic period is that the Vedānta tradition came increasingly under the sway of Sāṃkhyan thought-forms, the inclusion of which left little place for prāṇa. At the same time Sāṃkhyans were concerned to assert their orthodox status and demonstrate the compatibility of their views with Upaniṣadic teaching. In consequence, prāṇa/prāṇas found a place in their cosmology albeit a peripheral and precarious one.

The next system to be examined, the Pañcarātra, can be regarded as a genuine or conscious synthesis of Vedic and Sāṃkhyan teaching coupled with a distinctive form of theism. Perhaps surprisingly, it is here that the prāṇa concept seems to have retained some of its former scope and prestige.

REFERENCES

1. Hopkins (1901) p. 97, points out that Kapila is 'the only founder of a philosophical system known to the epic' and that his system is known in the epic as 'Sāṃkhyayoga' or, more specifically, 'Kapilam' (p. 99). He is also of the opinion that Kapila was 'a real (human) philosopher' (p. 98). Larson (1979) p. 139, doubts this last claim, arguing that the references point to Kapila being just a mythical figure. He is also doubtful about attributing the founding of Sāṃkhya to the great rājarṣi since, 'There are no sources other than popular tradition regarding the question of Kapila as the founder of Sāṃkhya' (p. 20). However, this claim has to be taken lightly for later in the same work he states that 'Kapila is considered by all texts to be the founder of Sāṃkhya ...' (p. 139).
2. Van Buitenen (1957) (2) p. 88.
3. For a thorough discussion of the meaning of this term see Van Buitenen (1957) (1).
4. op. cit. p. 16.
5. Larson (1979) pp. 78-79.
6. op. cit. p. 89.
7. Beidler (1975) p. 18.
8. Hume (1931) p. 242.
9. Larson (1979) p. 101.
10. See Hopkins (1901) p. 99.
11. Hume (1931) p. xiii.
12. Rao (1966) pp. 297-333.
13. Hopkins (1901) p. 27.
14. op. cit. p. 28.
15. Van Buitenen (1957) (2) p. 89.
16. Grierson (1909) p. 540 f.f.
17. e.g. Pande (1974) and Zimmer (1967).
18. Hopkins (1901) p. 98.
19. Roy (10) p. 453.
20. op. cit. p. 471.
21. op. cit. p. 621.
22. Hopkins (1901) p. 99.
23. Chakravarti (1975) p. 54.
24. Roy (9) p. 406. Larson, (1979) p. 123, provides the sanskṛt : vadanti kāraṇam cedam sāṃkhya samyagvijatāyaḥ vijñāyeha gatīḥ sarva virakto viṣayeṣu yaḥ.

25. Roy (10) p. 431.
26. op. cit. p. 422.
27. Roy (9) pp. 120-126.
28. Roy (10) p. 467.
29. op. cit. pp. 470-471.
30. Roy (9) pp. 120-121.
31. Roy (10) p. 478.
32. op. cit. p. 487.
33. Roy (9) p. 127.
34. Roy (10) p. 445.
35. loc. cit.
36. Roy (9) p. 310.
37. Larson (1979) p. 265. Larson takes 'the three' to mean buddhi, ahaṃkāra and the senses. Sinha, in his translation of the Sāṃkhya Kārikā, (1915) p. 27, takes it as a reference to the components of the internal instrument (antaḥkaraṇa): buddhi, ahaṃkāra and manas.
38. My translation.
39. My translation.
40. Sinha (1915). s.s. p. 495.
41. op. cit. p. 494.
42. Larson (1979) p. 190.
43. Sinha does not provide the sanskṛt for the bhāṣya of Vijñānabhikṣu and hence it is impossible to infer with any certainty whether antaḥkaraṇa or indriya is meant, though the former is obviously what is suggested.
44. Sinha (1915) s.s. p. 263.
45. op. cit. p. 248.
46. op. cit. Tattva Samāsa p. 12. Presumably samāna is omitted because of oversight. Narendra also presents an interesting objection that could have come from the mouth of a member of Deussen's 'older school': 'But Vāyu, Air, also may be regarded as causing all living beings to move or to shine, being itself sentient, moving, and the performer of vital activities in all bodies. Why then do you imagine a sentient Puruṣa diferent from it ?' Narendra's answer is essentially, 'Because Śruti says so'.
47. Chakravarti (1975) p. 268.
48. Details of this account can be found in Chakravarti (1975) pp. 265-270.

PART THREE : The Place of Prāṇa in the Pañcarātra System

The Pañcarātra is one of the most ancient identifiable schools of Vaiṣṇavism and the oldest now extant.[1] Grierson suggests that it is just one school of Bhāgavatism though the two are often identified.[2] According to him, its history can be divided into three stages. For his reconstruction of the first he finds himself in agreement with the conclusions of scholars such as Garbe and Bhandarkar, namely, that in origin Sāṃkhya (and also Yoga) were not brāhmanical systems but were developed in the 'Outland' around the 'Midland' (Madhyadeśa)–the area now occupied by and to the north of Delhi. This 'Outland', he argues, was dominated philosophically by kṣatriyas rather than brahmans and was the region where the Buddhist and Jaina traditions originated. Chattopadhyaya (1970) finds himself in general agreement with this picture, pointing out that the main centres of the Vāsudeva sect and of the Pañcarātra and Gopala Kṛṣṇa movements in both pre- and early post-Christian periods were Mathura, Nagri, Chitorgad, Rajasthan, Vidiśa and Ahicchatra, all of which are outside the Madhyadeśa. Even in the post-epic period only one of the principal sites for the worship of Viṣṇu's boar avatāra (the most popular form of Vaiṣṇavism in the Gupta period) was in the Madhyadeśa, 'showing evidently that the cult was not very popular there.'[3]

Grierson suggests that as the Bhāgavata movement developed from its simple beginnings, where it was concerned with the worship of a personal deity, bhagavat (the adorable), it required some kind of philosophical-cosmological framework for the expression of its theology. Sāṃkhya was the obvious source for such a framework and hence early Bhāgavatism, the nature of which is presumably inferred from an analysis of texts such as the Bhagavad Gītā and the Nārāyaṇīya section of the Mahābhārata,[4] was essentially Sāṃkhya plus god. The termination of this first and, it must be admitted, highly speculative and controversial period Grierson estimates to be the end of the fourth century B.C.E.[5]

The second stage, he suggests, 'is marked by the capture and absorption of Bhāgavatism by the Brahmaism of the Midland.'[6] The Bhagavad Gītā and Nārāyaṇīya are the primary expressions of this stage.[7] However, in Grierson's view, whilst the Bhāgavatas 'were stopped from denying the truth of Brahmaist pantheism [they] were still nominally professors of Sāṅkya-Yoga. The result was a series of attempts to unite the opposing lines of thought.'[8] A number of these can be found in book twelve of the Mahābhārata, associated with the names of teachers such as Pañcaśikha, Janaka and Sulabhā. 'These finally settled down into the form in which we find them in the third book (section 24 f.f.) of the Bhagavata Purāṇa'.[9] The philosophical result of these attempts to combine Sāṃkhya-Yoga with Brahmanism was, thinks Grierson, 'a medley of unrelated and mutually contradictory conceptions.'[10]

His third stage begins with the attempts by Rāmānuja and Madhva to refute advaitic interpretations of Vedānta. He regards the works of these teachers as differing Vaiṣṇava responses to the pantheistic inclinations of mainstream brāhmanical thought, Rāmānuja's trying to maintain the synthesis, Madhva's rejecting it.

Grierson thus proposes a fundamental tension between the essentially monistic Vedānta and the pluralistic Bhāgavata or Pañcarātra tradition. Implicit in this, of course, is the fundamental tension between monistic Vedānta and dualistic/pluralistic Sāṃkhya. Both tensions are indicated in orthodox literature.[11] Such a view of the radical dissimilarity between Sāṃkhya and Vedānta has been advanced by many scholars since the time of Grierson, e.g. G.C. Pande and H. Zimmer.[12] However, this is far from being a unanimously held opinion. Writers such as W. Beidler, G.J. Larson and K.B.R. Rao[13] have all argued for an evolution of Sāṃkhya from the Upaniṣads. Rao, in fact, goes further. He suggests that it is incorrect to think of the Pañcarātrins adapting a previously existing atheistic Sāṃkhya in the service of their own theism. He also claims that texts such as the Ahirbudhnya Saṃhitā, which contain developed versions of the Pañcarātra cosmology, predate the Sāṃkhya Kārikās of Īśvarakṛṣṇa.[14]

Whatever the origins of the Sāṃkhya system might be (and this remains a contentious issue at the present time) Rao's dating of the Pañcarātra material is unacceptable. Schrader fixes the date of the Ahirbudhnya Saṃhitā between 300 and 800 C.E. and there are at least two good reasons for inclining towards the later of these figures. First of all the cosmology of the Ahirbudhnya Saṃhitā is much more developed and complex than that of the Nārāyaṇīya. In the latter account it is clear that the process of interpretation is still in its early stages. Vāsudeva, also called 'the twenty fifth' [tattva] is the supreme soul, the eternal puruṣa. From him comes avyakta prakṛti, from avyakta prakṛti comes manas (mind), from mind space (ākāśa), from space wind (vāyu), from wind light (tejas), from light water (ap), from water earth (pṛthivī). The last five are called mahābhūtas and they are said to form the body of all creatures. Into each body enters the jīva, an individualised form of Vāsudeva known as Saṃkarṣaṇa (a name of Kṛṣṇa's brother). From Saṃkarṣaṇa comes Pradyumna (a name of Kṛṣṇa's son), and finally, from Pradyumna comes Aniruddha (a name of Kṛṣṇa's grandson) who is also called Īśāna and Īśvara though his place in the scheme does not seem clear. In this Nārāyaṇīya account the bhagavat generates prakṛti and Saṃkarṣaṇa from himself. It is from the association of these two that manas (= buddhi in the Sāṃkhya scheme) evolves. Saṃkarṣaṇa then evolves Pradyumna who, through association with manas, produces the mahābhūtas and the deity Brahmā, the fashioner of the material universe from the mahābhūtas.

The former account is immensely more complex than this and will be outlined below. The transition from the cosmology of the Nārāyaṇīya to that of the Ahirbudhnya Saṃhitā must have taken at least a generation, probably more, and since the Nārāyaṇīya is unlikely to have been composed before 300 C.E. the Ahirbudhnya Saṃhitā must have been written considerably later than that.

The second reason for thinking the Ahirbudhnya Saṃhitā account to be later than that found in the Nārāyaṇīya concerns the relationship between the Ahirbudhnya Saṃhitā and another, later, Pañcarātra work, the Lakṣmī Tantra. This text, dated by Gupta at some time between the ninth and twelfth centuries C.E., 'bears a close resemblance to the Ahirbudhnya Saṃhitā'.[15] Certainly the cosmologies of the two texts agree on fundamentals such as the division of creation into pure, mixed and impure and the location of principles such as vyūha, jīva and guṇa in each of these respectively. Such similarity would suggest that the date of

Ahirbudhnya Saṃhitā is likely to be closer to that of the Lakṣmī Tantra than to that of the Nārāyaṇiya. Hence, the likelihood of the Ahirbudhnya Saṃhitā being composed at a time prior to the writing of the Sāṃkhya Kārikā is extremely slight.

This, in turn, goes some way towards supporting Grierson's case for the Pañcarātra system being a synthesis of three distinct traditions: Sāṃkhya, Vedānta and Bhāgavata. Gupta too recognises that the Pañcarātra, as expressed in texts such as the Lakṣmī Tantra, is a complex synthesis of ideas. Nevertheless, she rejects the notion that it is 'a medley of unrelated and mutually contradictory conceptions'. Rather, at least as far as the Pañcarātra Saṃhitās are concerned, she feels that the various components of the synthesis 'are all fitted into a well balanced pattern'.[16] However, whilst this may be true at the general level, it is not the case at the specific, as I hope to demonstrate through the following investigation into the role of prāṇa in this scheme.

Pañcarātra Cosmology

In the Pañcarātra system as found in texts such as the Ahirbudhnya Saṃhitā and the Lakṣmī Tantra, the creation is divided into three levels: pure, mixed and impure, though there are different versions of the constituents of the pure creation.[17] According to the Ahirbudhnya Saṃhitā, a text chosen for analysis by Schrader because of its concern with the theoretical dimensions of Pañcarātra theology,[18] the end of the cosmic night is marked by Viṣṇu dividing his power (śakti) into two: kriya śakti and bhūti śakti. The former is unified whilst the latter is diversified in many ways. The former, called 'the prāṇa form of Viṣṇu's will (prāṇa-rūpo viṣṇoḥ saṃkalpa), can be regarded as the instrumental cause of the world.[19] Its symbol is the discus of Viṣṇu called Sudarśana.[20] This śakti also has a sound form (mantra mayi kriya śakti) which manifests on four levels: parā/śānta, paśyanti, madhyamā and vaikharī. The various letters/sounds of the sanskṛt alphabet correspond to the various sound manifestations of kriya śakti and, presumably, activate the principles contained within bhūti śakti. The latter is the material cause of the world and appears as the three creations.

The four above-mentioned levels of mantra mayi kriya śakti also correspond to four levels of consciousness. Parā or śānta corresponds to the turiya (fourth) state 'when the individual self is identical with the unpolarised consciousness of the supreme self';[21]

paśyanti corresponds to suṣupti the state of deep sleep where 'the knower is said to exist in the form of prāṇa (vital air), because during the state of puruṣa's deep sleep only prāṇa is manifested'.[22] This appears to be an echo of Ajātaśatru's teaching in the Bṛhadāraṇyaka and Kauṣītakī Upaniṣads. Madhyamā corresponds to svapna, the dream state where 'the knower is regarded as consisting of only eight cities (aṣṭapurī)' i.e. having eight parts.[23] Vaikharī, the level of articulated speech, corresponds to the waking state. The exact relationship between these fourfold manifestations and the three-fold creation is not, however, clear in these texts. In fact, as my comment under note 23 indicates, the compilers appear to have become confused by attempting to combine concepts from too great a number of diverse sources.

The pure creation (śuddhasṛṣṭi)

The first phase of the pure creation is called 'the appearance the guṇas' (guṇonmesadaśa), that is, bringing them from potentiality to actuality. These are jñāna (omniscience), aiśvarya (lordship) or icchā (will), śakti (power to become the material cause of the world), bala (strength–fatiguelessness in connection with the production of the world),[24] vīrya ('unaffectedness ... in spite of being the material cause of the world')[25] and tejas (splendour).

The six guṇas make up the body of Vāsudeva and Lakṣmī that is seen by liberated beings. The next stage is variously described in Pañcarātra literature.[26] In the Ahirbudhnya Saṃhitā it is the manifestation of the three vyūhas (emanations) that is described at this point. Each of these contains all six guṇas but actualises only two of them. The vyūhas are Saṃkarṣaṇa (also called Balarāma or Baladeva, the brother of Kṛṣṇa), who actualises jñāna and bala, Pradyumna (the son of Kṛṣṇa), who actualises aiśvarya and vīrya, and Aniruddha (the grandson of Kṛṣṇa), who actualises śakti and tejas.[27]

Each vyūha has a creative and a pedagogic role. Saṃkarṣaṇa brings the impure creation (aśuddhasṛṣṭi) into embryonic form through the power of the bala guṇa and teaches the way to liberation (ekāntika mārga) through the power of the jñāna guṇa. Pradyumna sows the potential for the later division of creation into prakṛti and puruṣa and teaches how to put the ekāntika mārga into practice (tat kriya). Finally, Aniruddha sows the potential for the evolution of prakṛti into manifest form (vyakta) and for the operation of time (kāla). He teaches about the fruits of practice (kriya phala = mokṣa). Each vyūha also emanates six vidyeśvaras (lords of knowledge) which superintend various parts of the creation and which are meditated on as parts of the ekāntika mārga.[28] Other creations at this level are the incarnations (avatāra–descent or vibhava–manifestation). These are of two kinds, primary and secondary. A primary avatāra is 'like a flame springing from a flame, that is to say Viṣṇu himself with a transcendent (aprakṛta) body',[29] whilst a secondary one 'is a soul in bondage with a natural body which, however, is possessed (āviṣta) or pervaded, for some particular mission of function, by the power (śakti) of Viṣṇu'.[30]

According to Schrader, different texts suggest different sources for the avatāras. For example, the Lakṣmī Tantra (4.29) derives all of them from Aniruddha[31] whilst the Padma Tantra has each vyūha manifesting a number of them.[32] In the Ahirbudhnya Saṃhitā, Aniruddha is also called antaryāmin (inner controller), thereby incorporating another prominent Upaniṣadic concept which, as we have noted above, is a synonym for prāṇa.[33]

Vaikuṇṭha (the highest heaven–parama vyoman) is also part of the pure creation. It is the tripad-vibhuti (manifestation of the three quarters of puruṣa (R.V. 10.90) that are beyond the material universe). It manifests at the time of the vyūhas and contains all the principles of existence, symbolised by Viṣṇu's ornaments and weapons. They are (1) jīva–symbolised by the jewel on Viṣṇu's breast (kaustabha); (2) prakṛti–symbolised by the curl of hair on his breast (śrīvatsa); (3) mahat (identified by Schrader as the mukhya prāṇa of the Upaniṣads)–symbolised by his club; (4) sāttvic ahaṃkāra–symbolised by his conch; (5) tāmasic ahaṃkāra - symbolised by his bow; (6) vidya–symbolised by his sword; (7) avidya–symbolised by its sheath; (8) manas–symbolised by his discus; (9) the indriyas–symbolised by his arrows, and (10) the mahābhūtas–symbolised by his garland.[34] Two types of jīva are found in Vaikuṇṭha : nityas (eternally free) and muktas (liberated). The former are all omniscient and can incarnate just as Viṣṇu can. They are divided into four classes according to their duties. Muktas are essentially bodiless though they can assume various bodily forms at will. However, they can have no effect on worldly events.

The mixed creation (śuddhāśuddhasṛṣṭi)

This evolves entirely out of Pradyumna and has two parts, both of which are manifestations of bhūti śakti : kūtastha puruṣa and maya śakti. The former is 'an aggregate of souls similar to a bee-hive',[35] the latter has three dimensions or components: niyati (destiny or fate), kāla (time) and guṇa (quality). Each of these evolves from the preceding one. Similarly, within the guṇa body of prakṛti (i.e. maya śakti) each guṇa evolves from a higher one in the following order: sattva, rajas, tamas. This diversified guṇa body is called avyakta (unmanifest) or mūlaprakṛti (the creative foundation). The manifestation of each guṇa is superintended by Aniruddha as Viṣṇu, Brahmā and Śiva respectively. Into this mixed creation come four pairs of Manus which issue directly from the mouth of Pradyumna. These descend, through the various tattvas of the intermediate and impure creations, eventually arriving at the coarsest level where they procreate and people the world. The jīvas of the Manu-descendents (mānavas), however, have their intrinsic omniscience obscured by the creation and hence the first Manus teach the religious path which leads to the eventual re-attainment of that sublime state.

The impure creation (aśuddhasṛṣṭi)

From the interaction of niyati, kāla and guṇa, mahat evolves.[36] This Schrader identifies with the mukhya prāṇa of the Upaniṣads, which is life (āyus), intelligence (prajñā), self (ātman), supreme power (brahman) and which is the master of the five sense faculties. Such an equation is supported, he argues, by the twelfth chapter of the Ahirbudhnya Saṃhitā where, in its discussion of the Sāṃkhya tattvas prāṇa is substituted for mahat.[37] However, as was observed under note 32 above, the Ahirbudhnya Saṃhitā (7.9-10) makes prāṇa one of the three divisions of mahat. A similar view is found in the Lakṣmī Tantra 5.27-33.[38] There we are informed that mahat is composed of prāṇa and the two principles which emerge from it : Hiraṇyagarbha (replacing the kāla of the Ahirbudhnya Saṃhitā account) and buddhi. The evolution of these two from prāṇa is not explicit in the Ahirbudhnya Saṃhitā account and hence the reference to prāṇa instead of mahat in chapter twelve may simply be the product of an un-acknowledged acceptance of the primacy of prāṇa among the three principles. Such an interpretation would make the different statements about prāṇa in the Ahirbudhnya Saṃhitā compatible rather than conflicting and this, in turn, would lend plausibility to Schrader's equation. Nevertheless, as I hope to demonstrate below, the Ahirbudhnya Saṃhitā's treatment of prāṇa is not internally consistent and hence, whilst it may be the case that the author of the text was thinking in terms of some kind of equivalence between the mukhya prāṇa of the Upaniṣads and the mahat of Sāṃkhya when he was writing, it is perhaps unreasonable to expect the synthesis to be without flaws as the concepts being combined are actually incompatible.

From mahat comes ahaṃkāra (I-ness), a synonym of which is Prajāpati. It has three forms. The sāttvic form is called vaikārika (that which is subject to modification). From this, with the aid of the rājasic form, taijasa (consisting of light), evolve the buddhīndriyas (organs of perception): śrotra (ear/hearing), tvac (skin/touching), cakṣus (eye/seeing), rasanā (tongue/tasting) and ghrāna (nose/smelling), and the karmendriyas (organs of action): vāc (vocal cords (?)/speech), pāṇi (hands/handling), pāda (feet/walking), upastha (genitals/generation) and pāyu (anus/excretion). The tāmasic form is called bhūtādi (the original element). From this, again with the help of taijasa, evolve the tanmātras: śabda (that which is audible), sparśa (that which is touchable), rūpa (that which is visible), rasa (that which is tastable) and gandha (that which is smellable). From each of these emerges, respectively, one of the mahābhūtas (great elements): ākāśa (space), vāyu (air), tejas (heat/fire), apas (liquid/water) and pṛthivī (earth).

At this point the Sāṃkhya account stops. The Pañcarātra system, however, adds a further stage of coalescing into a mass (saṃhatim vinā), i.e. a stage of the various buddhīndriyas, karmendriyas, tanmātras and mahābhūtas coming together to form the complex and variegated universe of our ordinary experience.[39] Within this universe are beings practising yoga for the purpose of attaining mokṣa. The details of this practice are set out in chapters thirty one and thirty two of the Ahirbudhnya Saṃhitā. It is described under the same headings that Patañjali employed in the aṣṭāṅga section of the Yoga Sūtras: yama, niyama, āsana, prāṇāyāma, pratyāhāra, dhāraṇā, dhyāna and samādhi.

In the section on prāṇāyāma (32.1-55) Nārada asks Ahirbudhnya (a name of Śiva) about the nāḍīs (channels) and vāyus (airs). He is told that such information is a supreme secret (paramam guhyam) but is nevertheless given an answer. Ahirbudhnya informs him that the seat of the nāḍīs is four aṅgulas high, four aṅgulas wide, oval shaped and covered with fat, flesh, bone and blood. It is nine aṅgulas higher than the penis, i.e. at the level of the navel. The navel cakra has twelve spokes. Kuṇḍalī is the place where it is situated, the medium in which it exists and the power by which it is sustained. She lives around the cakra and has eight openings. There are 72,000 nāḍīs in the body. The alamba and suṣumnā nāḍīs are situated in the middle of the cakra; the other twelve nāḍīs:

kuhu, varuṇa, yaśasvinī, piṅgala, pūṣan, payasvinī, sarasvatī, śaṅkhini, gāndhārī, iḍā, hastijihvā and viśvodarā, form the spokes of the cakra. Suṣumnā has five openings (randhra). Four are filled with blood. In the middle of them is the brahmarandhra, which is always shut off by Kuṇḍalī. Suṣumnā appears to be a composite nāḍī, different parts of it going to different parts of the body. Alambusā goes to the end of the feet, kuhu to the penis, varuṇa all over the body, yaśasvinī to the big toe of the right foot, hastijihvā to the big toe of the left foot, piṅgala to the tip of the right nostril, iḍā to the tip of the left nostril, pūṣan to the right eye, gāndhārī to the left eye, payasvinī to the right ear, śaṅkhinī to the left ear, sarasvatī to the tongue and viśvodarā to the stomach.

Ahirbudhnya Saṃhitā 32.31 informs us that vāyu exists in the body though it is not clear whether it moves in the nāḍīs or independently of them. This is not vāyu mahābhūta, however, for, as 7.42-3 informs us, the ten vāyus evolve directly from mahat (=prāṇa?).[40] Prāṇa-vāyu abides in the navel cakra and the jīva 'mounted on prāṇa, always moves to and fro in this cakra, like a spider in the middle of its web.'[41] Its activity is inhalation and exhalation (niśvāsocchvāsa). Apāna vāyu is located in the intestine, anus, thighs, knees, stomach, scrotum, buttocks, shanks and navel. The text does not mention the functions of apāna though it would seem reasonable to include digestion, a function attested in earlier literature, amongst them. Vyāna is located in the middle of the ears and eyes, in the joint of the neck, in both ankles and in the nose, throat and hips. Its function is learning to abandon (?) (hānopadāna). Udāna is located in every joint; its function is the elevation or making erect (unnayana) of the body. Samāna pervades all limbs and its function is to support the body. The other five vāyus are given functions but not locations. The function of nāga is eructation, that of kurma is the closing of the eyes, that of kṛkāra is sneezing, that of devadatta is fatigue and that of dhanañjajya is swellings.

Conclusion

The upshot of this investigation into the place of prāṇa in the Pañcarātra cosmology is that it seems to operate at all levels of creation and in a variety of ways. At the highest level it is an integral part of the supreme being Viṣṇu. In this context it is known as kriya śakti, his power to act, symbolised by the discus sudarśana. It is thus prāṇa which initiates and superintends the creation of the universe. However, it should be noted that the term 'prāṇa' is not prominent in descriptions of either the supreme principle or the pure creation. In other words, 'prāṇa' is a term and concept which seems to have been absorbed by and integrated into the Pañcarātra cosmology in a way that is consonant with statements found in the Vedic Saṃhitās, the Brāhmaṇas and the Upaniṣads, i.e. as a supreme principle, but is then virtually ignored as far as the distinctively Pañcarātra account is concerned.

In the same way, although the kriya śakti controls the creation, preservation and destruction of the universe at the level of the mixed creation and affects the destiny of puruṣas by obscuration (tirodhāna) or favouring (anugraha) the term prāṇa is never employed to refer to the power behind these activities. Hence, the comments made above about the place of prāṇa in the descriptions of the supreme being and the pure creation would also seem to apply here.

At the level of the impure creation 'prāṇa' is more prominent in the descriptions. It appears to manifest in two different ways. First of all, prāṇa is identical with, or is a primary constituent of, the cosmic mahat. Secondly, it manifests as the ten vāyus in the body of each individual, i.e. at the fourth level where the various constituents of the impure creation coalesce into physical objects and individual beings. However, both of these manifestations create problems for the overall coherence of the Pañcarātra account. Mahat and everything evolving from it, including the ten vāyus, are manifestations of bhūti śakti and not kriya śakti. Of course, it could be argued that both of these śaktis are ultimately one and this would be quite legitimate. But then one cannot help but wonder why prāṇa was identified with kriya śakti and not bhūti śakti in the account of the pure creation and why at no point is it explicitly stated that prāṇa is a constituent or evolute of bhūti śakti. A similar problem was noted above (note 23) in connection with the manifestation of kriya śakti at four levels of consciousness.

Another factor contributing to the coherence problems connected with this scheme is the relationship between the cosmic mahat and the ten vāyus. In the Upaniṣads the sense faculties and the vāyus all evolve directly from the cosmic prāṇa which, of course, is cast in the role of creator. Here, however, because of the fourfold division of the creation, the 'distance' between mahat, the cosmic principle, and the ten vāyus, as activities at an individual level, does not fit within the general evolutionary framework employed to describe the manifestation of bhūti śakti, and seems odd to say the least.

The reason for the lack of fit would seem to lie in the synthetic nature of the Pañcarātra doctrines themselves. Within the essentially monistic Vedānta tradition the mythological figures of the Vedas and Brāhmaṇas are easily related to the more abstract terms favoured in much Upaniṣadic discourse. Also, the fact that a particular principle manifests at both cosmic and individual levels does not present too much of a problem since there is a necessary continuity at a fundamental level.

The distinctive additions of the Pañcarātra such as the doctrines of vyūha and avatāra are also not too difficult to integrate with the Vedāntic scheme for the basic moves are essentially similar: the identification of personal deities with impersonal principles. Such a process has a well established and clearly identifiable history within the brāhmanical tradition.

In the case of the Sāṃkhya elements, however, such identifications are less common and less easy to establish. Even in the Pañcarātra-Sāṃkhya of the Nārāyaṇīya the personalised spiritual principles of Vāsudeva, Saṃkarṣaṇa, Pradyumna and Aniruddha are simply added into a scheme which would be quite coherent without them. Because of the fundamental dualism in classical Sāṃkhya, all components of the manifest world, including prāṇa, are evolutes of prakṛti. In the Pañcarātra scheme bhūti śakti takes the role of prakṛti in classical Sāṃkhya, hence at the level of the impure creation prāṇa has to evolve from bhūti śakti even though it was identified with kriya śakti at the levels of pre-creation and pure creation. It seems, therefore, that the identification of prāṇa with kriya śakti was made to square Pañcarātra theology with Vedāntic teachings whilst its derivation from bhūti śakti was included to square it with Sāṃkhya doctrine. The result was a mismatch that was not rectified. The reason why such an incompatibility was left unattended would seem to lie in the fact that by and large the Pañcarātra theologians were more concerned to present a cosmology which located their own foci of worship at the highest level whilst at the same time was consonant with widely accepted cosmological accounts of the time. The prāṇa concept had an obvious place in these accounts and hence needed to be included. However, it did not require careful integration because it was not a prominent feature in Pañcarātra thinking. Consequently, it remained an obscure testament to the crude and perhaps ultimately untenable fusion of Vedāntic and Sāṃkhyan teachings in the Pañcarātra cosmology.

REFERENCES

1. Gupta (1972) p. xv.
2. Grierson (1909) p. 540. For an example of the identification of the two, see Śaṅkara's commentary on Vedānta Sūtra 2.2.44.
3. Chattopadhyaya (1970) p. 62.
4. For a more detailed treatment of this issue see Bhandarkar, R.G. Vaiṣṇavism, Śaivism and minor religious systems, pp. 1-13 and 38-41.
5. Grierson (1909) p. 541.
6. Schrader (1973) p. 16 suggests that the Nārāyaṇīya is, in fact, 'our earliest source of information on the Pañcrātras ...'.
7. Grierson loc. cit.
8. op. cit. p. 543. This threefold combination is explicitly stated in a number of places in the Nārāyaṇīya, e.g. 12.340 where we read that the great secret teaching received by Nārada from Nārāyaṇa is perfectly consistent with the four Vedas, in harmony with Sāṅkhya-yoga, and called by him [Nārāyaṇa] by the name of the Pañcarātra scriptures' (Roy p. 558). In other places, however, e.g. the beginning of 12.350 (Roy p. 615), the difference between these three systems is acknowledged.
9. loc. cit.
10. loc. cit.
11. For example see Vedānta Sūtra 1.4.1-28 and 2.2.1-10, as commented on by both Śaṅkara and Rāmānuja, as rejections of Sāṃkhya. For rejections of Pañcarātra see Śaṅkara's commentary on Vedānta Sūtra 2.2.37-45; Manu Smṛti 10.23 designates Sātvatas as vrātyas, those who are excluded from the Sāvitrī ceremony. Pañcarātrins are also denounced as non-Vedic in the Aśvalāyana Smṛti and the following purāṇas: Kurma, Parāśara, Śāmba, Vṛhannāradīya, Vāyu, Liṅga, Āditya and Agni. Dasgupta Vol. 3 (1922) pp. 19-20.
12. Pande, G.C. (1974); Zimmer, H. (1967).
13. Beidler (1975); Larson (1979); Rao (1966).
14. For details see Rao op. cit. chapter 7.
15. Gupta op. cit. p. xx.
16. op. cit. p. xxiv.
17. See Schrader (1973) passim.
18. Gupta op. cit. p. 108.
19. op. cit. p. 36. The Lakṣmī Tantra both supports this equation of prāṇa and the kriya śakti and contradicts it. 54.20-29 presents Śrī (Lakṣmī) informing Śakra (Indra) that she 'consists of both pure

consciousness and the principle of life (prāṇa) ...' (Gupta op. cit. p. 364). This suggests that prāṇa is one of the two characteristics of the highest being for Lakṣmī, otherwise known as Nārāyaṇī, is 'the abiding quintessence of Nārāyaṇa, identical and at the same time not identical (with him) like the rays of the moon' (op. cit. p. 5). 51.24-32, however, presents her as saying 'with myself as substratum I voluntarily evolve this entire universe ... Consisting of pure knowledge, I first evolve into prāṇa' (op. cit. p. 358), which suggests that prāṇa, rather than being one aspect of her ultimate nature is, in fact, her first evolute. It can be noted, however that both of these passages and the Ahirbudhnya Saṃhitā account locate prāṇa higher than even the pure creation.

20. Sudarśana is, in fact, one of the synonyms for prāṇa. Ahirbudhnya Saṃhitā 12.53 tells us that 'The concepts of prāṇa, māyā, kriya, śaktirbhāva, unmeṣa, udyamaḥ and sudarśana are synonymous' (prāṇa māyā kriya śaktirbhāva unmeṣa udyamaḥ/sudarśanam ca saṃkalpa śabdāḥ paryāvācakāḥ//).

21. Gupa op. cit. p. 40.

22. loc. cit.

23. The Lakṣmī Tantra is somewhat confusing on this issue, perhaps because it is attempting to combine concepts from too many sources. The components of the aṣṭapurī are, according to 7.22-23 (p. 41), prāṇah (the vital airs), bhūtāni (the elements), karma (action), indriyāni (the senses), guṇāh (the qualities), prāgvāsanā (mental impressions), avidya (ignorance) and liṅga (characteristic)–here, according to Gupta, referring to the subtle body. However, 12.39-44 (p. 67) inform us that the liṅga consists of the eighteen individual (inner and outer) senses and kleśa [defilements], karmans, vāsanās and the prāṇas (vital airs)'. If these two references to liṅga are references to the same entity, as Gupta seems to think they are, liṅga cannot be a component of aṣṭapurī since, apart from bhūtāni and guṇāh, they are identical. Here I take avidya as equivalent to kleśa since, as Yoga Sūtra 2.4 informs us, avidya is the field (kṣetra) or 'breeding ground' of the other kleśas (see Feuerstein 1979 p. 62). Certainly the terms aṣṭapurī, liṅga and the related puryaṣṭaka are all commonly employed to refer to the same entity: the subtle body (the components of which vary from system to system), in different contexts. For example, the term 'liṅga' is favoured by the author of the Sāṃkhya Sūtras whilst puryaṣṭaka is preferred by the author of the Spanda Kārikās.

Another problem posed by this classification of the manifestations of kriya śakti is that a number of the items are evolutes of bhūti śakti, e.g. prāṇāḥ, bhūtāni and guṇāh, rather than of kriya śakti. Such mislocations are not easy to rectify though they are perhaps more easy to explain if one takes Pañcarātra to be an essentially synthetic system.

24. Schrader op. cit. p. 38.
25. loc. cit.
26. See chapter 51 of the Lakṣmī Tantra for an alternative version.
27. The Lakṣmī Tantra describes this in a rather different way. 2.52-56 explains that the vyūhas are simply another way of referring to the combinations of the guṇas, though 10.19-21, in conformity with Schrader's account, has the vyūhas possessing the guṇas.
28. For details see Schrader op. cit. pp. 48-49.
29. op. cit. p. 55.
30. loc. cit.
31. Gupta op. cit. p. 22. Schrader locates this information at 2.55. In Gupta's text, however, there is no mention of avatāras or vibhavas at this point.
32. Schrader op. cit. pp. 55-56.
33. See comments on B.A.U. 3.7.
34. We may note that this account of Viṣṇu's ornaments and weapons is one which Schrader has compiled on the basis of a number of Pañcarātra texts. However, the linking of manas with Viṣṇu's discus, sudarśana, conflicts with the statement in Ahirbudhnya Saṃhitā 12.53 that sudarśana is a synonym of prāṇa. In fact, the absence of prāṇa from this list reflects the general lack of concern for the prāṇa concept that is characteristic of Sāṃkhyan accounts.
35. Scrader op. cit. p. 70.
36. On pages 80-81 Schrader (op. cit.) notes that in the Ahirbudhnya Saṃhitā two incompatible descriptions of mahat are found one after the other. He writes, '... the first clearly shows that the Pañcarātra has drawn from an older form of the Sāṃkhya philosophy than the one which has survived in the kārikā and the sūtra-s. The mahat we are first told (7.9-11), is threefold in conformity with the three guṇas, its tamas element appearing as kāla (time), its sattva element as buddhi (reason, intellect), and its rajas element as prāṇa (vitality). The next statement, which would hopelessly conflict with the preceding one, unless we refer it not to the cosmic mahat but to buddhi as an individual organ ..., is essentially identical with the teaching of the twenty third āryā of the Sāṃkhya-Kārikā, namely that mahat manifests itself in four sāttvic and four tāmasic forms, being respectively good actions (dharma), knowledge, dispassion and might and their opposites'. These statements actually take up four verses: 9-12. They read as follows:

Kālo buddhistathā prāṇa iti tredha sa gīyate (9)

tamaḥsattvarajobhedāt tattadunmeṣa–saṃjñaya kālastruṭilavādyātma buddhiraghyavasāyinī (10)

dharmo jñānam virāgaścāpyaiśvaryamiti saṃjñayā (11)

mahataḥ sāttvikam rūpam caturdhā pravibhajyate adharmājñānāvairagyam–anaiśvaryam ca tāmasam (12)

'It is related in song that such is the threefold division: time (kāla), intellect (buddhi), breath (prāṇa).

From the division into tamas, sattva and rajas various appearances are acknowledged. The first one is time, divided into moment particles, [next] is intellect, destroying evil [next] is breath [having the nature of] form and activity. These are the divisions of mahat. Mahat is divided into four acknowledged sāttvic forms: dharma, jñāna, vairāgya and also aiśvarya. Addharma, ajñāna, avairāgya and anaiśvarya are the tāmasic ones'.

Rao (op. cit. pp. 360-361) disagrees with this interpretation arguing, essentially, that in the Ahirbudhnya Saṃhitā, which he regards as older than the Sāṃkhya Kārikās, there is still to be found a cosmic function of buddhi/mahat which is later lost in the kārikās. In fact, the opposite would seem to be true: the Ahirbudhnya Saṃhitā has added a cosmic dimension to buddhi/ mahat in order to accommodate it into the wider, more complex and ultimately monisic Pañcarātra cosmology.

37. Schrader also feels that this equation between prāṇa and mahat casts light on some of the connections between Sāṃkhya and Buddhism. In particular he argues that the cosmic mahat is to the individual buddhi what vijñāna-dhātu is to vijñāna skandha. For details see op. cit. pp. 85-86.

38. Gupta op. cit. pp. 29-30.

39. See Schrader op. cit. pp. 91-98 for details.

40. Schrader op. cit. pp. 82-83.

41. Chapter 32 verse 22 prāṇarūḍho bhavjjīvascakre'smin bhrante sadā/urṇanābhiryatha tantupañjarāntarvyavasthitaḥ//

[illegible]ātmā buddhirnighṛṣavāsyāni (10)

dharmo jñānaṃ [illegible] [illegible]vāryamiti sammitāḥ (11)

38. Gupta, op. cit., p. 29.

sadā tvaṃ nābhinyasya tanmapañjarā sarvasaṃmitaḥ //

Conclusion

In the foregoing study of the prāṇa concept it has been suggested that the pre-Upaniṣadic Vedic tradition evolved within itself a contemplative movement which developed distinctive techniques of spiritual uplift. Methods of chanting and visualization appear to have produced, for the members of this movement, insights into what they regarded as the pattern or scheme underlying the world of ordinary experience. The universe, particularly the living universe, was seen to be in a constant state of flux. Life was followed by death, the eater of food became the food of another eater. Copulation produced offspring, which became eaters and eaten in turn. Hence vitalistic concepts came to occupy an important place in the Vedic world-view. Alongside this it was recognized that words brought order into existence, facilitating the structuring of experience. In many places these two principles: vitality and speech, were combined to provide a bi-polar image of the fundamental reality behind the changing world. Examples, would be the puruṣa-Virāj conception of the Ṛgveda and the prāṇa-Vāc concept of the Śatapatha Brāhmaṇa. Elsewhere, however, a more unitary conception prevailed and just one principle was presented as the source and foundation of all. The treatment of Vāc in R.V. 1.164 and that of prāṇa in A.V. 11.4 are both indicative of this tendency.

By the time of the Upaniṣads the bi-polar view was dwindling in significance whilst the unitary one was becoming more prominent. Two of the terms used frequently in the Upaniṣads to denote this unitary source and foundation of existence have clear vitalistic connotations. They are prāṇa and ātman. In the pre-Upaniṣadic period these were just two out of a number of vitalistic concepts which do not appear to have acquired a fixed meaning by that time. Some, such as asu, āyu and vāta, declined in importance during the

Upaniṣadic period whilst others, like vāyu, prāṇa and ātman, continued to play a prominent role in religious and philosophical thinking.

In the Upaniṣads the two principal concepts are ātman and brahman, both of which developed primary meanings as the source and foundation of all the universe and the immortal essence of the individual. In the later Vedānta tradition these terms came to acquire a monopoly on statements about the ultimate principle of existence and hence scholars have devoted considerable energy in plotting the history of their usage. However, if the Upaniṣads are examined in isolation from the interpretative structure of the Vedānta, it becomes clear that in many Upaniṣadic texts the concept of prāṇa occupies the position accorded to ātman/brahman in others. This concept has not, however, received anything like the amount of attention that has been devoted to the other two.

As far as I am aware, the study of Ewing is the only detailed scholarly work on the subject. His investigation provides an indispensible foundation for work in this area, though it is by no means the last word. Although detailed, it is not comprehensive. His comments on the early material deal more with what might be called the more concrete meanings of the terms in the prāṇa series: prāṇa, apāna, vyāna, udāna and samāna, rather than with their place in the wider Vedic world-view. The same is true of his treatment of prāṇa in the singular. Although he acknowledges both the cosmic (as the creator and foundation of the universe) and individual (as the inner controller) dimensions of this concept he does little to explore their ramifications.

Most other scholars who have given some consideration to the place of prāṇa in Indian thought have been more concerned with the Upaniṣads than with earlier literature. All have noticed that in these texts prāṇa does have a cosmic/ultimate status in a number of places though the general trend seems to be one of its subordination to the concept of ātman and brahman. However, none offer anything like satisfactory explanations of the reason for and mechanics of this process.

Consequently, one of the first concerns of the present study was to plot the development of the prāṇa concept in pre-Upaniṣadic Vedic literature. What emerged, in brief, was that even before the time of the Upaniṣads the term 'prāṇa' was seen by a number of Vedic thinkers to carry many of the connotations later associated with the terms 'ātman' and 'brahman': it was the source and foundation of all existence and the immortal inner essence of a person. Outside the body it was unitary, inside it divided itself into the various vital energies: prāṇa, apāna, etc., and the sensory faculties, including mind and speech. It also appears to have acted as a kind of 'inner controller', knowledge of which bestows immortality. In the pre-Upaniṣadic period then, the prāṇa concept attained a much clearer definition than did its principal competitor, that of ātman, which in the Śatapatha Brāhmaṇa ranges in meaning from 'spirit' through 'self' to 'body' or 'organism'.

In the Upaniṣads the trend seems to have been reversed. Whilst it is the case that many passages continue to present prāṇa in a way similar to that found in some pre-Upaniṣadic texts, they repeatedly occur juxtaposed between others presenting ātman or brahman or both as the supreme principle. In other cases, there are clear statements to the effect that prāṇa is a principle which is derived from the ātman/brahman. Only in a very few places are clear and strong statements that prāṇa is the supreme principle found in the Upaniṣads. The Kauṣītakī Upaniṣad is probably the best example of such a statement.

Deussen suggests that there is clear evidence in the early Upaniṣads for the existence of a polemic between schools of the white Yajurveda and schools of the Sāma Veda, since teachers who are exhalted in one are often denigrated in the other. He also notes the existence of two schools of thought on the nature of the ultimate principle. One, which he regards as the more ancient and calls 'the older school', takes this principle to be prāṇa (understood by Deussen as 'unconscious life'); the other, 'younger school', takes it to be ātman (the subject of cognition). Though he provides no further details on these 'schools' it seems reasonable to link the older one with the view of prāṇa identified in chapter one. There also seemed to be some connection between the Yajurveda-Sāmaveda dispute and the one between Deussen's older and younger schools, since one of the concerns of the redactors of the Chāndogya Upaniṣad, the principal Upaniṣad of the Sāmaveda, appears to have been the downgrading of the prāṇa principle. This is evident in a number of C.U. passages, though perhaps most apparent in the udgītha vidyā (C.U. 1.2.1-14), Uddālaka's teaching (C.U. 6) and Sanatkumāra's teaching (C.U. 7). The first and last of these betray clear signs of redactions, which appear to have been undertaken for the express purpose of lowering the status of the prāṇa principle.

It was these same Chāndogya redactors who appear to have been responsible for the hermeneutical stance taken by the compilers of the Brahma Sūtra and hence by the mainstream of later Vedānta philosophy. Consequently, we witness in the Brahmasūstra and the bhāṣyas of its principal commentators the same dislike of a world-view in which the prāṇa concept has any degree of prominence that is found in the arrangement of the above mentioned C.U. passages.

By the time of Śaṅkara and Rāmānuja, however, Vedāntins could not simply rework older material to make it fit with their own views. The texts of the Veda had acquired a fairly fixed form and were regarded as inerrant revelation (śruti). Hence, all Upaniṣads, even those like the Kauṣītakī which preserved the teaching of 'the older school' in a fairly systematic form, were deemed to be both true and in accord with each other. Consequently different methods for dealing with material preserving 'the older view' had to be adopted.

It is clear in both the Brahmasūtra, and the C.U. that one motive for taking prāṇa to be a purely derivative principle was to restrict the number of terms which could be used to denote the supreme principle, which, in turn, rendered the task of characterizing it much easier. In the Brahmasūtra, we also find evidence of a desire to employ Sāṃkhyan concepts in the articulation of the Vedāntic world-view and this required a further degree of marginalization for prāṇa. Even though the ultimate status of prāṇa is disputed in a number of Upaniṣads it is often found to be the source of both vital breaths: prāṇa, apāna etc., and the faculties. In the Brahmasūtra it is denied even this latter association since such a doctrine does not mesh very easily with the Sāṃkhya-derived concept of eleven indriyas.

It was thus suggested that as far as the concept of prāṇa is concerned, the Vedāntic claim that it represents the true meaning of the Upaniṣads is totally without foundation. In fact, the principal Vedāntin thinkers were shown not to be interpreters of the Upaniṣads but manipulators and distorters of them.

The fact that Sāṃkhyan concepts tended to displace Upaniṣadic ones in the system of the Vedānta suggests that the Sāṃkhya tradition had little room for this prāṇa concept in its scheme. That such is the case was demonstrated by a consideration of references to prāṇa in both epic and classical versions of Sāṃkhya. When arguments to account for the seeming lack of fit between the Sāṃkhyan cosmology and the Sāṃkhyan view of the prāṇas were examined they were found to be both unconvincing and at variance with the general tenor of Sāṃkhyan thinking, thereby underlining the fact that the tattvic cosmology of Sāṃkhya and the Vedic/ Upaniṣad doctrine of prāṇa/prāṇas are essentially incompatible.

This conclusion was given further support by the results of an investigation of the prāṇa concept in the synthetic Pañcarātra system. There, much of the early status of the Vedic concept of prāṇa was preserved through the identification of prāṇa with the kriya śakti of the supreme being–Viṣṇu. At the level of the diversified prāṇa, however, the Pañcarātra cosmology is dominated by Sāṃkhyan concepts. These are incorporated into the scheme by making them evolutes of Viṣṇu's bhūti śakti. At the phenomenal level, therefore, prāṇa, as a component of mahat and as the ten vāyus in the body, is an evolute of bhūti rather than kriya śakti. The prāṇa concept is thus not very well integrated into the cosmology of the Pañcarātra. This is primarily because the Vedic and Sāṃkhyan schemes are not really compatible. 'Prāṇa' is a central concept in the former and essentially alien to the latter. In fact, it would not seem too unreasonable to claim that where the orthodox religious and philosophical systems of India preserve a world-view in which prāṇa plays a prominent part they are likely to apprehend the universe in a manner which resonates in essential harmony with that of the ancient ṛṣis. Where the prāṇa concept is marginalized or abandoned, however, the vision of the later acāryas has deviated considerably from that of many Vedic poets and Upaniṣadic teachers.

Bibliography

Barua, B.: *A History of Pre-Buddhistic Indian Philosophy,* Motilal Banarsidass, 1970 (re-print of 1921 edition).

Beidler, W.: *The Vision of Self in Early Vedānta,* Motilal Banarsidass, 1975.

Bhandarkar, R.G.: *Vaiṣṇavism, Śaivism and Minor Religious Systems* Indological Book House, Varanasi 1965 (reprint of 1913 edition).

Bhattacharji, S.: *The Indian Theogony,* Cambridge University Press, 1970.

Brown, W.N.: 'Agni, Sun, Sacrifice and Vac: A Sacerdotal Ode by Dirghatamas (Rig Veda 1.164)' in *Journal of the American Oriental Society,* Vol. 88, 1968, pp. 199-218.

Bühler, G.: *The Laws of Manu* Dover 1969 (reprint of Clarendon Press 1886 edition: Sacred Books of the East, volume 25).

Carmen, J.B.: *The Theology of Rāmānuja,* Yale University Press, 1974.

Chakravarti, P.: *Origin and Development of the Sāṃkhya System of Thought* (2nd ed.), Oriental Books Reprint Corporation, Delhi, 1975.

Chattopadhyaya, S.: *Evolution of Hindu Sects,* Munshiram Manoharlal, 1970.

Cowell, E.B. & Gough, A.E.: *Sarva-Darśana-Saṅgraha of Mādhavāchārya,* Parimal Publications, 1981.

Dasgupta, S.: *A History of Indian Philosophy,* Vols. 1 and 3. Cambridge University Press, 1922.

Deussen, P.: *The Philosophy of the Upanishads* (trans. Geden, A.S.), Dover 1966 (reprint of '1906 edition).

Deussen, P.: *The System of the Vedānta* (trans. Johnston, C.), Dover 1973 (reprint of 1912 edition).

Deussen, P.: *Sixty Upanishads of the Veda* (2 vols.) (trans. Bedekar, V.M. and Palsule, G.B.) Motilal Banarsidass, 1980.

Edgerton, F.: 'Prāṇa and Apāna' in *Journal of the American Oriental Society*, Vol. 78, 1958, pp. 51-57.

Eggeling, J., *The Śatapatha Brāhmaṇa* (5 vols.), Motilal Banarsidass, 1963 (reprint of 1882 [1], 1885 [2], 1894 [3], 1885 [4] and 1900 [5] editions).

Ewing, A.H.: 'The Hindu Conception of the Functions of Breath (Part 1)' in *Journal of the American Oriental Society*, Vol. 22, 1901 pp. 249-308.

Ewing, A.H.: *The Hindu Conception of the Functions of Breath* (Part 2), Liddell's Printing Works, Allahabad, 1903.

Falk, M. (1): *Nāma-Rūpa and Dharma Rūpa*, University of Calcutta, 1943.

Falk, M. (2): 'The Oldest Psychology: Terminus A Quo and Aspects' in *Indian Journal of Psychology* (Sept. and Dec.), 1943, pp. 106-116.

Feuerstein, G. & Miller, J.: *A Reappraisal of Yoga*, Rider, 1971.

Feuerstein, G.: *The Yoga Sūtra of Patañjali*, Dawson 1979.

Feuerstein, G.: *The Bhagavad Gītā*, Arnold-Heinemann, 1980.

Frauwallner, E.: *History of Indian Philosophy* (2 vols.), (trans. Bedekar, V.M.), Motilal Banarsidass, 1973.

Gonda, J.: *The Vision of the Vedic Poets*, Mouton, 1963.

Grierson, G.A.: 'Bhakti Mārga' in Hastings, J. (ed.) *Encyclopaedia of Religion and Ethics*, Vol. 2, T. and T. Clark, 1909, pp. 539-551.

Griffith, R.T.H.: *The Hymns of the Ṛg Veda*, Motilal Banarsidass, 1973 (revised edition).

Griffith, R.T.H.: *The Texts of the White Yajurveda* (4th edition), The Chowkhamba Sanskrit Series Office, 1976.

Gupta, S.: *Lakṣmī Tantra,* E.J. Brill, 1972.

Herman, A.L.: *The Problem of Evil and Indian Thought,* Motilal Banarsidass, 1970.

Herman, A.L.: *Introduction to Indian Thought,* Prentice Hall, 1976.

Hopkins, E.W.: *The Great Epic of India,* Punthi Pustak, 1969 (reprint of 1901 edition).

Hume, R.E.: *The Thirteen Principal Upanishads,* Oxford University Press, 1931.

Jacob, G.A.: *A concordance to the principal Upanishads and Bhagavadgītā,* Motilal Banarsidass (reprint), 1985.

Johnson, W.: 'On the Ṛg Vedic' Riddle of the Two Birds in the Fig Tree (R.V. 1.164.20-22) and the Discovery of the Vedic Speculative Symposium' in *Journal of the American Oriental Society,* Vol. 96, 1976, pp. 248-258.

Keith, A.B.: *The Aitareya Āraṇyaka,* Oxford University Press, 1969 (reprint of the 1906 edition).

Keith, A.B.: *The Religion and Philosophy of the Veda and Upanishads* (2 Vols.), Motilal Banarsidass, 1970 (reprint of the 1925 edition).

Keith, A.B.: *A History of Sāṃkhya Philosophy,* Nag Publishers, 1975 (reprint).

Krishnamacharya, V.: *Ahirbudhnya Saṃhitā of the Pañcarātrāgama* (2 vols.) Adyar Library 1966 (revised version of M.D. Rāmānujāchārya's 1916 edition).

Larson, G.J.: *Classical Sāṃkhya* (2nd. edition) Motilal Banarsidass, 1979.

Mayeda, S.: *A Thousand Teachings: The Upadeśasāhasrī of Śaṅkara,* University of Tokyo Press, 1979.

Miller, J.: *The Vedas,* Rider, 1974.

Monier Williams, M.: *A Sanskrit-English Dictionary,* Oxford University Press, 1976 (reprint of 1899 edition).

Müller, F.M.: *The Upanishads* (2 vols.), Dover, 1962 (reprint of the 1829 and 1884 editions).

Nakamura, H.: *A History of Early Vedānta Philosophy* Motilal Banarsidass, 1983.

O'Flaherty, W.D.: *The Rig Veda,* Penguin, 1981.

Oldenberg, H.: *Vedic Hymns,* Motilal Banarsidass, 1967 (reprint of 1897 edition).

Pande, G.C.: *Studies in the Origins of Buddhism* (2nd edition), Motilal Banarsidass, 1974.

Pandey, S.L.: *Pre-Śaṃkara Advaita Philosophy,* Darshan Peeth, Allahabad, 1983.

Panikkar, R.: *The Vedic Experience,* Darton, Longman and Todd, 1977.

Radhakrishnan, S.: *Indian Philosophy* (2 Vols.), George Allen and Unwin, 1929.

Radhakrishnan, S.: *The Principal Upanishads,* George Allen and Unwin, 1953.

Radhakrishnan, S.: *The Brahma Sūtra* George Allen and Unwin, 1960.

Raghavachar, S.S. (trans.): *Vedārtha-Saṅgraha of Śrī Rāmānujācārya,* Sri Ramakrishna Ashrama, Mysore, 1978.

Rao, K.B.R.: *Theism of Pre-Classical Sāṃkhya,* University of Mysore, 1966.

Reat, N.R.: *The Origins of Buddhist Psychology,* Ph.D. thesis, University of Lancaster, 1980.

Roth, R. and Whitney, W.D.: *Atharvaveda Saṅhitā,* Berlin Ferd Dummler's Verlagsbuchhandlung, 1856.

Roy, P.C.: *The Mahabharata,* Vols. 9 and 10, Oriental Publishing Co., Calcutta, No date.

Sastri, P.S.: 'The Vision of Dirghatamas' in *Prabuddha Bharata,* Vol. 62, 1957, pp. 63-66.

Sastry, A.M. (trans.): *The Bhagavad Gītā with the commentary of Śaṅkarāchārya,* Samata Books, 1981.

Schrader, F.O.: *Introduction to the Pañcarātra and the Ahirbudhnya Saṃhitā* (2nd edition) Adyar Library, 1973.

Singh, J.: *Spanda Kārikās* Motilal Banarsidass, 1980.

Singh, J.: *Vijñānabhairava or Divine Consciousness* Motilal Banarsidass, 1979.

Sinha, N. (trans.): *The Sāṃkhya Philosophy containing (1) Sāṃkhya Pravachana Sūtram, (2) Tattva Samāsa, (3) Sāṃkhya Kārikā, (4) Pañcaśikha Sūtram* A.M.S. 1974 (reprint of 1915 edition).

Srinivasachari, P.N.: *The Philosophy of Bhedābheda,* Adyar Library, 1972 (reprint of 1934 edition).

Thibaut, G.: *The Vedānta Sūtras of Bādarāyaṇa with the commentary by Śaṅkara* (2 Vols.), Dover, 1962 (corrected version of the Clarendon Press, 1908 and 1968 editions). S.B.E. vols. 34 and 38.

Thibaut, G.: *The Vedānta Sūtras of Bādarāyaṇa with the commentary by Rāmānuja,* Motilal Banarsidass, 1962 (reprint of Oxford University Press, 1904 edition). S.B.E. vol. 48.

Van Buitenen, J.A.B.: *Rāmānuja on the Bhagavadgītā,* Motilal Banarsidass, 1968.

Van Buitenen, J.A.B.: 'Studies in Sāṃkhya', Part 1. *Journal of the American Oriental Society,* Vol. 76, 1956, pp. 153-157. Part 2. *J.O.A.S.* Vol. 77 (1957) (1) pp. 15-25. Part 3. *J.O.A.S.* Vol. 77 (1957) (2) pp. 88-107.

Werner, K. 'Yoga and the Ṛg Veda: An Interpretation of the Keśin Hymn (Ṛ.V. 10.136)' in *Religious Studies,* Vol. 13, 1977, pp. 289-302.

Whitney, W.D.: *The Atharva Veda Saṃhitā* (2 Vols.), Motilal Banarsidass, 1971 (reprint of the 1905 edition).

Zaehner, R.C. (trans.): *The Bhagavad Gītā,* Oxford University Press, 1969.

Zimmer, H.: *Philosophies of India,* Routledge and Kegan Paul 1967

Sinha, N (trans.): *The Sāmkhya Philosophy containing (1) Sāmkhya Pravachana Sūtram, (2) Tattva Samāsa. (3) Sāmkhya Kārikā. (4) Pañcaśikha Sūtram* A.M.S. 1974 (reprint of 1915 edition).

Srinivasachari, P.N.: *The Philosophy of Bhedābheda*, Adyar Library, 1972 (reprint of 1934 edition).

Thibaut, G.: *The Vedānta Sūtras of Bādarāyaṇa with the commentary by Śaṅkara* (2 Vols), Dover, 1962 (corrected version of the Clarendon Press, 1903 and 1968 editions). S.B.E. vols. 34 and 38.

Thibaut, G.: *The Vedānta Sūtras of Bādarāyaṇa with the commentary by Rāmānuja*, Motilal Banarsidass, 1962 (reprint of Oxford University Press, 1904 edition). S.B.E. vol. 48.

Van Buitenen, J.A.B.: *Rāmānuja on the Bhagavadgītā*, Motilal Banarsidass, 1968.

Van Buitenen, J.A.B.: "Studies in Sāṅkhya", Part 1, *Journal of the American Oriental Society*, Vol. 76, 1956, pp. 153-157. Part 2, *J.O.A.S.* Vol. 77 (1957) (1) pp. 15-25. Part 3, *J.O.A.S.* Vol. 77 (1957) (2) pp. 88-107.

Werner, K: 'Yoga and the Ṛg Veda: An Interpretation of the Keśin Hymn (R.V. 10.136)' in *Religious Studies*, Vol. 13, 1977, pp. 289-302.

Whitney, W.D.: *The Atharva Veda Samhita* (2 Vols.), Motilal Banarsidass, 1971 (reprint of the 1905 edition).

Zaehner, R.C. (trans.): *The Bhagavad Gītā*, Oxford University Press, 1969.

Zimmer, H.: *Philosophies of India*, Routledge and Kegan Paul, 1967.

Index

A